Social Economics

By the same author

Taxing Personal Wealth, George Allen and Unwin, 1971

Case Studies in Economics, Macmillan (with M. S. Bradbury et al):
Principles of Economics, 1971, *Role Playing and Projects*, 1971,
Economic Policy, second edition 1977.

Hidden Costs of Taxation, I.F.S., 1973.

An Accessions Tax, I.F.S., 1973 (with J. R. M. Willis and D. J.
Ironside).

An Annual Wealth Tax, I.F.S./Heinemann Educational Books, 1975
(with J. R. M. Willis and D. J. Ironside).

National Economic Planning, Heinemann Educational Books, second
edition 1976.

Economics of Public Finance, Pergamon, second edition 1977.

Social Economics

Cedric Sandford
Professor of Political Economy,
University of Bath

Heinemann Educational Books · London

Heinemann Educational Books Ltd

LONDON EDINBURGH MELBOURNE AUCKLAND TORONTO
HONG KONG SINGAPORE KUALA LUMPUR NEW DELHI
NAIROBI JOHANNESBURG LUSAKA IBADAN
KINGSTON

Cased edition ISBN 0 435 84780 5
Paper edition ISBN 0 435 84781 3

Published by Heinemann Educational Books Ltd
48 Charles Street, London W1X 8AH
Printed and bound in Great Britain by
Morrison & Gibb Ltd, London and Edinburgh

Contents

General Introduction

This book arose out of a lecture course currently given at Bath University to first year students reading for degrees in sociology (and social work), economics, government, business administration and social science. The course and the book assume no prior knowledge of economics, but seek to introduce such economic concepts and principles as are necessary to enable students to appreciate the economist's perspective, and to apply his way of thinking to social problems and policies. Although designed particularly for students who might undertake little or no further formal study of economics, it is valuable to those who will subsequently study economics at greater depth because it covers many economic aspects of social policy which do not enter mainstream economics as generally taught. It is hoped that the book will be found useful by 'A' level students and students on professional courses as well as by undergraduates. Because it is not dependent on previous training in economics, it is also the author's hope that the book will prove attractive to the general reader who seeks to understand more about the economy in which he lives and, in particular, the social policies which governments do or might follow. It is no exaggeration to say that the subject matter is crucial to the health and possibly the continued existence of the kind of economy and society in which we live in Britain.

Separate introductions describe the coverage and objectives of each part of the book, but two characteristics common to the work as a whole might be indicated here. Firstly, the book is concerned essentially with the 'mixed' economy, and the economy of the United Kingdom in particular. Secondly, there is a common pattern in each chapter: the penultimate section poses and attempts to answer a question of particular relevance to the subject matter of the chapter; the final section is a brief summary. The question is intended to stimulate and often to crystallize thinking on the subject, whilst the summary serves to reinforce the main lessons of the chapter.

Acknowledgments

My thanks are due to a large number of my colleagues who have assisted me in various ways, principally by commenting on all or part of the typescript; in particular I must mention Nancy Burton, Mary Couper, John Cullis, Ann Robinson and Willie Seal. I am especially indebted to Mike Godwin, who, besides making many valuable comments which enabled me to improve the text, prepared much of the statistical material. I am also most grateful to Jacqui Knight and Sue Powell who between them typed the bulk of the manuscript with speed and efficiency.

Cedric Sandford
November 1976

Part I

SOCIAL ECONOMICS IN A MIXED ECONOMY

Introduction to Part I

In this first part of the book we seek to lay the essential groundwork for what is to follow. In Chapter 1 we discuss the meaning of economics and of social economics and the contribution the economist can make to social policy. In Chapter 2 we look at the methods of the social sciences and in particular the uses and misuses of statistics. Then follow three chapters which provide the general groundwork for understanding the workings of the mixed economy. Chapter 3 looks at the economic system as a whole, classifies goods, indicates the relationship between income, output and expenditure, explains how the figures of national output are compiled and considers the uses and limitations of those figures. Chapter 4 examines the private sector in the mixed economy, the merits and defects of the market mechanism, how the market works, and the implications of state intervention in the market. Then, in Chapter 5, we examine the public sector: its nature and characteristics, the methods of state intervention in the economy, the problems of measuring the public sector and the growth of public spending including the development of the welfare state in the United Kingdom. This chapter on the public sector ends with a brief analysis of the merits and defects of the extreme form of command economy. Finally, in Chapter 6, we conclude this part of the book by considering the 'social balance', the optimum size of public and private sectors, and ask the question 'Where does the social balance lie?' We can point to biases in the mixed economy of the United Kingdom, some working in the direction of less, some of more government spending. We conclude that it is not possible to specify what is the social balance, but we can highlight some of the most relevant considerations. The analysis in this chapter, though based on economics, necessarily takes us beyond its confines to consider aspects of political behaviour and value judgments.

The lessons of this part of the book need to be thoroughly grasped, for throughout the remainder of it we shall be making frequent reference to them, explicitly or implicitly. These include the essential nature of economics, the limitations of the statistical tools available to the social scientist, Gross National Product (GNP), the working of the price system including specific concepts such as the income and substitution effects of price changes, and the growth, characteristics and problems of the public sector of the economy.

1 What is Social Economics?

Meaning of Economics

If someone were to ask you 'What is your economic problem?' you would probably say 'Money'. If pressed to define this more precisely, you might amplify by saying 'Lack of money income'. This is a perfectly reasonable and accurate answer for an individual to give to the question. It follows that your economic problems could be solved by a benevolent uncle who made you an allowance of, say, £100 per week.

But, whilst accurate, the answer is superficial. Let us transfer it to a larger scene. Suppose the state acted as a benevolent uncle to everyone and a well-intentioned government set the printing presses to work and sent each person £100 a week in the post. Would all our economic problems be solved?

The answer is clearly 'No'. As everyone tried to spend this additional money the stocks of goods in the shops would start to run down and the prices of goods to rise. Shortage of money would have been replaced by shortage of goods and services. If, at the time the government started to act as the benevolent uncle, there were unemployed men and women seeking work and unused machines, then we could expect some increase in goods and services as these resources were taken into employment following the extra spending. But this additional source of supply of goods and services would soon be taken up. The scarcity of goods and services would then be seen to result from the scarcity of resources to make them.

Thus, what is seen by the individual as a scarcity of money is underlain by a scarcity of real resources. There is, indeed, normally a connection between the money income of an individual or family unit and the amount and value of the real resources it supplies to the productive process. A person's income from work is a reflection of the value society puts on the quality and quantity of labour power that person supplies to the productive system. Similarly, income from property is a reflection of the contribution of the property owner in lending the property to assist in production. (The income from uncle was not like this; there was no economic service rendered by you in exchange. But there is an important difference between uncle's action and the government's. When uncle gave you £100 per week he reduced his own capacity to demand goods—he was sharing with you the fruit of his contribution to the productive system. When the state gave everyone £100 per week by printing it, there was no corresponding reduction in its demand on resources.)

Money, though important, is less significant than the real resources of which it is usually the reflection. Primarily, though not exclusively, money is a medium of exchange which enables us to avoid the disadvantages of barter. Most economic issues can be looked at in both real and money terms but often we get a clearer understanding of a problem by examining it in real terms.

Economics, then, might be broadly defined as a study of how man uses (or fails to use) the resources at his disposal to satisfy his wants. Let us amplify this. By wants we mean objectives of all kinds, both material and immaterial. The wants may be those of an individual, a family unit or a nation. Wants are characterised by being virtually unlimited. The economist takes these wants or ends for granted in the sense that, as an economist, he does not seek to judge their desirability or morality. By resources we mean what the economist usually calls the factors or agents of production. These are conventionally grouped under three broad headings: labour—the immediate human element in production; capital—man-made equipment; and land which consists of resources provided by nature and covers not only land as normally understood but also resources such as mineral deposits. Time can also be regarded as a resource. These resources which can be used to satisfy wants, or as means to achieve desired ends, have two main characteristics. They are scarce in relation to the demand for them; indeed, scarcity is always relative to demand; as Professor Robbins put it, 'There are more good eggs than bad eggs but only good eggs are scarce'. The second essential characteristic of resources is that they are capable of alternative use. Labour, for instance, can be used to make a variety of different products or to provide a variety of different services, and, given time, workers can be trained in a variety of different skills. Similarly, equipment can be used in making different products and in the long run, when it wears out, can be replaced by different kinds of machines.

Because our wants are virtually unlimited and because resources are scarce and capable of alternative use, economic life is permeated with choice. We have to choose which of the wants to satisfy or how fully to satisfy them. This is true of the individual and of the community. Mostly these choices are not of an absolute kind but are choices 'at the margin'. For example, as individuals the choice is not between having food and no clothes or clothes and no food, but rather whether to have some extra food at the cost of doing without some additional clothing. As a nation the choice is not between hospitals or schools, but whether to have an additional hospital and postpone the building of a new school or vice versa. An important choice is that between the present and the future. By saving, an individual can improve his future living standard at the cost of a lower living standard now. Similarly, a community can devote more of its current resources to investment in new equipment having a lower living standard in the present so as to enjoy a higher one in the future.

This economic problem of how to satisfy manifold ends with scarce means and what choices to make in the process is valid for most forms of activity and all national economies. The methods by which a nation seeks to solve the problem may differ, but the problem is the same.

The term 'economizing' can now be seen in its true sense of using scarce resources to best advantage; to satisfy as many wants as possible, or to satisfy any given want with the least resources so that more are available to satisfy other wants. An economist is sometimes thought of as a professional conserver of candle ends; but economizing does not mean pinch-penny saving. As a famous classical economist put it, 'Economy should not be confused with parsimony'. Some illustrations of what economists study may help to make the point clearer. Economists analyse the causes of unemployment because unemployment constitutes a failure to use scarce resources. They examine foreign trade because, if nations concentrate their production on those goods in which they have the greatest comparative cost advantage and exchange them for other goods, total output can be increased and living standards raised, i.e. more wants can be satisfied. Similarly, economists study the location and size of firms and industries because an economy of scarce resources may be obtained from a particular location or a particular scale of operation.

Meaning of Social Economics
What of social economics? There is no precise, clear cut, compre-

hensive definition of social economics. The term is sometimes used in a very wide sense to cover virtually the whole of economics except the theory of consumer behaviour and the theory of the firm. But there is a narrower sense in which it is becoming accepted as a convenient, if somewhat imprecise, phrase to cover the economist's approach to, or economic aspects of, social problems and policies. This is the sense in which we are using it in this book. It includes some aspects of the economics of population, partly by way of background but also because of the relevance of the size and composition of the population to a whole range of social policies such as education, health, pensions and housing. It includes economics of employment and unemployment. It comprehends economic aspects of the social services, the economics of poverty and the related problems of the distribution of income and wealth. It can also be taken to cover environmental economics.

Characteristics of Social Economics

Social economics has certain characteristics. It is concerned with all matters fairly directly relating to the standard of living and the quality of life. It is intimately connected to the public sector of the economy, especially aspects of government expenditure, and it raises questions of the extent and form of government expenditure in a mixed economy. The topics it considers are those where other social scientists, especially sociologists and psychologists, have much of relevance to say. At times the border lines between the contributions of the different social scientists are blurred if not fluid; but whilst this book seeks to create an awareness of where the contributions of other social scientists may be particularly helpful, our prime concern is with the economist. A further characteristic of social economics is that it is concerned with policy issues where moral or value judgments often have to be made. We have already said that the economist, as such, does not judge the desirability of particular objectives (although, of course, as a citizen he is just as entitled to his judgment as anyone else). His approach primarily takes the form of saying that if you want to obtain this end, here are some of the implications of this choice and these are the appropriate means. The necessity to make value judgments in policy issues does not preclude the participation of the economist, but the economist (and the student) should cultivate an awareness of when value judgments are being made or implied, and should not claim the support of economic science for such judgments. A value judgment might be said to be one the validity of which cannot be determined as a result of an objective empirical test; that is to say, it cannot conceivably be verified by an appeal to fact. For instance, if I say that I believe in capital punishment because it is just that those who take life should themselves pay the supreme penalty, this is a value judgment which no amount of empirical investigation will affect. But we must beware, for sometimes what sounds like a value judgment is not necessarily one. The simple statement 'I believe in capital punishment' does not stand as a value judgment until we have found out why. If 'I believe in capital punishment' because I think capital punishment is a deterrent, then the statement rests on a view which, in principle, it is possible to test against the facts.

The Contribution of the Economist to Social Policy

We have already said that the issues with which social economics deals are also those where other social scientists have contributions to make, and the voice of the economist should not necessarily dominate. What the economist offers is a perspective which is significant for all such issues—a perspective which seeks to identify the objectives of social policy, and to achieve those objectives with the least expenditure of scarce resources. The economist has a pervading awareness of costs, in the sense of 'opportunity cost'. He is continually conscious that, because of the scarcity of resources, the cost of one good or service is the next best alternative sacrificed in order to achieve it. There is nothing ignoble in this contribution although it is concerned with means rather than ends; economizing enables us to attain more ends or attain existing ends more fully.

Besides this perspective on problems, the economist brings particular contributions to their solution. Firstly, there are some developed tools of economic analysis which can be very helpful in dealing with issues of social policy. These points will become clearer in the course of the book but it may be useful to list one or two of them here. We have already mentioned the concept of 'the margin' to which we shall frequently refer and which can help to illuminate particular problems. The economist's analysis of the substitution and income effects resulting from a change in price helps in assessing the disincentive effects of both taxation and welfare payments. The concept of education as an investment in human capital may clarify certain aspects of educational policy. In addition, some newer techniques such as cost-benefit analysis and output budgeting may sometimes be fruitfully applied to practical policy issues in the social services.

Secondly, the economist has an appreciation of the workings and characteristics of the price system. As we shall see in Chapter 4, one of the essential features of the price mechanism is the inter-dependence of prices; indeed, it is a truism that in the economic system 'everything depends on everything else'. This realization makes the economist aware of the less obvious repercussions of government policy so that he can better judge whether a particular government intervention in the economy is likely to achieve its objective. For example, rent control, as we shall see in later chapters, does not necessarily help the less well-off who seek houses to rent or buy; nor may a legal minimum wage be the best means of aiding those on low earned incomes.

Thirdly, economics is the oldest and most fully developed of the social sciences and the economist brings to the consideration of social policies a long experience of problems of measurement. His training makes him conscious not only of the uses but also of the limitations of statistics and of the other quantitative tools in his kit. Such an understanding is vital to the successful application of various techniques in the field of social policy.

What is meant by 'the economics of a church'?
The student may well ask what the economics of a church has to do with our theme. The answer is 'Not much directly'; some of the charitable work of churches may be relevant to the economics of social policy but this is not why we consider the church here. Our purpose is to demonstrate how the approach of the economist can be applied to a wide variety of situations and institutions and a church has been chosen as the illustration precisely because, on the face of it, a church with its spiritual connotations seems unlikely ground for the economist with his emphasis on material things.

We are not attempting a comprehensive analysis of the economics of a church but rather seeking to indicate the kind of issues which would be raised by such a study. We define a church as a group of people who meet together for religious worship in a building designed for that purpose. What are its objectives or ends? This kind of question might well provoke theological argument amongst church members, but most would agree to something like the following as a statement of objectives:

1. To maintain a meeting place for church members primarily for the purpose of sustaining their corporate faith (which might be called, for convenience, the 'fellowship' objective);
2. to seek to convert others to that faith (the 'missionary' objective);
3. to help those in need both in the local community and in the world at large regardless of their religious affiliations (the 'caring' objective).

To achieve these aims a church disposes certain real resources which consist of a building and site, an ordained full-time minister and the part-time labour of lay members. In money terms the expenses might consist of the costs of heating, lighting and maintaining the building (and possibly interest on money borrowed to construct it), the upkeep of the site, the payment of the minister's salary and financial contributions to good causes. The money income consists of what the members give from their own incomes or raise by various church 'efforts' (e.g. an annual Spring Fair), and possibly rents from occasional lettings of the premises.

The main economic issues regularly faced by the church members revolve around the use of the buildings, the minister and the lay talent. Thus, premises will be used for fellowship for only a few hours per week; indeed, church buildings are probably the most under-utilized 'plant' in the country. The church buildings may be capable of use as part of the caring function of the church, for example, a 'Senior Citizens' Club', set up by the church, which regularly meets in the church parlour. Otherwise, the most obvious way to use the premises economically is to try to let them to other bodies whose use does not clash with church activities. If the church can 'spread its overheads' in this way, it releases resources to increase its effectiveness elsewhere. The church's 'labour' as well as its 'capital' can be used efficiently or inefficiently. The full-time minister, as well as being the spiritual leader, is expected to combine the capabilities of scholar, teacher, social worker and administrator; to equip him he has received a long and specialist training. It is good economics to try to ensure that the minister spends his time in ways which use his trained skills. Thus, if ministers are expected to visit members of their congregation, which necessarily entails much travelling, a sensible church minimizes travelling time by helping its minister to run a car. Similarly, it may be an uneconomical use of ministerial time and church resources not to provide secretarial assistance for a minister whose job entails much correspondence and other writing. Economical use of its resources requires also that the varied skills of the ordinary church members should be carefully employed. Thus, for example, laymen should be selected for church offices so that their capabilities closely match their functions.

These are relatively simple and obvious economic considerations; but a wider perspective raises more complex issues. Thus, the site of a city-centre church may have risen enormously in value. Should such a church building and site be sold to a developer and a new church built on cheaper land outside the town centre? To do so might release resources for the more effective pursuit of the missionary and caring activities of the church. Sometimes a conflict between objectives may emerge. For many a local church the effort to maintain the fabric monopolizes, or at least dominates, its activities to the neglect of the other objectives. Yet for some members the missionary and caring objectives are paramount; hence some may take the radical view that fellowship should be sustained by members meeting in each other's homes or occasionally hiring a hall, while the church premises should be sold to provide funds to help the needy.

Another dimension is given to the economics of a church when it is appreciated that most local churches are members of a denomination (such as the Church of England or the Methodist Church) and all, or nearly all, churches see themselves as members of a world-wide Christian Church. With declining church membership and changing living patterns in the population, the economic problem of under-utilized church plant has been accentuated. One answer is for neighbouring churches (of the same or of different denominations) to unite. To dispose of one of the buildings provides a capital sum from the sale proceeds and saves running costs which are not restricted to the reduced heating, lighting, cleaning and maintenance; with one local church and one congregation instead of two there is also saving in the time taken in church government and even in preparing and preaching sermons. On the other hand, there may be some disadvantages in closing one church, such as extra travelling time and costs to some church members.

We are not seeking to suggest that only economic factors are relevant in determining matters such as the amalgamation of local churches; nor, to repeat an earlier point, do we pretend to have touched on, let alone examined thoroughly, all the economic aspects of a church. But perhaps enough has been said to demonstrate two principles. Firstly, that economics is a study of how means or resources can best be used to secure objectives or ends; as such it is applicable not only to an individual, a household, a firm, a country, but also to almost any kind of institution or organization. Secondly, where the individual or organization seeks to achieve multiple objectives, as is generally the case, opportunity cost comes into play: because resources are scarce, the fuller attainment of one objective requires some sacrifice of another.

SUMMARY AND CONCLUSIONS

Economics is a study of the use of scarce resources to satisfy wants or attain objectives. Economic comprehension is often helped by considering 'real' resources (land, labour, capital) rather than money, which is primarily a means of exchange. Social economics is concerned with matters directly affecting the standard of living and the quality of life. Social policy measures necessarily entail value judgments; this should not debar the participation of the economist but he should be clearly aware that they are being made. The economist brings to the study of social issues a particular perspective, some developed tools of analysis, an appreciation of the workings of the market mechanism and an experience of problems of measurement.

2 Methods of the Social Sciences

Characteristics of the Social Sciences

Economics is the scientific study of an aspect of human behaviour. Because its subject matter involves behaviour of human beings it is called a *social* science, in the same way as sociology, politics or psychology. Science is sometimes defined as a systematized branch of knowledge; but it is more than this. A science seeks to explain the relationship between observed phenomena and to draw up laws or generalizations by means of which we can make forecasts or predictions about what will happen under certain circumstances. Science proceeds by means of two methods which, in practice, are inextricably inter-connected: deduction and induction. Deduction implies the logical working out of the implications of certain definitions, and the formulation of hypotheses or theories. Induction comprises experimentation, observation and the testing of theories against facts. In the simplest terms, these two methods might be said to be on the one hand thinking, and on the other looking at the real world.

The usefulness of a scientific theory or hypothesis rests on its applicability: the essence of science therefore is the appeal to fact. The more precise and quantitative are the generalizations of science the more useful they are likely to be; hence it has been said that 'science is measurement'.

Social sciences have particular characteristics. Because they are concerned with human behaviour and because human beings are not homogeneous but have their own individualities and eccentricities, prediction in the social sciences is more difficult than in the natural sciences. However, despite individual exceptions, generalizations about human behaviour can be made because such generalizations are about aggregates rather than individuals.

An example may help to illustrate the point. Some of the best known laws of economics relate to supply and demand. We could, for instance, draw up a law or prediction which said that 'If Baker A in a particular town raised the price of his bread, the quality remaining the same, whilst other bakers in the town kept to the old price without changing quality, then baker A would sell less bread'. Now this prediction, 'Baker A would sell less bread', would still hold true if some customers bought as much bread from Baker A as before for reasons of ignorance, loyalty or habit; and it would even still hold if one customer (Mr B) bought more bread from Baker A because B fell in love with the baker's daughter who served in the shop and he kept buying bread as an excuse to see her. These exceptions would not nullify the aggregate effect.

Another feature which makes prediction more difficult in the social sciences is that the social scientist can rarely if ever conduct experiments of the kind carried out by the natural scientist. In the physical sciences experiments can be conducted in the laboratory where the environment (temperature, humidity, etc.) can be carefully controlled so that reactions to a change in one variable can be isolated. In the social sciences this cannot be done; moreover, it is probably true that, in the social sciences as compared with the physical sciences, there are more 'other things' affecting the outcome which, ideally, we should wish to keep constant.

To illustrate this point, suppose that the Chancellor of the Exchequer wanted to know if a reduction of income tax by 5p in the £ would stimulate work effort. He would like to be able to try out this tax change on a small scale in carefully controlled conditions to see what happens before deciding to reduce tax in the country as a whole. But this he cannot do. He therefore reduces income tax for everyone and decides to observe the results so that he can use them for future policy. What he requires is some statistical indicator of changes in work effort following the tax reduction. An adviser might point out that in the coal mining industry there are some reliable statistics of absenteeism; if the tax reduction stimulates work effort, the absenteeism in the mines can be expected to drop. Unfortunately for the Chancellor, however, absenteeism is affected by many issues other than the rate of income tax and the Chancellor cannot hold these other things unchanged whilst he observes the effect of the tax reduction. Thus absenteeism may fall because of a growth of unemployment (which may make those in jobs work harder to save against a rainy day or may lead to a tightening of discipline in the mines); or because of a change in the age structure of the mining labour force, e.g. more younger miners; or because football teams from mining towns are doing particularly badly in the cup final; or because of bad weather, so that fewer miners take days off to go fishing; indeed it may change for a whole host of reasons outside the Chancellor's control. By advanced statistical techniques an attempt can be made to isolate a variety of different factors affecting the situation so as to obtain a measure of the tax effect; but the results from this method of testing the hypothesis (that reducing the basic rate of income tax increases work effort) have not the same degree of reliability as the physicist's laboratory experiment.

Another feature of the social sciences, which adds to their fascination but also their difficulty, is that people learn from past experience and adjust their reactions in a way which does not apply to inanimate objects. For example, suppose the government pursued a policy of assisting industries facing temporary depressions by reducing taxes on (or subsidizing) their products to lower prices and thus increase sales. This might work very well on one or two occasions. But it might then happen that a slight downturn in the sales of that industry stimulated a depression, because the public, noticing the downturn, postponed their purchases in anticipation of government intervention leading to lower future prices. A policy designed to stabilize sales would then become de-stabilizing because the expected policy measures have generated a new response.

It is a characteristic of the social sciences that what happens may have happened simply because enough people thought it was going to happen and acted accordingly. Thus, for example, the expectation of inflation breeds inflation. If people expect that prices are going to rise they will take this expectation into account in their economic bargains: they will seek extra large wage increases to offset the effect of the inflation they anticipate; if they lend money they will seek an extra high rate of interest as an insurance against inflation; and if they anticipate an early and speedy price rise they will hurry to buy goods to stock up before the rise takes place. But these increases in the costs of labour and capital and the extra demand for goods will all raise prices. Thus, if enough people expect prices to rise and act accordingly, prices will rise.

A related but different complication in the social sciences is that the very process of investigating human behaviour may alter it. For example, there is some evidence that public opinion polls on voting intentions at the time of a General Election alter the results of the election.[1] The party which was in the lead in the polls does less well in the election; its supporters may be more subject to apathy, whilst

[1] See, for example, a letter by Mr James Rothman, 'Voters and opinion polls', *The Times*, 12 March 1974.

the supporters of the party which is behind in the polls are more likely to turn out to support it.

The inability of the social scientist to conduct experiments of the laboratory type forces him into a heavy reliance on statistics. The word statistics is used in two senses. It can be broadly synonymous with numbers and refer essentially to a numerical record of past happenings. It can also be used to describe the discipline concerned with the techniques of quantitative measurement, so that the testing of hypotheses can be more rigorously carried out. The social scientist needs to employ statistics in both these senses. We shall not in this book be concerned with advanced statistical techniques; but the use and interpretation of even elementary statistics is so important in social economics that it is worth spending some time considering their value, and, in particular, the limitations, abuses and pitfalls associated with them.

Uses and Abuses of Statistics

Statistics are an essential component of social economics and social policy. They provide a basis of fact indispensable for explanation, diagnosis or policy formulation on social issues. By means of statistics we can obtain a summary picture of a situation which is more comprehensive than we would get from many pages of words. For example, if we want a broad view of the educational system, a single page of statistics could provide us with information such as the number of schools and colleges of various kinds; the number of universities and polytechnics; the number of students attending certain courses; the mode, median and mean sizes of each type of institution, and so on. Further, as we have seen, in the social sciences particular reliance has to be placed on statistics because of the impossibility of conducting controlled experiments under laboratory conditions.

But statistics have limitations and their use creates pitfalls for the unwary. Statistics may give misleading impressions either unwittingly or because the user deliberately seeks to mislead. It has been said by one of the more honest politicians that 'Politicians use statistics as a drunken man uses a lamp-post—for support and not illumination', and this failing is not confined to politicians. There is a story (doubtless apocryphal) of a rather subtle Russian economic adviser who was asked by his political boss for his forecast of the Russian economy for the following year. He considered that the economy was moving into a slump, but aware of the disfavour attaching to those who brought bad tidings, he replied, 'About average'. The politician questioned him further: 'What do you mean by average?' The adviser replied, 'Next year will be worse than this year but better than the year after.'

We can group the pitfalls of statistics under six or seven separate heads, although they overlap somewhat.

1. *The danger of a misleading impression because of the particular way (one might say the emotional overtones) in which the statistics are presented.* Different impressions may, for example, be created by the use of an adjective. Suppose that 10 per cent of those who enrol for degrees in a particular university fail to complete the course successfully. Then to say that: '*Fully* 10 per cent did not complete the course successfully' creates a somewhat different impression from saying that '*Barely* 10 per cent did not complete the course successfully'. To give a different example, in the United Kingdom a million unemployed corresponds to approximately 4 per cent of the work-force. A somewhat different impression is created by each of the following statements, even though they give precisely the same information:

'There are one million unemployed.'

'Four per cent of the workforce is unemployed.'

'Ninety-six per cent of those seeking work are in employment.' Even more subtly, different impressions may be conveyed by the kinds of approach illustrated by the reaction of the optimist and the pessimist to half a glass of beer: the optimist regards his glass as half *full*, whilst the pessimist regards his as half *empty*.

2. *The danger of generalizing on the basis of an inadequate sample.* This is a pit into which all but a few of us fall on occasion. We know a few instances of something, perhaps even quite a large number, and we assume that they are typical and generalize accordingly. In fact, they may not be typical either because our sample was not sufficiently large or because there was some particular bias in it, or both.

Such insufficiently supported generalizations are the vice of the casual TV reporter/pollster who asks the first twenty people he meets in the streets of a particular town their opinion about some topical issue, claims that he has questioned a random sample of the population, and assumes that the views given are representative of the nation. In fact, not only is his sample too small, it is necessarily biased in that the people in the street of a particular town at a particular time on a particular day cannot be representative of the community at large. Such a sample overweights housewives who do their own shopping and probably underweights those who go out to work, the old, those who have shopping delivered, country dwellers and people who prefer to shop in the suburbs or in other towns. There is no reason to believe that the few people interviewed have the same characteristics as those who are underweighted in the sample. In fact, the sample was not random in the statistical sense in that it did not offer every member of the population an exactly equal chance of appearing in the sample.

Another illustration of bias is provided by the problem faced by the historian of, say, wheat prices in the sixteenth century. Although there are many surviving price quotations, most of them necessarily refer to institutions, for they kept records; but institutions might buy or sell on different terms from those of ordinary people. Also, because these institutions often grew their own wheat, many quotations might be accounting prices only. Further, there might be seasonal bias in the figures because they survive from a time when price variations were much greater between seasons than now, or a locational bias because town and country prices, and prices between one town and another, differed more markedly than they do today because of poorer transport facilities.

3. *Too ready an assumption of a causal relationship.* A notable danger is that of jumping from a statistical relationship to the assumption of a causal connection. For example, in 1973 the death rate (measured as so many deaths per thousand population) was 11.9 for England and Wales, 12.8 for Bristol, and 13.5 for Bath. There might be a temptation to conclude that Bath was a relatively unhealthy place to live compared with Bristol or that its health services were inferior to those of Bristol, which in turn were inferior to those of the country as a whole. If we include the figure for Bournemouth at 18.8, however, it is clear that this cannot be the explanation. Indeed, this probably suggests the answer to the reader. Differences between death rates in towns in England and Wales are likely to depend mainly on variations in the age structure of their populations. Bath and Bournemouth have a relatively high proportion of older people who are subject to higher death rates; in other words, they are retirement areas—people go there to die! If we apply an 'area comparability factor'[1] which allows for the differences in the age

---

[1] The area comparability factor also makes allowance for the uneven dispersion of certain types of hospital throughout the country. One town may have a higher death rate than another simply because it happens to contain more of certain kinds of hospitals.

and sex structure, then we find that the death rate for Bristol is lower than that for England and Wales, whilst Bournemouth and Bath have lower death rates still (Table 2.1).

Table 2.1

	Crude death rates, 1973 (per 1000 population)	Area comparability factor	Ratio of local adjusted death rate to national rate*
England and Wales	11.9	1.00	1.00
Bath	13.5	0.81	0.91
Bristol	12.8	0.89	0.95
Bournemouth	18.8	0.58	0.91

* A figure of less than 1 implies lower death rates than the national average; the lower the figure the lower the rate when allowance is made for the age structure of the population.

Similarly, the death rate of a national population may vary as a result of changes in age structure, e.g. it is possible for the overall national death rate to be rising when the death rate at each age group is falling, simply because there is an increasing proportion of the population in the older age groups.

In fact, statistics can suggest causal relationships though they can never prove them. The most statistics can do is to establish the degree of correlation, i.e. to demonstrate how closely one variable changes with another. The relationship is asymmetrical. It may be possible by statistics to *dis*prove a supposed causal relationship because a causal relationship may imply a correlation—which can be shown not to exist. But demonstrating a statistical correlation does not prove the existence of a causal relationship (although this may often be the most plausible explanation).

To illustrate this point, we can look at an industrial example. The National Coal Board in a 'Pit Profile' once published some figures comparing the output per man shift (OMS) in a group of highly mechanized mines with the OMS in a group with little mechanization. As was to be expected, the first group had the higher OMS But the author was wrong to conclude that the whole of the difference was due to mechanization. There are reasons for believing that the pits lending themselves most to mechanization would also be those where the OMS would be higher even if they were not mechanized. This is because mechanization is more likely in mines where coal seams are wide rather than in mines with narrow seams and in new mines rather than in those nearing exhaustion. Thus the factors promoting mechanization would also favour a higher OMS even without it.

4. *Often our statistics do not measure exactly what we wish to measure but only something near it.* This deficiency may be because what we seek to measure is really incapable of precise measurement. Thus, suppose we want to assess whether the health of the nation has improved between two years. We can look at certain relevant statistics, for example, changes in death rates and life expectations; variations in time lost from work because of sickness; numbers of visits to the doctor; changes in the proportion of the population annually suffering from particular diseases; and so on. Each measure could be elaborated to a high degree of sophistication, but none of them, nor even all of them taken together, quite give us what we want.

Alternatively we may be unable to measure exactly what we want because the available statistics have been compiled for particular administrative purposes and/or arise out of particular administrative procedures. For example, our statistics of income and wealth distribution are derived from data compiled by the Inland Revenue in the process of tax collection. Such data have deficiencies arising from their source, e.g. they do not allow for tax evasion and avoidance, or for incomes or wealth which for one reason or another may be exempt from taxation. A notable example of statistics which do not meet the requirements of the social economist are the official unemployment figures. The economist wants to know the number of people who are out of work and who would like to be employed at the current wage rates. The official figures show the numbers of people who have registered as unemployed. The two measures may be different. The biggest incentive to register as unemployed is to collect unemployment pay; but some people, e.g. many married women, are not eligible to receive it and therefore may not trouble to register. Again, the economist's concept would include people who have unwillingly retired early because, having become unemployed towards the end of their working lives, they have felt that their chances of obtaining another job in their own trade are small; but such people would not appear in the official unemployment statistics. On the other hand students on vacation may register as unemployed. If they are genuinely seeking work their unemployment is clearly of a different nature from that of the majority on the register; and some students may be less interested in taking a job than in securing an entitlement to supplementary benefit. Again, the significance of the unemployment figures may change over time because of changes in the relationship between take-home pay when unemployed and take-home pay in employment; this relationship may alter for a number of reasons including changes in the nature and rates of benefit, in wage rates, and in income tax thresholds and rates (wages being taxable but not unemployment benefit). The higher the take-home pay in unemployment as a proportion of take-home pay in work, the less incentive there is for unemployed workers to take a job soon; hence, on average, they may stay longer on the register, which causes a rise in the unemployment figures. Because these figures are used as indicators of the state of the economy, such changes in their underlying meaning may mislead the policymakers seeking to regulate the economy.

5. *Pitfalls associated with a change in base or difference of base.* Many examples under this head arise from the use of percentages. It is often over-looked that if, for example, an increase in production of 50 per cent between one year and the next is then followed by a reduction of 50 per cent the following year, this does not bring you back to the same level of production from which you started. To take another example: misleading conclusions may readily be drawn from voting figures such as those set out below:

| | *Percentage of poll* | | |
	Conservatives	*Labour*	*Liberal*
General election	70	25	5
By-election	49	15	36

Political commentators might argue that in the by-election the Conservative Party had fared worse than the Labour Party because the Conservative vote had dropped by 21 per cent of the poll whereas the Labour vote had dropped by only 10 per cent of the poll. A more convincing argument is that the Conservatives did less badly than Labour. The falling away of Conservative support had been 30 per cent (21 on 70) whilst Labour had lost 40 per cent of its support (10 on 25). The reduction in Conservative support only looks bigger because they started off with a much larger proportion of the total vote. (If the reader is in doubt, imagine voting figures where the Conservative vote had dropped from 90 to 70 per cent of the poll and the Labour vote from 10 per cent to nothing: it would be absurd to argue that Labour had done better than the Conservatives because their vote had only fallen by 10 per cent of the poll whilst the Conservative vote had fallen by 20 per cent.)

Another frequent illustration of this point arises from the relationship between prices and wages. Not infrequently, in wage negotiations, trade unions and employers appear to be presenting mutually incompatible arguments. Trade unions argue that prices have risen more than wages whilst employers maintain that wages have risen more than prices. Both may be right. The validity of the statement depends on the time period taken and each may choose a different period. For the past 30 years or so the movement of both prices and wages has been consistently upwards, although the rate of increase has varied. But whereas price increases have been more or less continuous each month, wage increases for any particular group of workers have been discontinuous, taking place at intervals of perhaps a year. This difference provides almost endless scope for choosing time periods, according to inclination and interest, where prices can be shown to have risen more than wages or vice versa. To take an extreme illustration, suppose that wage negotiations are taking place on 1 January 1973; that the last wage increase was of 15 per cent on 1 January 1972; and that prices have been rising at the rate of 12 per cent a year. Employers, taking a starting point of 31 December 1971, can argue that wages (15 per cent increase) have risen more than prices (12 per cent increase); whilst trade unions starting from 2 January 1972 can argue that prices (12 per cent increase) have risen more than wages (zero increase). Various other time periods (less extreme than that beginning immediately before or immediately after the last wage increase) could be taken to yield one or other result.

6. *Difficulties arising from differences in definition.* It is essential, if correct conclusions are to be drawn from statistical comparisons, that like is compared with like, or in other words that the user appreciates the definitions of the entities being compared. In comparisons over time, for administrative, legal or economic reasons the basis of a series of statistics may change thus affecting the validity of the comparison (e.g. the coverage of unemployment statistics before and after the Second World War). Even the geographical coverage may alter—thus the definition of the United Kingdom changed significantly in 1922 when Southern Ireland ceased to be a part of it. It is particularly important in international compariso

to ensure the equivalence of what is being compared; for example, it was a regular pastime of politicians in the sixties to compare the annual 'output' of technologists in the USSR, the USA and the UK; but care was not always taken to adjust the figures to ensure comparison of like with like. To mention one discrepancy, the Russians counted economists amongst their technology graduates, not so the Americans or the British.

7. *The need to 'break down' aggregates.* Finally a brief warning that aggregates can be misleading and hide more than they reveal. For example, an index of total production might remain constant one year with the next; but the constant aggregate might conceal very considerable variations between industries, with substantial expansion in one industry being offset by contraction in another. Similarly, as Chapter 5 will demonstrate, a rise in total government expenditure tells us little until we know whether the increase is government spending on goods and services or on cash transfers (which leave the actual spending to the individual); whether on capital or current account; or whether it simply results from an administrative rearrangement by which a cash grant replaces a tax concession.

Inconclusion, in case the emphasis on the dangers and limitations of statistics has created a misleading impression, it must be stressed that statistics are an indispensable aid to the study of social economics and to social policy-making. They enable us to measure, if not always exactly, at least the order of magnitude. The lesson to be learnt from this catalogue of the misuse of statistics is that they should be employed with due appreciation of definitions used and the method of compilation; and hence with due appreciation of their limitations.

Is Economics Really a Science?

It is sometimes asserted of economics (and indeed of social science as a whole) that it is not really a science at all; that it lacks the essential hallmarks of science. Those who argue thus often themselves misunderstand the nature of science. But controversy on whether economics should or should not be called a science is not very fruitful. More useful is to discuss the similarities and differences between the physical sciences and economics (as the most developed of the social sciences).

Both the physical sciences and economics have a similar methodology: each is concerned to study data, to formulate hypotheses and to test these hypotheses against the facts—the simplest hypothesis consistent with all known facts being accepted. Both seek to propound laws or generalizations with as wide an applicability as possible, and much of economics is concerned with abstract model building aiming at widespread applicability. Both economics and the physical sciences seek to develop a predictive capacity, the purpose of prediction being to control.

What of the differences? Firstly, it is sometimes said that science is 'certain' and economics is not. But this is not so. The generalizations of each are statements of probabilities. The history of science abounds with examples of theories which at one time fitted all known facts and were held to be valid but which subsequent facts refuted. However, there is a difference. Science (at any rate middle order science as distinct from theories about whether the universe is expanding or contracting) can use controlled experiments to validate a hypothesis and the experiments are repeatable. The economist can rarely do that. At best he may be able to compare the reactions of two groups of people similar in certain respects and different in one important respect; and he can conduct opinion samples and the like. But much of his testing is concerned with the correlation between two 'time series' (i.e. sets of data recorded over a period of time) and we have already said something of the dangers of assuming that a correlation implies a causal relationship. In other words, the scientist's theory is of a higher order of probability than an economist's because of the superiority of his testing procedures.

Secondly, it is sometimes argued that science is objective and economics is not. But the objectivity of science is not absolute. A subjective element enters into the formulation of an experiment, into the reading of the results and perhaps particularly into the source of the 'hunch' which may constitute the creative leap of the imagination which generates a new hypothesis to fit the facts. Economists claim for their science a 'positive' as distinct from a 'normative' role and much of the model-building of economists may be as free of value judgments as that of the scientist. Nonetheless, because economics is concerned with human beings, subjective valuations are more likely to intrude into the economist's work especially when he deals with economic policy. As we argued in Chapter 1, the necessity of value judgments does not preclude the economist from a policy role, although it is important for the economist to make such judgments explicit.

Thirdly, it is argued that science is exact and economics is not.

Again, the issue is one of relative rather than absolute difference. Science has grown in precision as it has developed. The mathematical model-building of economics is exact, although often not very useful, whilst many of the more useful predictions of economics are qualitative rather than quantitative.

The main differences between natural science and economics stem from two features. Firstly, the nature of the subject matter. Because economics is concerned with human behaviour it faces limitations both in its methods of testing and in its predictive generalizations not faced by a science which deals with the physical universe. Secondly, economics, to quote an eminent economist, 'has hardly yet reached its seventeenth century',[1] and is as yet 'underdeveloped'.

SUMMARY AND CONCLUSIONS

Economics is a social science. Like the physical sciences it is concerned with formulating and testing hypotheses with the object of deriving generalizations by means of which prediction is possible. But because economics is still relatively underdeveloped and because its subject matter is human behaviour, the formulation of reliable predictions is more difficult. Social economics, in common with economics as a whole, relies heavily on statistics, but there are many pitfalls associated with their use.

[1] Phelps Brown, E. H., 'The underdevelopment of economics', *The Economic Journal*, 325, **82**, March 1972, p. 10.

3 The National Output

The Economic System

Probably the most important single economic statistic for any nation is the figure of national output, usually quoted in the form of GNP (Gross National Product). Our two final comments in the previous chapter on the pitfalls of statistics apply to this figure with particular force. It is an aggregate which can mislead if we pay no attention to its components; and similarly, if we are to use it in a meaningful way, we must understand the basis on which it is compiled and the definitions which underlie it. Our object in this chapter is to achieve that understanding and at the same time to learn something more about how the economy works.

Professor Sir John Hicks, in his admirable book *The Social Framework*,[1] has defined the economic system in two ways. Firstly, as an association of producers to satisfy the wants of consumers. Secondly, as a system of mutual exchanges. These two definitions are not alternatives, but rather two complementary ways of looking at the economic system.

We work in order to gain the means to satisfy our wants. Employers employ workers either because the workers directly satisfy the wants of the employers (for example, a gardener may satisfy his employer's desire for an attractive environment) or—as in most cases—because the employers consider that the product the workers help to make will satisfy the wants of some third person who is willing to pay for it. Hence, although the description may sound a little grand for an arrangement which may sometimes be inefficient, and where some of the wants satisfied are trivial or even harmful, an economic system can be thought of as an association of producers with the objective of satisfying consumers' wants.

But, of course, the producers and consumers are to a large extent

[1] Hicks, J. R., *The Social Framework*, Clarendon Press, 1971. The author's treatment of the subject of this chapter owes much to the work of Professor Hicks.

the same people. In advanced economies, people do not work to satisfy their own wants directly; each family does not grow all its own food, build its own house or make its own clothes. To enable people to work in ways which suit their inclinations and abilities and so that they can improve their skills by training and practice, they specialize in making only one product or part of a product; then, in effect, they exchange the products they help to make for the goods and services they wish to consume. Hence, as well as an association of producers to satisfy the wants of consumers, the economic system is an arrangement of mutual exchange.

These exchanges are generally accomplished not by barter but through the medium of money, which enormously facilitates the exchange process. Besides those who contribute to the productive process by using their labour, we can also include as producers those who lend their property to help to satisfy consumers' wants and who get a share of the product by so doing. (This does not pre-judge the issue of whether private ownership of the means of production is desirable, or whether the share of the output going to property owners is appropriate; it simply recognizes the situation which exists in an economy with a private enterprise sector.) There is one further complication which must be taken into account, namely the economic activities of government. Many of the activities of government, for example the provision of defence forces, do not seem to fit into the pattern of a system of production to satisfy the wants of consumers. However, we can fit them into this framework if we think of them as contributing to the satisfaction of collective wants, the wants of the community as a whole.

Definitions

This picture of the economy provides us with a set of mutually consistent definitions which are important in themselves, as indicating the meaning which economists attach to particular words, and because they provide the foundation on which British national income and output statistics are constructed. It is a little unfortunate that many terms used in everyday speech are also used by economists' but with a different—and invariably more precise—meaning. Hence, if we are to avoid confusion, we must define terms carefully. Thus, 'production' is the process of satisfying wants through exchange; a 'producer' is a person engaged in satisfying wants through exchange; and 'consumption' describes the satisfaction of wants of all kinds, not just hunger or thirst. Two points about the definition of production need to be stressed. First, it includes not only the supply of material goods but also of services. A retailer, a doctor, or a teacher each provides a service, and each can be regarded as a producer just as much as a miner or a factory operative. They all help to satisfy wants. Indeed, the distinction between those who 'make material things' and those who provide services is less clear cut than is often thought. Essentially, for example, both the miner and the retail coal merchant help to move coal from where it has less use to where it has more use. The second point is that we only count as production those things which are exchanged in the market, i.e. which are sold. The justification for this procedure is expediency rather than logic. In practice, when we want to add up the national output, it is very difficult to allow for, or to put a value on, goods and services which are not sold. Moreover, if we once started to include such services, it would be very difficult to know where to draw the line. For example, we clearly count as part of national output the value of the services a man buys from the barber who shaves him or the services of the shoe-shine boy whom he pays to brush his shoes. Should we then also count the services a man renders himself in shaving himself and cleaning his own shoes? The implications of defining production to include only those goods and services exchanged (sold) in the market is that some very important services in the community do not enter into official figures of output, in particular the services rendered by the housewife to her family in the home. Also, vegetables and flowers grown for home consumption, and 'do-it-yourself' work in the house, do not count as part of production.

Classification of Goods

The goods which result from the productive process can usefully be classified into consumers' and producers' goods. Consumers' goods are those which satisfy consumers' wants directly, e.g. food or clothes. Producers' goods are those goods which are stages on the way to the satisfaction of consumers' wants, which help to make consumer goods, e.g. raw materials or factory machines. Professor Hicks also makes a useful distinction (which applies to both producers' and consumers' goods) between single-use and durable-use goods. Single-use goods are those which, once used, are completely used up (such as items of food), although with producers' goods this may simply mean that they are passed in another form to the next stage of production. Durable-use goods are goods which can go on being used for a considerable period of time, such as a TV set or an automatic loom.[1] This distinction is of considerable importance when we come to consider the control of the economy in Chapter 15. Single-use goods tend to be quickly consumed and are therefore produced in fairly regular quantities. Durable-use goods, especially durable-use producers' goods, are subject to much greater fluctuations in demand, partly because they can always be made to last a little longer, if necessary, by some patching and extra maintenance. It follows that the production of them will also be more irregular than that of single-use goods. This distinction is therefore important for understanding causes of unemployment.

This picture of the economic system that we have presented is summarized in Figure 3.1.

Figure 3.1   The Economic System.

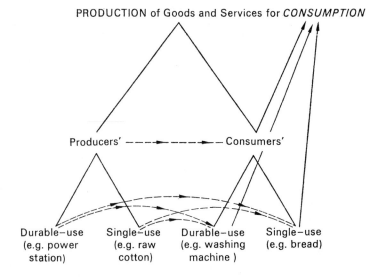

PRODUCTION of Goods and Services for *CONSUMPTION*

Producers' — — — ▶ — — — ▶ — Consumers'

Durable—use (e.g. power station)   Single—use (e.g. raw cotton)   Durable—use (e.g. washing machine)   Single—use (e.g. bread)

Production in the Annual Period

We can only talk about production in any meaningful way as a 'flow' over a period of time. When we are talking of national output

---

[1] Note that a durable-use good is not the same as a durable good. A durable good is non-perishable; it will last for a long time if *not* used, but it may not be capable of being used over a considerable period of time, e.g. a piece of coal. In general, when people speak of 'consumer durables' they have in mind what we have called 'durable-use consumers' goods'.

the most usual period to take is a year. At the beginning of a year there will be a stock of capital consisting of goods of all kinds, but especially durable-use goods, and also of land and other natural resources. Labour will work in conjunction with the capital and land to produce a stream of goods and services. All the services and most of the goods will be consumed during the year and will largely determine the living standards of the members of that community in that year. Some of the goods will be producers' goods which are both used and used up during the year, and some other goods will be produced during the year and remain in existence at the end of the year to add to the stock of goods in the following year. This addition to capital is called investment. Part of the capital with which the year had started will also have been used up during the year; this we call capital consumption or depreciation. New capital produced and available at the end of the year, minus the depreciation of the initial capital stock, gives us a figure of net investment for the year.

The proportions in which output goes to consumption and investment strongly affect current compared with future living standards. The more output going to net investment in a year the less will go to consumption in that year, but the larger will be the initial stock of equipment in the next and subsequent years and hence, other things being equal, the larger will future living standards be.

Besides goods and the services of labour there is one other item which is counted as part of output and of consumption—the use of house room. There is a basic problem of how to treat all durable-use consumers' goods arising from the very fact they can go on being used for a considerable period of time: at what point should we count them as output and consumption? Should it be when they are purchased or should they be regarded as making a continuing contribution to output throughout their usable life? The point can be made clear by an illustration. Supposing there was some national emergency such as a war and the government introduced clothes' rationing of such an extreme kind that the ration for the first period was zero. This would not mean that nobody received any satisfaction from clothes over that period, even though the amount of satisfaction would diminish. We would go on using our old clothes, patching them and darning them to see us through. Should all consumer durable goods, then, be treated as providing a continuing output throughout their lives?

This might be the most logical decision to take, but in practice what happens is that only the output of houses is treated in this way. Houses are the most important type of durable-use consumers' goods, and it is common practice for the use of houses to be paid for each week in the form of rent, just as each week there is a food bill. Hence, in British national output statistics, an annual value is attributed to all house room, which counts as part of the output and consumption of the year. No other consumers' durable-use goods are treated in this way; all others are treated as contributing to output and consumption only in the period in which they are purchased.

We can thus produce a new diagram amplifying Figure 3.1.

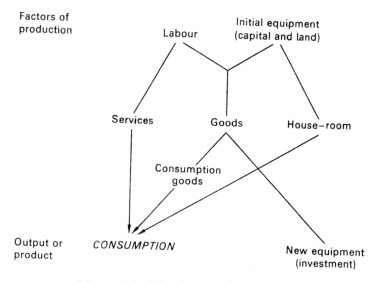

Figure 3.2   The Production Process.

It is useful at this point to pull together a few more definitions arising from the previous paragraphs. *Capital* is a stock of goods of all kinds existing at a particular point in time which can be used to satisfy wants in the immediate and more distant future. In ordinary speech we usually think of capital in terms of money, or paper assets such as stocks and shares, but, as we indicated in Chapter 1, underlying money concepts are real concepts. The two are related. Money, as the medium of exchange, is the means by which capital goods are acquired. Also, when we think of capital, we have in mind pre-eminently producers' durable-use goods, such as industrial buildings and machines; and these are the real assets which underlie the paper assets of the shareholders. When a shareholder lends to a firm by buying a share he pays in monetary terms and this money is likely to be used for the acquisition of producers' durable-use goods or perhaps producers' single-use goods in the form of stocks of materials. Although he cannot readily get his hands on them, these 'real' assets really belong to the shareholder. *Investment* constitutes the addition to capital over a period of time. Capital used up in a period of time we call *depreciation* or capital consumption. Whereas capital itself can only be measured at a point of time, investment and depreciation must necessarily relate to a time period.

From Figure 3.2, we can see that (*gross*) *output* or *product* consists of the value of consumption goods and services plus the value of new equipment. We can distinguish between gross investment and net investment. *Gross investment* is all the new equipment produced during a year with no allowance for depreciation. *Net investment* takes account of the depreciation during the period. Gross output can be defined as consumption plus gross investment and *net output* as consumption plus net investment.

In calculating the total of output we exclude those producers' goods which are used up during the year—which may in fact simply mean that they are passed on to another stage of production. These goods are all embodied in the consumers' goods which form part of the year's consumption and if we were to count them as producers' goods as well as consumers' goods we would be double counting. Thus, for example, we count as part of output the loaves of bread produced during the year. But we do not also count the wheat and the flour that went into those loaves. The bread incorporates these other single-use producers' goods which have become embodied in the final consumers' goods.

This account of the productive process and the definitions arising out of it are central to the idea of what constitutes the national output, and indeed to an appreciation of the limitations of the measure. But, before we proceed to see how national output is measured in practice, we need to explore certain inter-relationships.

Income, Output and Expenditure

Central to an understanding of the national output and its method of compilation is an appreciation of the basic inter-relationship that exists between output, income and expenditure. We can understand this most easily if we take a simplified picture of the economic system assuming a self-contained community, no government activity and no saving, i.e. that everybody always spends the whole of their current income on consumption. In this situation there is a simple equality between income, output and expenditure. Households provide the services of labour to firms and in exchange receive a payment in money terms. Firms produce a flow of goods and services which are bought by households. The total receipts of firms are paid out in either wages or profits and become somebody's income. All incomes are spent on goods and services produced by firms. So we have the equality where—in aggregate—expenditure, income and the value of output are the same. We can make our model slightly more realistic by assuming that households have some savings which take the form of lending to firms, which the firms in turn use to provide investment. The basic equality remains the same, but now some firms will be making equipment which is bought by other firms. A new equality emerges from this model, namely that between saving and investment. This interrelationship between income, output and expenditure in our simple model is shown in Figure 3.3.

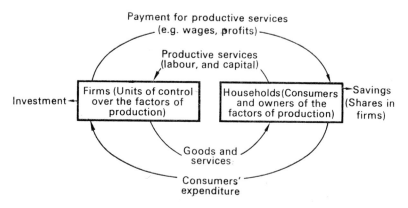

Self–contained community with no government activity and all saving in the form of shares in firms

Figure 3.3   Circular Flow of Output, Income and Expenditure.

If we take other complications into account such as the existence of financial intermediaries, other forms of saving, e.g. home ownership, profits made by firms but not distributed, the existence of non-profit-making bodies such as charities owning property and lending it to the productive system, it still remains true that, for the community as a whole, the equality between income, output and expenditure holds exactly for a wholly self-contained community with no government activity. The basic equation can be set out as follows:

INCOME	=	OUTPUT	=	EXPENDITURE
Earnings of labour, land and capital (wages, salaries, rent, profit, interest)		Consumption + Net investment		Consumption + Saving

When we take into account government activity and allow for international trade, including international lending and borrowing, then certain questions are raised and certain adjustments become necessary.

Allowing for Government Economic Activity

Let us start by considering government activity. The first question is whether we should regard all the services provided by government as part of national output or whether some of them should be considered as a necessary cost of producing the rest of the output. Consider, for example, the costs of the police force. Some of the duties of the police are the protection of property and in that respect their duties are similar to those of a nightwatchman privately employed by a firm. We do not count the value of the nightwatchman's services as contributing to output over and above the product of the factory in which he is employed. For example, suppose a nightwatchman is employed at a factory making matches; then the watchman's wage is a cost of making matches which is embodied in the value of the total output of matches produced by the factory. There is no additional output over and above the value of the matches as a result of the nightwatchman's activities. In the same way it would be logical to regard police activities concerned with the protection of property as a necessary cost of the production of the remainder of output, and not as contributing to output over and above the rest. Similarly the whole of the defence services could be regarded as a necessary cost incurred for the protection of the community, which makes possible the production of the rest of output. Or again, take the case of a minister, say the Minister for Energy. Should we regard him as contributing to output over and above the supply of electricity, gas, and other forms of energy in the community, or should we regard his services (and the salary he is paid) as being a cost of producing this supply of energy? This dilemma does not apply to all public sector output. Thus the State education system and the National Health Service clearly provide identifiable benefit over and above the remainder of output.

In practice, whatever may be the logic of treating the defence services and the services of the police as necessary costs of the remainder of output, all services provided by government are regarded as additional services to the community over and above the rest of output. This is clearly of considerable importance in assessing changes in the national output, because the police, the defence forces, the services of ministers and civil servants do not, on the whole, create benefits resulting in *individual* improvements in welfare. Thus, for example, if there is an increase in expenditure on defence paid for by additional taxes which reduce the private citizen's ability to buy goods and services in the market, the total national income and national output may remain the same, but the volume of goods and services that individuals personally enjoy has been diminished.

A second problem relates to transfer incomes. Transfer incomes are regular receipts which citizens obtain by cash transfers from the government without an equivalent economic service being generated. Examples are family allowances, retirement pensions, and interest on the national debt. These are incomes not derived from economic activity. The funds are obtained by the government from some people, in the form of taxes or loans, and passed to other people who do not render an economic service in exchange. When we are looking at the total value of incomes we must deduct such transfer incomes, otherwise the total of the incomes column would come out higher than that of the value of output. To put it another way, if we did not deduct transfer incomes we would be double-counting; we would be counting the same income both when it was generated by economic activity on the part of the taxpayer, and again as the income of the beneficiary of the state transfer where there was no output generated.

A third problem relating to government activity arises from the valuation of output. The market prices paid by consumers may differ from the value of the product measured at the cost of the factors of production embodied in it, because of the existence of taxes on expenditure and of subsidies. In order to find the 'factor cost' value of expenditure, we need to deduct from the expenditure column what might be called net outlay taxes; that is to say, we need to deduct the total of taxes on expenditure and add subsidies on expenditure. This will give us an aggregate value of the expenditure column equal to the value of the income and output columns.

Allowing for International Economic Relations

Allowing for international economic relations means further adjustment. The *composition* of expenditure and output will differ because part of output will now be exported and part of expenditure will be spent on imports. Similarly, net investment may now mean foreign investment, and saving may take the form of saving in overseas assets. The main adjustments, however, are required to take account of the position of creditor and debtor nations. Creditor nations are those with a net income from foreign assets; the income from past overseas lending exceeds that from overseas borrowing, so that the citizens of the country receive an income against which there is no corresponding output within their own country. The output which generates that income is an output within another country from assets owned by the nationals of the lending country at which we are looking. Thus, in order that the three columns of income, output and expenditure should be equivalent in value, with creditor nations we need to add to the value of (home produced) output their net income from foreign assets. With debtor nations the reverse is true; their income will be less than the value of their output because some of that output is due to foreigners. The same formal adjustment to the equations will serve as for creditor nations if we recognize that the item 'net income from foreign assets' may be negative.

These various modifications to allow for government activity and international economic relations are summarized in Figure 3.4.

INCOME	=	OUTPUT	=	EXPENDITURE (at factor cost)
−		+		− Taxes on goods and services
Transfer payments		Net income from foreign assets		+ Subsidies on goods and services

Figure 3.4 Adjusting Income, Output and Expenditure to Allow for (i) Government Economic Activity and (ii) International Economic Relations.

Adding-up the National Income

The total of the national income (output or expenditure) can, of course, be obtained by any of three routes: by collecting data on income, output or expenditure. The method (or methods), chosen in practice depends on the statistical material available. In the United Kingdom the most regular data is provided by the income method, where information on incomes collected by the Department of Inland Revenue for income tax purposes, together with material collected by the Department of Employment on wages, provides the statistical basis for an estimate of incomes. The output method yields particularly good results in years in which there is a census of production and a census of distribution, and these form the basis for output estimates in intermediate years. Data on expenditure is less complete, but can be used as something of a cross-check on estimates of particular components derived by the other methods.

In this book we have frequently stressed the significance or 'real' as against 'money' entities. Income and output consist basically of a flow of goods and services enjoyed or produced respectively. But in order to aggregate the goods and services and reduce them to some manageable form we need to value them in terms of a common denominator, i.e. money. Thus we measure the national income and national output in monetary terms. This gives rise to its own problems when the value of money changes. To some extent this can be allowed for, and in any case there is no practical alternative to using money as the means of adding together the vast list of goods and services which constitute income and output.

Concepts of the National Income

Our analysis enables us to distinguish different measures of national income and output according to what we include in it. Thus we can distinguish gross domestic product (GDP), which is the total output of the residents of a country, say the United Kingdom, and equals the value of income less net income from foreign assets. Gross national product (GNP) represents the total value of the domestic output of UK residents (GDP) plus net income from abroad (equivalent to the net output derived from overseas assets). The term 'gross' in both cases implies that no allowance has been made for depreciation or capital consumption; if we do make that allowance, then we reach the figures of net domestic product (NDP) or net national product (NNP) respectively. There are two sets of prices which we can use in valuing output: factor cost (FC) or market price (MP), the difference between them being taxes and subsidies on goods and services. Thus we have, in all, eight concepts as follows:

GNP at FC or MP

NNP at FC or MP

GDP at FC or MP

NDP at FC or MP

The most suitable measure to use in any particular case depends on the purpose in view and also to some extent on the accuracy of the statistics. In principle, perhaps the most meaningful measure for most purposes would be the net national output at factor cost (also referred to as *the* national income). This can be defined as the flow of goods and services available to members of the community, over a period of time, whilst maintaining capital intact. Using factor cost instead of market prices avoids distortions arising from changes in the structure of the tax system. But sometimes getting market price data may be easier than getting factor cost data; and the measure of depreciation, by means of which we obtain net product from gross product, is deficient and so a better series can often be obtained by using gross national product or gross domestic product. Probably the concept most frequently used is that of gross national product at factor cost.

When economists talk about economic growth they are normally referring to the growth of the national product.

The Uses of National Income and Output Statistics

The statistics of national output and income, and also the expenditure equivalents, provide a basic set of national accounts which are valuable for a variety of purposes. These figures are the essential components of economic planning and of government attempts to control the economy. The figures are important not only for the totals, but for the components, which can themselves be used for all sorts of purposes. We can, for instance, look at the distribution of income between factor shares (the proportion of income going to the owners of property and that going to labour), or between persons. We can see what proportion of output is being consumed, compared with that invested; how much consumption is private and how much public; what proportion of output goes for exports, and so on.

Despite their imperfections, the figures of national output from year to year provide probably the best single index of the economic progress of a country. They provide an overall figure of the changes in the value of goods and services available to the inhabitants of that community.

More generally, the methods used to explain the background to the national output provide a basis for considering problems of efficiency. Thus it is clear from our analysis that the volume of national output will depend on the quantity of the resources available, their quality, the way in which output is divided as between consumption and investment, and by implication the effectiveness with which the various factors of production are combined.

Is GNP a Good Measure of National Welfare?

The first point to make here is that GNP is not a measure of welfare at all. Welfare is concerned with well-being or happiness; the national output only tells you the total quantity of goods and services available to a community in a particular period of time. Even in this respect there are deficiencies and limitations which need to be borne in mind and which can conveniently be listed.

1. *Price changes.* In comparing national output over a period of years, we must allow for changes in prices if the comparison is to be meaningful. This can be done by valuing the goods and services of all the years we are comparing in the prices obtaining in one year. But it is easier to say this than to do it satisfactorily. For example, in the later years of the comparison there may be new products available which had not been invented in the earlier years, for instance colour television. Conversely, if one is looking at a substantial period of time, then in earlier periods there will have been possibilities open to people, such as a ride in a stagecoach, not available in later years.

2. *Population changes.* We need to allow for changes in the population if some comparisons are to be helpful. For some purposes an average figure of *per capita* GNP, obtained by dividing the total national output by the total population, may be the most useful index. However, this tells us nothing about the distribution of income amongst the population; it only gives us an average.

3. *Hours of work.* Figures of national product tell us nothing about the input required to obtain the output and hence reveal nothing about hours of work or the amount of leisure enjoyed. Between two years of similar GNP hours of work may have fallen, so that the population could properly be regarded as better off in the year of shorter hours. Similarly, with the timing of work; we could increase GNP by using capital more intensively by the widespread adoption of shift working. But this would not be an unmitigated advantage, because it would involve many people working unsocial hours.

4. *Changes in habits.* Changes in habits may affect the size of GNP. It should be remembered that we only count as part of output those things which are paid for in the market. The services of the housewife, for example, are not included, however valuable they may be. Thus if all housewives went out to work and neglected their homes the GNP would rise by more than the proportional increase that there would be in real goods and services. To put the point in another way: if a man employs a housekeeper and pays her for looking after the house, then her services count as part of the national output; if he marries her and she continues to do the same services as before, the national output goes down! Changes in shopping habits may similarly affect the level of national output. For example, a switch to supermarkets may cause the national output to rise more than is justifiable in terms of the additional services gained because some services which were previously provided in the market would then be provided by the customer himself, and not paid for. For example, the customer may collect goods from the shelf instead of an assistant doing it for him and he may have no option but to convey them home himself because deliveries have been discontinued.

5. *Public sector goods.* Another important qualification arises from the treatment accorded to the public sector. Because the services of civil servants and the defence forces and so on all count as part of the national output, if we were to transfer a larger proportion of our resources to defence from the making of consumption goods then the national output might remain unchanged in statistical terms, but the individual consumer would be significantly worse off.

6. *Changes in quality.* Another possible deficiency is that changes in the quality of goods may not be reflected in the GNP figures. For example, if the daily newspaper were to be halved in size this would not be reflected in the statistics. This kind of change may take

place particularly in war time when there is restriction of choice and a considerable decline in the quality of goods, e.g. less alcohol in the beer and a decline in the service going with goods, e.g. long queues for service in shops.

7. *Environmental factors.* Because GNP is concerned simply with the output of goods and services it may not adequately reflect, or indeed reflect at all, a deterioration in the environment which may result from making these goods and services. Thus GNP would not measure the loss to the community from the pollution of water or air as a result of economic production. This pollution would only be taken into account if the costs were imposed on the producer himself. Indeed, the position can be more distorted than that. Take, for example, the situation in a large city which is congested with road traffic as a result of people commuting to and from work. People may not like commuting; it reduces the income they can spend on things they enjoy. However, because the car and the petrol, the rail ticket and the bus ticket are things that they buy in the market, these transport goods and services are all counted as contributing to the national output as though they provided a series of consumption benefits to the purchasers, when in more meaningful terms they might be regarded as a cost of producing output. It would be possible to adjust the figures to allow for such costs, but this is not normally done.

8. *International comparisons.* Particular problems arise when we take account of international factors. Thus there are special difficulties about making international comparisons of GNP per head. In converting the figures into a common currency it must be recognized that exchange rates are a very imperfect measure of the relative values of all the goods and services which people in each country buy. Again the needs in different countries vary. Thus in a cold country people will need to spend a great deal on fuel, whereas in an African country they would not. These differences in needs cannot adequately be taken into account in comparisons. Again the prices of goods in different countries differ accordingly to whether they are typical or not: the Frenchman's breakfast may be more expensive in England than in France while the Englishman's breakfast may be more expensive in France than in England.

9. *Terms of trade.* Finally, besides the difficulties of international comparisons, changes in international price levels may reduce the standard of living in a country even thought its own output is going up. The measure of the imports that a country can get in exchange

for a unit of its own exports is called the terms of trade. If import prices rise more than export prices, then the terms of trade move against a country and it may suffer a fall in its standard of living even though its own output has increased.

Having said all this it remains true that statistics of GNP are a very useful measure of economic progress—but, like all statistics, they must be used with understanding and care.

SUMMARY AND CONCLUSIONS

In essence the economic system is both an organization of producers to satisfy the wants of consumers and a system of mutual exchanges. Provided the terms are defined appropriately to allow for the complications of government economic activity and international economic relations, the total value of income, output and expenditure are the same for the community taken as a whole. Figures of national income and output are vital to the control of an economy and are probably the best single index of economic progress. The way they are compiled needs to be thoroughly understood if their limitations are to be appreciated and they are not to mislead.

4 The Market Mechanism

Solving the Economic Problem

In Chapter 3 we explained what constitutes the national output and the relationship of output to income and expenditure. But only by implication, if at all, have we answered three vital questions affecting all national economies: *What* shall be produced? *How* will it be produced? *Who* will get the product? These fundamental questions all arise from the nature of the economic problem, as outlined at the beginning of Chapter 1: wants are virtually unlimited; resources to satisfy them are scarce and capable of being used in different ways; hence the need for choice (which permeates all aspects of economic life) and the three vital questions of 'What', 'How' and 'Who'.

Whatever the form of socio-economic system the problem is the same, but the way in which answers are reached to the three questions may be different. Broadly speaking there are two directions in which solutions are sought: the command system and the market system. In the extreme form of command economy an economic dictator or economic committee would determine, in a gigantic national plan, what should be produced, what methods should be used and what incomes people should receive (i.e. who should get the product). At the opposite extreme is the laissez-faire economy where millions of consumers and producers acting individually through the market and responding to price changes, determine what should be produced, by what methods and how much each shall benefit.

The command economy relies primarily on coercion for the fulfilment of the plan; the laissez-faire economy rests mainly on mutual self-interest to secure a non-coercive cooperation. But this is an overdrawn contrast. Thus the market economy requires a framework of rules and conventions, like the laws of property and contract, which ultimately rely on the force of the state. Command economies invariably make some use of markets. Moreover a minimum of mutual goodwill is required to operate either system. In the last resort state force itself is dependent on goodwill, even if it is only the goodwill of the Praetorian Guard, the KGB, or, in Britain in the mid 1970s, the trade unions.

The extent to which an economy is a command or a market system is closely related to the ownership of the means of production, i.e. whether it is a socialist economy (used in the sense of state ownership of the means of production, distribution and exchange) or a capitalist economy (in the sense of private ownership of the means of production). But it is possible to have many of the attributes of the command economy whilst retaining private ownership of resources (as in Nazi Germany); and many socialist countries use the price mechanism in a limited way—for example, to ration available goods amongst consumers, though not as the prime determinant of *what* should be produced.

In a mixed economy like the United Kingdom the majority of resources are privately owned, but there is a substantial public or state ownership mainly through the nationalized industries. The determination of what shall be produced is partly through the market mechanism (for the private sector of the economy) and partly through the political machinery (for the public sector). But when a United Kingdom government determines what shall be produced (e.g. how much of the national output should be in the form of state-provided education), much of the 'how' may be left to the market mechanism. For example, the government education authorities may 'buy' new schools, desks, blackboards, etc. by seeking the lowest price from private suppliers in the market. The nationalized industries, also, may follow 'commercial' principles, sell their products in the market and determine their investment policies much as large private corporations, save that the injunction may be laid upon them to balance their books rather than to make a profit.[1] As to the determination of who should get the product in the mixed economy, the position is complex. If we leave on one side (for later consideration) all questions of incomes policies, then incomes in the private sector of the economy are largely determined through the market mechanism. But what of the public sector? The state in the United Kingdom is the employer of something like one in four of the labour force (including local government and

---

[1] In practice ministers seem to have found it impossible to refrain from interfering in the day-to-day running of the nationalized industries, and other requirements have been superimposed on the general directive.

nationalized industries). In some cases, especially where it employs in small numbers workers of a kind more numerously employed in the private sector, the rate paid by the state may follow the market; but where the state is the sole employer (e.g. defence forces) or the main employer (e.g. teachers) the state will play the major role in determining the rate of remuneration. Even so, in the absence of direction of labour, it must have some regard to pay in the private sector. Whilst the state can pay a price higher than is required to man its services, it cannot pay less (or, more accurately, offer a less attractive package of pay, pensions provision and other conditions of work) if it wishes to obtain the staff it needs and maintain the quality.[1]

In the next chapter we shall look in some detail at the public sector of the economy, much of which is an integral part of the subject matter of social economics. In the remainder of this chapter we examine briefly the way the market mechanism or price system works, its characteristics and its limitations. This analysis provides us with a framework of reference against which to set the characteristics of the public sector; and exploring the limitations of the price system gives us a partial explanation of, and rationale for, the growth of the public sector.

Operation and Characteristics of the Price System

In the market sector of the economy the actions of numerous persons, making their own decisions in the light of the information available and relevant to them, determine what shall be produced, how it will be produced and who will get the product. The solution is reached through the operation of prices, not only the prices of consumers' goods and services, but also the prices of producers' goods of all kinds, the price of land (which can be regarded as a particular kind of durable-use good) and the price of labour. In other words the price system embraces both the products and the factors of production. Prices serve a number of functions, all closely interconnected.

Firstly, they act as a rationing mechanism for the scarce products and resources available. They ration consumers' goods in such a

---

[1] This description takes no account of the many ways in which government policies may indirectly affect incomes and modify the distribution generated by the market, either to reduce incomes by taxation or supplement them by welfare benefits. We shall have much to say about this especially in Parts III and IV.

way that each household is able to obtain that combination of goods and services which, within its budget limitations (an important qualification about which we shall have more to say later), enables it to maximize its satisfaction (or, more accurately, expected satisfaction). This assertion becomes clearer by reference to the alternative, physical rationing, where each person irrespective of tastes receives the same physical quantity of a good. With physical rationing, if I like eggs but detest bacon I nonetheless receive my allocated quantity of each, no more and no less. I might manage to find someone whose tastes were the exact reverse of mine, but Jack Spratt and his wife were exceptional, and to succeed in my quest requires an abnormal amount of good luck and an entirely disproportionate expenditure of time. Further, the wider the range and variety of products available, the less satisfactory is a physical rationing system.[1]

Prices ration the scarce factors of production as well as products. Just as the prices of consumers' goods serve to distribute them in accordance with the relative preferences of consumers, so the prices of the factors of production help to ensure that they are used in the production of those goods preferred by consumers (a point which links up with the third aspect of the price system below).

Secondly, prices act as signals and guides to firms about what should be produced in the future. If consumers wish to consume more of a particular commodity then its price will tend to rise. This indicates to firms that more should be produced; at the same time it provides an incentive for more factors of production to move into that line of production. Firms making the good will be earning high profits. They will wish to expand output. To obtain more of the new materials, machinery and workers wanted they will be prepared to offer higher prices and thus more resources will be drawn to this line of production to meet the increase in demand. In this process we see the operation of what to Adam Smith was like an 'invisible

---

[1] The system of 'points' rationing introduced in the United Kingdom during the Second World War—which applied to a wide range of tinned food stuffs—is a remarkable recognition of the merits of this function of the price system. The points required for each commodity could be periodically adjusted according to the demand and supply conditions and the total points allocation could also be changed. In effect, variations in points values served the same purpose as changes in relative prices, whilst the total points allocation was akin to income—with the vital difference from money income that the points income was the same for all.

hand', by which individuals, following their own self interest,[1] were *ipso facto*, led to pursue the interests of the community.

The validity of 'consumers' sovereignty' has sometimes been questioned. It certainly does not imply that consumers initiate new products. Such innovation rests with producers. But, unless consumers are prepared to accept what producers provide, at prices which cover costs of production, then production of that good will cease. In other words, consumers' determine what is produced in the sense that they exercise a continuous right of veto.

Thirdly, the price system acts as a guide to the organization of production. If the price of a particular factor of production rises (e.g. a raw material which has become more scarce) this is a sign to producers to use that factor more economically. Each entrepreneur faces a number of possible ways of producing a given level of output; he will usually be able to vary his input mix of factors of production quite considerably. When one factor of production rises in price relatively to the others he will seek to substitute other factors for that which has risen in price in order to produce any particular level of output at minimum cost. This way the entrepreneur maximizes his profit. At the same time his action helps to ensure that this particularly scarce factor will be left for use in those products where substitution is costly or impossible.

Expressed in a slightly different way,[2] the price system can be said to do five things: it provides *information* about people's preferences; it *allocates* men, machines, land, buildings and other resources in accordance with these preferences; it influences *decisions* on which production techniques to use; it creates *incentives* to avoid unnecessarily costly methods, to invest, to develop new technologies and products; and perhaps most important of all, it *coordinates* the desires of millions of individuals, firms and households.

At its best the price system enables the economic problem to be solved in a way which combines efficiency and freedom. Efficiency, because individual preferences determine what is produced; because the profit motive promotes enterprise; because movements in the relative prices of the factors of production stimulate entrepreneurs to economize in the use of the scarce factors. Freedom, because the

---

[1] The market economy is often condemned as materialist and based on selfishness. But this by no means follows. The altruist, who is concerned to maximize his giving, can only do so if he first maximizes his income.

[2] Following Professor A. Lindbeck, *The Political Economy of the New Left*, Harper and Row, 1971.

price system is a remarkable device for dispersing economic decision-making and therefore economic power; because individuals are free to choose what goods they want and to work where they want.

In fact, although these points contain a vital component of truth, this picture of the price system is somewhat idealized; the uncontrolled price system does not always work as perfectly as we have described; moreover it has inherent limitations and some positive disadvantages. To these we now turn.

Limitations and Defects of the Market System

1. *The market mechanism is unable to cope with the supply of those goods or services where the benefit is diffuse or indiscriminate.* These are 'goods' such as defence or the services of the police force. Individuals purchasing in the market cannot buy their own quota of defence forces or of police protection; for this they need some sort of communal or political organization. These are the kind of goods which we define in the next chapter as 'pure public goods'.

2. *The uncontrolled price system does not take account of externality or spill-over effects.* The purchase of a good in the market may have spill-over detriments or benefits for other consumers. Similarly a producer may use resources in such a way as to cause detriment or benefit to others. Thus the heavy drinker may cause additional work for the police and put up the costs of the police services and annoy other people by his noisy behaviour. A producer may cause detriment to others by using processes which pollute air or water, by generating excessive noise, or by creating eyesores such as slag heaps. Without some form of government intervention in the market these processes of consumption or production would involve cost to the community which would not be taken into account by the private consumer or producer. Thus, without some intervention in the market mechanism, more of these products would be produced than is justified by their cost to the community. Conversely there are some products which give rise to benefits to the community not taken into account by the individual producers or consumers. For example, as we shall see in later chapters, some expenditures on education and on health services provide benefit to the community over and above that to the individuals most directly concerned.

However we must be careful of assuming that any externality effect justifies state intervention in the market. Firstly, we must recognize that almost any activity does have some external effect.

For example, if I keep my garden tidy and beautiful this gives benefit to others, whilst if I neglect it, it is an eyesore to them. However it would be absurd to suggest that the state should intervene in such a situation. Before state intervention is justifiable the external effect must be substantial and if possible must be capable of being measured so that there is no danger of an over-reaction by the state which could be as bad as no reaction at all. Secondly, by appropriate regulation it may often be possible to turn an externality effect into an internal cost. For example, the state may lay down certain rules about pollution of water or air so that producers are obliged to use equipment which stops the pollution. In this way external effects are internalized and become part of the private costs of production.

3. *The effectiveness of the price mechanism is reduced by the existence of various imperfections in the market.* The response mechanism to changes in price implies the existence of effective competition. Where there is monopoly, or restrictive practices exist, supply is not responsive to price changes in the manner we have described. Again, imperfections in the knowledge of consumers mean that consumers' sovereignty may result in mistakes. The presence of a high degree of uncertainty may make for inappropriate decisions. Thus the market may not be able to cope with providing investment funds for highly techno-logical processes where the risk factor is difficult to calculate.

4. *The market mechanism depends on and generates inequality in the distribution of incomes.* The prices obtained for goods determine the incomes of the factors of production which help to make those goods. The price of labour is the income of the worker, the price of capital the income of the property owner. Peoples' incomes will depend on the value which society puts on their productive services. Not only that, the incentive mechanism of the market depends on changes in the price of the factors of production. Thus, if there is an increase in demand for a particular product, there will be an increase in the demand for the labour making that product and the return to that labour will rise. Elsewhere in the system there will be a reduction in demand leading to a reduction in wages. These changes in relative incomes bear no relationship to the merit or effort of the people concerned. Differences in income likewise tend to generate differences in amounts of wealth because the higher a person's income the easier it is for him to accumulate wealth. Such wealth may then be passed to successive generations by inheritance.

5. *The free operation of the market tends to generate instability and unemployment.* Experience before the Second World War suggested

that market economies suffered from trade cycles characterized by fluctuations in income, output, prices and employment.

6. *It may be doubted if the market system can cope adequately with the existence of unique resource scarcities.* If there is a possibility that a particular resource, such as coal or oil, may be completely exhausted within a foreseeable timespan, it may be doubted whether a mechanism which reflects the interest of those alive today can adequately protect the interests of future generations.

To nearly all these issues we shall be returning later in the book and examining how far the limitations and defects of the market system can be rectified by state intervention within a mixed economy. However, let us conclude this chapter by considering a question which demonstrates the nature of the market mechanism and bears directly on some aspects of government economic and social policy.

Why Not Introduce Price Control?

A truism about the economic system is that 'everything depends on everything else'. It is this inter-relationship which gives such importance to the coordinating function of prices. Some of the inter-relationships are brought out by this illustration of government intervention in a particular market.

Let us suppose that the price of a particular product has recently risen markedly and that this product (e.g. bread) is one that the government regards as especially important in the poor man's budget, consequently the government introduces price control to hold the price below what it would be in a free market. What happens?

We can show the effects most clearly using a simple diagram with demand and supply curves (Figure 4.1). A *demand curve* shows the amount of the commodity which would be purchased at each possible price per period of time. The lower the price, the more will be purchased. When price is lower, consumers will tend to substitute this commodity for other goods, whilst if its price rises the reverse will be true. This *substitution effect* will usually be reinforced by an *income effect*. When price falls the consumer is better off (he has had the equivalent of an increase in income) and unless the good is an 'inferior' good, he will tend to purchase more of it. Should it be an inferior good (one such that, as people become better off, they spend a smaller percentage of their income on it, e.g. potatoes or bread), it is still likely that more will be purchased when the price falls because the income effect of the change in price of a good is usually very small, and is outweighed by the substitution effect.

A *supply curve* shows the total amount that firms, in aggregate, will offer for sale at each of a range of prices per period of time. A supply curve normally slopes upward to the right indicating that more will be offered for sale at a higher price than at a lower. Short-period supply curves, which show the response of existing firms with a given amount of fixed capital (plant and machinery) to the increase in price, always slope upwards. Existing firms can only increase the supply of a commodity by incurring additional cost, e.g. by working machinery above the optimum operating level, paying overtime rates to its workers or paying higher wages to attract new labour. In the long period, however, when the firm has had time to adjust the level of its fixed capital to the new price level and when new firms have had the time to come into existence, the supply curve may become horizontal or even fall in extreme cases where there are external economies of scale.[1]

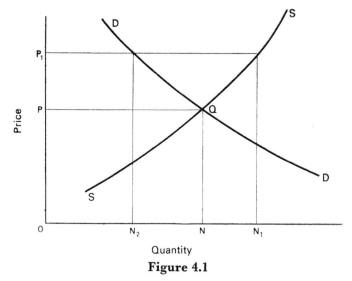

Figure 4.1

[1] External economies of scale are economies dependent on the growth of the industry as a whole, irrespective of the size of individual firms, as distinct from internal economies which are economies resulting from the growth of the individual firm. To give some examples of external economies: as an industry grows improved transport services might be developed to meet its needs; specialist financial services might grow up; and at some size of industry it might be worthwhile for a firm to set up to process waste products of the industry.

Figure 4.1 shows a short-period supply curve (SS) and a demand curve (DD) for a particular product. In a free market the price which would come to rule if these supply and demand conditions persisted would be OP. At that price—the market-clearing price—the amount supplied and the amount demanded would be the same. If the price were anything other than OP then, in a free market, forces would come into play to restore the price OP. For example, if producers anticipated a price of OP$_1$ then they would supply an output of ON$_1$. But at price OP$_1$ consumers would only be willing to buy ON$_2$. Suppliers would be left with a surplus which they could only dispose of at a lower price. As price fell, so the amount consumers were willing to purchase would rise and the amount that suppliers were willing to supply would fall until, possibly after some oscillations, the equilibrium at Q (where the demand and supply curves cross) would be established and price OP would rule.

Now let us return to the question we posed earlier; what happens if the government introduces price control in a particular market?

Let us reproduce again in Figure 4.2 the demand and supply conditions of Figure 4.1. OP is again the equilibrium price which would rule in a free market, at which price ON would be purchased. The government then decrees that the price must be OC.

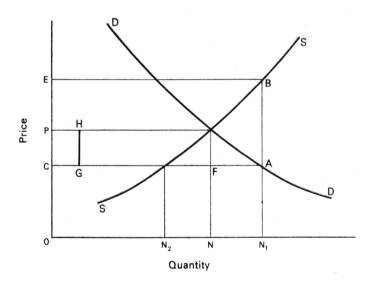

Figure 4.2

At price OC the amount that would be supplied would be ON_2 (less than the amount in the free market); the amount that consumers would wish to purchase would be ON_1 (more than the amount in the free market). There would be a deficiency in supply represented by the distance N_2–N_1 on the horizontal axis. Let us look at the possible consequences and further government responses.

Price Control Alone

In the absence of further government action, then four consequences are likely.

1. There will be a haphazard distribution of the available supplies. Because supplies are so much less than the amount demanded at that price, they will quickly disappear from the shops and as new supplies come in they will be snapped up. The supplies will tend to go (a) to those who have most time to spend hunting the shops and joining every queue; and (b) to those with influence with the suppliers, e.g. many shopkeepers may put the good 'under the counter' and offer it only to regular customers with large orders.

2. There will be some breach of the law, through the growth of black (or grey) markets. Control price OC leaves many consumers short of the good for which they would willingly pay a higher price; and there are suppliers who would willingly supply more if the price were higher. Thus there are strong forces in play to establish a black market. (In a black market price could well be above the equilibrium price OP, for there are some consumers who would pay more than that price for some of the good in question, and suppliers in the black market are likely to seek higher prices if only to compensate for additional costs and risks). A black market does not have to take the form of high-powered crooks operating at night. A higher price can effectively be paid for a good by associated transactions; for example, suppliers may release the price-controlled product to customers with large orders and over-price other goods to these customers to compensate for the favour.

3. Another possible consequence depends on the nature of the good. It may be possible to change its form somewhat to sell it in another market which is not price controlled, e.g. to sell parts rather than an assembled product if only the completed product is price-controlled; or to convert unfurnished to furnished accommodation if only the unfurnished is rent controlled.

4. A further likely consequence is that resources will move from

the production of this good to the production of other goods not subject to price control. As price-controlled goods are likely to be those regarded as 'essential', the consequence of extensive price control could well be that the economic system is increasingly encouraged to produce things people want less in preference to things they want more.

It is very dubious whether controlling the price of a particular product, with no further government action, will help the poor in whose interests the policy was introduced.

Price Control with Rationing

It is very unlikely that price control of a 'necessity' would stand by itself. In the face of the consequences we have outlined further government action would be called for and one possibility would be to support price control with physical rationing. This would secure an orderly distribution of the supplies becoming legally available and so partly remedy the first consequence of price control outlined above. But a physical ration takes no account of tastes and can only to a limited extent be modified to cater for special needs. Furthermore the other consequences of price control above would still apply; black markets and the diversion of supplies to related markets, or of resources to different uses. Also operating the rationing system incurs administrative costs.

Price Control with Subsidization

Another possibility would be for the government to combine price control with subsidization. If the subsidy was set at an appropriate level, then consumers could be left free to purchase as much as they wished without the danger of haphazard allocation or of black markets. The required level of subsidy would be that at which suppliers would supply the amount which consumers wished to purchase at the control price. The amount can be read off from Figure 4.2: it would be a subsidy per unit of AB, with the total level of subsidy represented by the rectangle CEBA (which is the subsidy per unit multiplied by the number of units supplied and demanded at the control price). The main disadvantage of this solution is the cost. This cost is much higher than is necessary to compensate the poor for the extra they would have had to pay for the good in a free market (a) because the benefit of the subsidy goes to all purchasers irrespective of size of income and (b) because consumers, at all income levels, tend to purchase more of the good than they would have done at the free market price. In addition the price control still introduces a distortion into the economic system, though not in the direction of inducing the production of less essential goods. One of the ways prices promote efficiency is by reflecting costs of production. The price of a good represents the 'opportunity cost'[1] to the community of using resources in that way rather than in an alternative way. When a good is subsidized, it no longer reflects true opportunity costs. People are then encouraged to buy more of it than if they were paying the full cost. Finally there is some cost incurred, though probably a minor one, in operating the subsidy system.

An Alternative Strategy

A completely different strategy, which in general has much more to commend it than price control combined with either rationing or subsidization, is to leave the price to the free market and compensate the poor for the high price by increasing their incomes by such means as raising social security benefits, family allowances, income tax thresholds or, if there is one in existence, the level of negative income tax. Provided that the increases in income can be directed fairly precisely to the poor whom it is sought to protect, this has a number of advantages: (a) there is no distortion of relative prices and hence of opportunity costs; (b) the beneficiaries are left free to spend the additional income as they wish—the benefit is not conditional on purchasing that particular good; (c) most important, the cost is much less. Suppose, for example, that the government's intention was to compensate the poor for the extra they would have to pay at the free market price over and above what they would have to pay at the control price; and suppose that the poor, whom it is desired to help, would have purchased 20 per cent of the total supplied at the market price. Then the amount required to compensate them, if it could be perfectly allocated, can be respresented on Figure 4.2 by the rectangle CPHG (CG being one-fifth of CF). This is very much less than 20 per cent of the total subsidy, which was equal in area to CEBA. Considerably more than CPHG could be distributed to allow for the imperfections in the mechanism of raising the incomes of the poor consumers, whilst still allowing a very large total

[1] See Chapter 1, p. 7.

saving in cost over the subsidy. Moreover we must consider what this cost is. The cost of a subsidy (or of increasing the incomes of the poor) will normally have to be met from taxation. In practice, in the United Kingdom, a substantial proportion of tax revenue is paid by the poor—the tax system as a whole is only mildly progressive. If the taxes to meet the subsidy had the same incidence as the tax system as a whole, the poor would find themselves paying an additional amount in tax not much less than their benefit from the subsidy. If, alternatively, their income is increased to compensate for the high price, they will gain relatively more because (assuming the same distribution of tax incidence as for taxes as a whole) their additional tax bill will be less than it would have been with the subsidy in operation.

Some Caveats and Qualifications

Our analysis has brought out the inter-relationships in the economic system and emphasized that a government policy of intervention in the market needs to be carefully thought through, with a full appreciation of all the inter-relationships, if it is to meet its desired objectives. It is easy for ill-considered action not only to fail to benefit, but actually to harm, those whom it was intended to help.

Having said that, however, we must introduce some qualifications to avoid misleading. Our analysis implicitly assumed the existence of effective competition; if the supplier of a good was a monopolist making high profits there might be a strong case for price control. Again there may be a case for price controls with subsidization if this will help to check the growth of inflationary expectations.[1] A government may wish to subsidize a particular product on paternalist grounds, because it considers it desirable that consumers should have more of it. Finally there is a case for subsidizing particular products to offset a distortion already existing in the economic system—that is to say, to compensate for the existence of a substantial externality effect.

SUMMARY AND CONCLUSIONS

In any economy, three vital questions are: what should be produced, by what methods and who should get the product. The answers are

[1] See Chapter 15.

sought along two directions—the command system associated particularly with state socialism, and the market system, associated particularly with capitalism. The United Kingdom is a mixed economy with a large market sector but also with a large public sector in which many decisions are made through the political machinery rather than markets. Markets provide information, offer incentives and coordinate the activities of millions of people as consumers and producers. At their best they combine efficiency and freedom. But the unregulated and unsupplemented market system suffers from inherent limitations and defects. State intervention in markets must take into account the inter-relationships of the economic system if it is not to do more harm than good.

5 The Public Sector

The Nature of the Public Sector

In general terms we speak of public goods,[1] or publicly provided goods, as goods provided by the state, paid for mainly by taxation, and sold at a nil or nominal price to the user. Private goods are goods sold in private markets, where the price has to be at least equal to the marginal cost of production if the long-term supply of those goods is to be maintained. However, it is sometimes useful to identify goods not in relation to the method by which they are actually provided, but according to their inherent characteristics affecting the necessity or suitability of the form of provision. Such a distinction links with our analysis of the deficiencies of the price system in Chapter 4. On this basis we can distinguish three categories of good: pure public goods, pure private goods, and an intermediate category of quasi-public/quasi-private goods.

Pure public goods are goods the benefit of which is diffuse or indiscriminate; the benefit received by each citizen is not precisely allocatable to him, nor is it possible to exclude from benefit those who make no contribution to cost (the 'free-riders'). Examples are defence services, police forces and the other services necessary for the maintenance of internal order, e.g. a uniform legal system and courts of law. We can also include in this category other goods with predominant externality effects such that, although it would be possible to allocate benefit and charge individual users in relation to their use, it would be absurdly expensive to do so, e.g. street paving and lighting in towns. On economic criteria these pure public goods should be publicly provided.

At the other extreme are pure private goods. The benefit from these is precisely allocatable; the exclusion principle applies—the owners can exclude others from the consumption of the goods; the goods are competitive in the sense that more consumption by one

[1] For convenience we use the term 'good' in this chapter to comprehend services as well as material products.

person implies less by others; and externality effects are nil or negligible. The majority of goods fall into this category, e.g. an apple, a fountain pen. There is a clear economic case for private sector allocation.

In between come the quasi-public/quasi-private goods. With these there is a precise and allocatable private benefit, so that the goods could be provided through private markets, but also there are significant externality effects. Particular examples are education provision and aspects of health care. These goods may be either publicly or privately provided and which method to adopt is a matter of much contemporary controversy. Non-economic criteria tend to determine the outcome.

There are some significant differences between the methods of choosing private and public goods. With private goods the bene-ficiary pays—there is a direct relationship between cost and (ex-pected) benefit. Further, although the purchaser may allow himself to be persuaded by advertising, there is no compulsion. In the last resort the choice is a free one. With public goods there is no direct relationship between cost and benefit. Citizens in a democracy are likely to be offered alternative 'packages' of public goods to choose between at election times, but it is an all-or-nothing choice—they cannot opt for part of the package of one political party and part of that of another, nor indeed can they be certain that the successful party will fully implement its promises. Still less are the parties likely to specify the precise tax changes to meet the costs. Moreover the election options are presented in very broad terms, e.g. increased nursery school provision. The detailed decisions—of how many nursery schools, where, and with what facilities—will be made by ministers and officials. Further, save in the unlikely case of unanimity, there is an irreducable element of compulsion in publicly provided goods—the difference, indeed, between a price and a tax. Thus, if I am an out-and-out pacifist, I may object to any public expenditure on armaments; but I am nonetheless compelled to pay taxes to meet defence costs. Or I may see no reason why my local authority should offer a 'free' library service, which I do not wish to use; but I am legally constrained to pay local rates to support it.

In practice experience suggests that governments often have pre-dilections for particular kinds of public spending irrespective of the wishes of the bulk of their citizens. Governments are attracted to prestige projects. Thus every state, however poor or small, feels it must have its own national airline; and projects like Concorde, especially where the interested experts can gain the ear of a minister, are often favoured. Also, in a democracy based on territorial representation a government is often sympathetic to interests which are concentrated in particular constituencies (especially if they happen to be marginal). Thus it may provide subsidies to particular firms in order to maintain local employment even though this is at the expense of the general taxpayer and possibly to the detriment of other producers who are more dispersed or whose interest is less obvious.

Methods of State Intervention

It would be misleading, however, to see state intervention solely in terms of public provision. In attempting to remedy the various deficiencies of the price system the state may intervene in a variety of ways, which may be used in combination. The methods can be grouped under three main heads: regulation, fiscal measures and provision.

Examples of *regulation* are numerous. The state may recognize the social benefit arising from a literate population by requiring all children of certain ages to attend school. It may endeavour to control the social costs which can be associated with drinking by imposing licensing regulations and the social harm of smoking by restrictions on cigarette advertising. It may seek to preserve the attractiveness of the environment by a variety of planning controls, and to restrict pollution in its many forms by regulations on clean air, acceptable noise levels, and the disposal of industrial waste in sea and rivers.

Fiscal measures can likewise take a variety of forms. The most general is a policy of taxation and cash transfers to alter the distribution of income so that everyone can afford the goods they are considered to need. The state may seek to influence the production and consumption of particular products by taxes or subsidies. Thus products which pollute (such as oil) may be heavily taxed, whilst others which provide social benefits (such as education) may be subsidized. Finally under this head the state may prefer to encourage the consumption of particular goods not by a cash subsidization but by means of vouchers—coupons encashable only against a particular product or service. In this way the state can try to ensure that at least a specified minimum (the value of the voucher) is spent on that service. Thus some American states have distributed food vouchers rather than cash as part of their poverty programmes, and experiments have been tried or suggested for education vouchers and vouchers for the purchase of medical insurance.

Provision, the third category, is also more complicated than at first appears. Whilst it is not feasible to charge user costs for pure public goods, quasi-public goods can be supplied with different amounts of user cost or nil. (The term 'nil' user cost is preferable to 'free' because it avoids the impression that there is no cost involved— to quote an economic aphorism, 'There is no such thing as a free meal').

Even this oversimplifies the real situation, however, because where there is state provision, the extent to which the state controls the resources used can vary. Thus the state may provide for defence, but buy all weapons and equipment from private contractors in the market and recruit its soldiers, sailors and airmen by offering high enough wages and sufficiently attractive conditions of service to secure all the manpower it requires. At the other extreme the state could own all the establishments making munitions and military equipment and obtain its personnel for munitions' production and for the armed services by conscription. Such complete public sector allocation of resources would, in a mixed economy, be restricted to war-time emergencies. Usually, in a mixed economy when the state provides a good, whether it be defence services or education, it controls the end product, but many or all of the resources used are purchased in the market.

These three methods of state intervention—regulation, finance and provision— are not mutually exclusive and it is common for the state to use them in combination. Thus a government may restrict cigarette advertising and also tax cigarettes. It may regulate school leaving ages, subsidize some forms of adult education, and provide education itself. The number of possible 'mixes', with or without user costs for publicly provided services, is very large. The question of the form or forms which state intervention should take lies at the heart of many contemporary political issues.

Measuring the Public Sector

The form of state intervention used also vitally affects the size and nature of the public sector of the economy. But before we can examine the situation in the United Kingdom, we need to say something on the problems of measuring the public sector. No set of statistics can adequately convey the degree of influence and control a government may exercise over the economy. If a government used predominantly the method of regulation rather than finance or provision, then a small sector measured in terms of the amount of public spending or the proportion of the labour force employed, could be compatible with overwhelming government control. Having made this *caveat* we shall now concentrate on public expenditure as a measure of the size of the public sector. Even government intervention in the economy in the form of regulation involves some increase in public expenditure (the costs of the bureaucracy required to operate the controls and ensure their effectiveness); and inverventions by means of finance and provision are likely to require substantial public spending.

Any measure of public spending is to some extent arbitrary. Prices change, sometimes very rapidly; the population grows (or may even fall); national output changes. A monetary measure of public expenditure is practically meaningless in making comparisons over time. A 'real' measure (one which takes account of changes in the price level) is better, especially if expressed on a per capita basis, but it makes no allowance for changes in national output. The most convenient single figure, despite imperfections, is public spending presented as a proportion of national output. This measure not only incorporates some automatic allowance for price changes (albeit an imperfect one, because the prices of the goods the government buys change in somewhat different proportions to the average of all goods and services), but gives an indication of the relative size of the public sector compared with the private. But this measure immediately presents two problems to which there are no wholly satisfactory answers: what do you include within public expenditure and which measure of national output do you use as the denominator?

There are at least three measures of overall public expenditure which possess a certain logic.

1. The combined spending of central and local government (including the national insurance fund) and the capital expenditure of public corporations. This gives the biggest total and can be taken as some approximate measure of the total spending influence of the government in the economy.
2. As 1, but omitting altogether the nationalized industries, on the grounds that these are best regarded as more or less autonomous bodies.
3. As 2, but omitting from the combined expenditure of central and local government capital expenditure on 'financial assets',

which comprises net lending by local and central government. This item consists mainly of loans to private industry and public corporations where the government can be regarded as acting as an intermediary in the provision of capital.

Each of these measures is valid in its own right and the choice should depend largely on the purpose in hand.

As to the second problem, it is usual to employ Gross National Product or Gross Domestic Product. Ideally Net National Product (or National Income) is preferable to Gross National Product, but because of the unreliability of the figures of capital consumption—which represent the difference between the gross and net figures—a more consistent series is likely to be attained by using GNP. The factor cost measure is preferable to the market price measure of GNP to minimize distortions arising from taxes on expenditure.[1]

Public expenditure is made to appear at its largest by including the capital expenditure of nationalized industries and using Net National Product as the denominator.

Three further conceptual points should be mentioned. Firstly, in calculating the total of public expenditure there remains an element of arbitrariness arising from the relationship between income and expenditure—the same policy effect may be achieved by adjustments to either side of the government's accounts. Thus a government can provide benefits to a particular category of taxpayer by explicit expenditure or by tax concessions which leave expenditure unchanged. For example, a government may offer investment incentives by cash grants or by tax allowances; it may relieve the cost of parenthood by family allowances in cash form or by child allowances in the form of tax relief. Adopting the first method each time raises public spending, whilst the second reduces tax revenues whilst leaving spending unaffected.

Secondly, expressing government spending in the form of a percentage has the consequence that the outcome is affected by changes in the denominator as well as by changes in the numerator. Thus, if government expenditure were constant or even falling in real terms, our measure would show an increase in expenditure if GNP was falling more than expenditure. This result is meaningful—it would imply a rise in the relative size of the public sector—but the point needs to be realized.

Thirdly, the figure of public expenditure as a proportion of GNP

[1] For more details on these alternative concepts, see above, Chapter 3, p. 36.

must be interpreted with care. If, for example, the figure is 50 per cent, this does not mean that the government pre-empts half the national output for its own purposes, for public expenditure includes transfer payments, where, in most cases, the recipients and not the state determine what goods and services are bought (and hence produced).

Putting the point in another way: in Chapter 3 we explained how GNP is arrived at by excluding transfer payments—transfers of income, brought about by the state, where the recipient has not rendered an economic service in exchange for the income (e.g. a family allowance). Thus, our measure excludes from the denominator items included in the numerator. GNP is a convenient datum line to which to relate total public expenditure, thus giving an indication of changes in the size of the public sector. It does not, however, as is commonly assumed, indicate the proportion of national output which the government directly controls by its spending. To find an approximation to that figure we must look at the components of public spending.

The Growth in Public Spending

Table 5.1 gives an indication of the trend in public expenditure since 1790. The third of the measures outlined earlier has been adopted: the figures show local and central government expenditure excluding expenditure on financial assets with nationalized industries left completely out of account. Transfers between central and local government (mainly grants to local authorities) are deducted to avoid double-counting (i.e. counting the grant both as central government spending and as the expenditure of local governments when they spend the grant). This particular measure of public spending has been chosen because it gives the most continuity over the period. Had expenditure on financial assets been included the 1975 figure would have been 55; if the capital expenditure of public corporations were also added then the figure for 1975 would be 58.

The particular years in the table have been selected to bring out the long term trend. This they do well, but they hide a pattern of growth which was apparent until the middle 1950s. The years in the table are all peace-time years. The full data since 1790 shows expenditure rising to a peak in times of emergency (notably wars, but also the Great Depression of 1929–33), falling back after the emergency but not to its pre-emergency level, and then settling on to a plateau until the next emergency. Thus wars had a ratchet effect, jacking up public expenditure to new levels; but in peacetime, public expenditure remained roughly constant as a percentage of GNP.

Table 5.1   Government Expenditure in the United Kingdom Expressed as a Percentage of GNP at Factor Cost (Selected years, 1790–1975).[1]

Year	*Expenditure as % of GNP*	*Year*	*Expenditure as % of GNP*
1790	12	1964	38
1840	11	1966	40
1890	8	1968	45
1910	12	1970	45
1932	29	1972	45
1951	40	1974	49
1961	38	1975	50

[1] Local and central government minus spending on financial assets. No nationalized industry expenditure is included. Financial transfers between local and central government have been deducted.

Sources: for 1790–1961, J. Veverka, 'The Growth of government expenditure in the United Kingdom since 1790', *Scottish Journal of Political Economy*, 1, **X**, 1963. *National Income and Expenditure*, 1964–74, HMSO 1975, and 1965–75, HMSO 1976.

Professors Peacock and Wiseman[1] evolved a 'working hypothesis' to explain this growth pattern of public expenditure. They argued that wars created the need for emergency expenditure and emergency taxation, upsetting established ideas of what were 'reasonable' tax burdens. This they named a 'displacement' effect. The wars accustomed people to the idea of higher tax levels (an 'acceptance' effect). Also wars revealed new needs for government expenditure, hitherto only half-realized (an 'inspection' effect). At the same time the wars themselves might generate some long-term expenditure commitments (e.g. on debt interest and war pensions). As a result, although expenditure dropped back from its peak, it remained at a higher level than pre-war. This level was maintained until the next emergency because, in normal times, people's ideas of what were

[1] A. T. Peacock and J. Wiseman, *The Growth of Public Expenditure in the United Kingdom*, Allen and Unwin, 2nd edition, 1967.

reasonable tax burdens were more important in determining public action in a democracy than ideas about desirable forms of expenditure. In peacetime public expenditure could grow as national income grew, but a rate of growth of public spending above that of national income was unlikely.

This hypothesis correlates well with the statistical data until the middle 1950s but it fails to account for the growth of public spending since. Between the mid-1960s and the mid-1970s public expenditure grew from 38 per cent of GNP to 50 per cent without a war-time emergency to explain it—an unprecedented peace-time growth.

In the next chapter we present some arguments which suggest that, beyond a certain size of public sector, forces come into play which provide a built-in bias to public sector expansion and that, in the United Kingdom at the time of writing, those influences are reinforced by certain institutional features. If correct, these arguments go a long way to explain the recent growth of the public sector.

For the moment let us turn to examine the composition and changes in the composition of public expenditure, as set out in Table 5.2. This table shows a three-fold division of public expenditure for some of the years included in Table 5.1. Expenditure is broken down by function, by economic category and by level. The functional breakdown is a little arbitrary. The categories of national debt interest and defence are straightforward. The social services are taken to include education and housing expenditure. Economic and environmental services include subsidies to industry and agriculture whether paid direct to the producers or consumer subsidies, the provision of roads, public health, sewage, and various urban amenities. 'Administration and other' is a residual category covering not only costs of administration by departments like the Inland Revenue, but police, the courts and, indeed, any expenditures which do not readily fit into the other categories.

The division between expenditure on goods and services (sometimes called 'exhaustive' expenditure) and that on transfers and subsidies distinguishes spending by which the government directly controls resources, from transfers of cash (not in exchange for services rendered) where the recipient usually determines what shall be consumed and produced. With transfer payments, such as family allowances, debt interest and retirement pensions, the recipient has unfettered use of the cash transferred. But with some transfers there is an element of state control. Thus student grants must be used for the maintenance of the student at an approved educational

Table 5.2   Government Expenditure by Level, by Economic Category, and by Function, as a percentage of Total Expenditure.[1]

Year	By function[2]					By economic category		By level	
	Administration and other	National Debt interest	Defence	Social services	Economic and environmental services	Goods and services	Transfers and subsidies	Central government	Local government
1790	17	39	26	9	9	57	43	83	17
1840	16	42	23	9	9	53	47	78	22
1890	22	15	28	20	15	80	20	59	41
1910	14	7	27	32	20	81	19	50	50
1932	7	25	10	45	14	48	52	65	35
1951	6	11	25	43	15	62	38	77	23
1961	7	10	20	47	16	61	39	73	27
1966	7	11	16	51	14	60	40	68	32
1974	7	10	12	53	17	57	43	67	33

[1] Definition of government expenditure as Table 5.1.
[2] Columns 2–6 do not always total to 100 for each year because of rounding.
Sources: as Table 5.1.

establishment, and part of the grant is specifically for spending on books. Subsidies or grants to firms are sometimes still more circumscribed, e.g. specifically for expenditure on investment in new equipment or buildings.

The third division is simply the governmental level concerned—how the total divides between central and local expenditure (counting grants by central to local governments in local spending).

The three categories are inter-linked. Thus, for example, defence spending, interest on the national debt and most other transfer payments are centralized forms of spending; when these are high, local spending tends to be low. Environmental services on the other hand have a high local expenditure content. It is therefore no mere coincidence that the year with the highest proportion of expenditure on economic and environmental services also has the highest proportion of local government expenditure (1910).

Let us now briefly comment on some of the salient comparisons over time. The reduction in the proportion of expenditure on 'administration and other' probably reflects an increased efficiency of administration, partly as a result of improvements in technology, such as typewriters and computers, and partly economies associated with a larger scale of operations. But we should be wary of reading over much into the figures: they tell us nothing about the efficiency of the public sector relatively to the private, and in any case the picture is confused because the category is something of a ragbag.

The decline in national debt interest as a proportion of total expenditure reflects the growth in expenditure, not any reduction in debt in later years, and also the tendency for interest rates to lag in times of inflation, so that the real burden of the national debt falls for any given size of debt.

Apart from 1932—an exceptional year of unemployment crisis with various effects on the components of public expenditure—the proportion of expenditure going on defence remained between 20 and 28 per cent in all the selected years between 1790 and 1961. Since 1961, however, this proportion has shown a very marked decline. But this generalization understates the transformation which has taken place in the share of defence in public expenditure. In the early years in our table war-related expenditures accounted for over two-thirds of total expenditure and possibly nearer four-fifths, for, besides direct expenditure on defence, the national debt was almost entirely a product of past wars, whilst administration and social service expenditures were also partly generated by war or the preparations for it. In contrast is the rise in social services expenditure from under 10 to well over 50 per cent of public spending. The transfer/subsidy column reflects these changes. By coincidence the same proportion of public spending went on transfers and subsidies in 1790 as in 1974, but the content had changed. In the earlier year all but 4 of the 43 per cent was debt interest. In the later year debt interest accounted for only 10 of the 43—the predominant form of transfer had become social security payments of one kind or another.

Growth of the Welfare State

The most striking feature of Table 5.2 is undoubtedly the growth of expenditure under the heading of the social services. It would be inappropriate to embark on a detailed historical account of the growth of the social services but we shall try to say enough to provide a background to our studies in later chapters. In particular we shall attempt to trace out two major changes of principle which have taken place in the provision of social services over this period and to high-light the turning points.

The first change is that from mere relief of poverty to an attempt to deal with its causes—the change from a remedial to a preventative and curative policy. At the end of the eighteenth century and until well into the nineteenth, the main social service expenditure was on poor relief, administered with varying degrees of harshness. The approach of 'relief from destitution within a framework of repression' was particularly embodied in the 1834 Poor Law Amendment Act, which enshrined the principles that relief to the able-bodied should only be given in well-regulated workhouses and that conditions in workhouses should be less comfortable than those of the lowest paid independent worker. In fact these principles were never rigidly applied and, as the century progressed, the emphasis gradually if implicitly changed, moving towards an attempt to deal with the causes out of which poverty arose—old age, sickness and unemployment. This new principle received explicit support in the recommendations of the Royal Commission on the Poor Law, 1905–09. It was also embodied in the social legislation of the Liberal governments just preceding the First World War, which introduced non-contributory old age pensions for the over seventies in 1908, established Labour Exchanges and introduced an experimental scheme of unemployment insurances, and made a start with a scheme of national health insurance.

The second change was from services for the benefit of limited categories of needy persons to welfare services for all citizens. The legislation of the Liberal government before the First World War was very much concerned with identifying particular needs and seeking to meet them. Thus the national health insurance as first introduced was a scheme restricted to most manual employees and lower paid non-manual employees, and the 1911 unemployment insurance scheme was confined to certain industries characterized by unemployment. In the inter-war years provisions of this kind were gradually extended, and there was also a particular development in local authority house-building aimed at slum clearance. According to one authority 'By 1939, Britain had developed a system of social services as good as that of any country in the world at that time.'[1] But it had grown up piecemeal on a somewhat ad hoc basis. Whilst the range had widened considerably from pre-1914 days, the social services in 1939 were not comprehensive in their coverage and the underlying concept was still that of limited and partial provision.

We have already noted how, according to Professors Peacock and Wiseman, wars through their displacement, acceptance and inspection effects generated permanently higher levels of public spending. Much of this higher spending was applied to social services. The Second World War was particularly notable for the influence it exerted towards the universal social service, especially through the medium of the Beveridge Report on *Social Insurance and Allied Services*, published in November 1942, which fired the popular imagination. Its essential recommendation was the introduction of a single comprehensive scheme of national insurance, replacing all existing schemes and covering virtually everybody. It was based on the principle of flat-rate benefits and contributions for all regardless of income, thus, in Sir William Beveridge's view, strengthening the sense of participation in common rights of citizenship. Benefits were intended to be adequate for subsistence but not more. Sir William held that anything above subsistence level should be provided by the individual, not the state. The scheme was to be financed by compulsory contributions from employees, employers and the self-employed and by a general Exchequer contribution. The scheme was to provide unemployment benefits, sickness benefits, retirement pensions, widows' and orphans' pensions as well as training benefits

[1] J. F. Sleeman, *The Welfare State, its Aims, Benefits and Costs*, Allen and Unwin, 1973, p. 33.

and maternity and death grants. A system of social insurance which made payments to those who satisfied contribution conditions could not cover all cases of need. Beveridge therefore proposed the replacement of existing public assistance schemes by a nationally administered scheme of National Assistance making payments on uniform scales of benefit subject to uniform tests of needs and means. Once the comprehensive insurance scheme was fully in operation he envisaged a very much reduced role for National Assistance—which should act, indeed, simply as a safety net.

Sir William saw the national insurance provisions as only a part of the attack on poverty and its causes. In particular, the success of the attack implied a system of family allowances, the introduction of a comprehensive health service, and government acceptance of the responsibility for maintaining a high and stable level of employment.

The war-time coalition government or the Labour government which followed took action on all these fronts. But one important divergence from Beveridge must be noted, to which we shall need to return later: the principle that national insurance benefit levels should be set at subsistence was never accepted.

There was one further social service the scope of which was much widened during the Second World War—education. In the 1830s the state had made small financial contributions towards the cost of education provided by voluntary agencies. The 1870 Education Act was a landmark which laid the foundations for (though it did not immediately introduce) a system of compulsory and free primary education. The 1944 Education Act is especially noteworthy as explicitly embodying the principle of secondary education for all.

Before we leave this brief review, one other distinction of importance should be made. With social security benefits the emphasis of state provision is on minimum levels below which people shall not be allowed to fall. With the national health service and with the state educational service, the aim is not a 'minimum' but an 'optimum' provision. Since an optimum is even less easy to define than a minimum,[1] the problem of how many resources should be devoted to each of these services, compared to other services in the public sector and compared to the private sector, is acute. We shall be looking at some aspects of it in Chapters 12–14.

[1] We look at some of the difficulties of defining a minimum (e.g. a poverty level) in Chapter 10.

Why Not a Command Economy?

In Chapter 4 we considered the market mechanism and the limitations and defects of the uncontrolled price system. To some extent the public sector has developed to remedy the defects. For example, to provide communal services like defence, which could not be provided by individuals, to expand services like education and health where there are strong externality effects and to put limits on the extremes of income distribution generated by the free market. If the price system has these defects, it may be asked, why not have all public sector? Why not a command economy?

Some part of the answer has been hinted at in our consideration of the characteristics of public goods and the way they are chosen. But it is worth closing this chapter on the public sector by considering the matter a little further.

At the opposite extreme to the capitalist laissez-faire economy, consisting of the market system with minimum government intervention, is the socialist command economy, resting on a system of complete central administrative planning, which, in its extreme form, does not include prices. Information has to be collected about the resources available, the alternative uses to which they can be put, the alternative production techniques and the community's preferences. In the light of this information the central planning committee decides what should be produced and who should get the product and its commands are executed and implemented in physical terms, i.e. a physical allocation of resources to units of production and a physical ration of food, clothes, etc. to consumers.

Advantages of the Command Economy

The command economy has a particular appeal to those with a strong concern for economic equality and who are attracted by the idea of 'scientifically controlling' an economy as compared to leaving it, in part at least, to 'blind market forces'. More specifically three main advantages can be claimed for a socialist command economy.

1. As people are not permitted to own wealth in productive resources there is much less scope for inequality in the distribution of wealth. Such inequality of wealth-holding as does exist, does not carry with it power over others.
2. The degree of inequality of income can be controlled. Such

inequalities as do exist are deliberate. They are not the result of chance or impersonal factors.[1]

3. As the whole economy is centrally planned, waste of resources which may result from competition is avoided.

Disadvantages of the Command Economy

Against these advantages have to be set some fundamental disadvantages.

1. *Such an economy is likely to suffer from extreme inefficiency* for a variety of reasons, partly interconnected.

(a) It is characterized by apoplexy at the centre. The magnitude of the task of administratively planning a complete economy is huge. With a modern economy a large number of pieces of information have to be fed into the system and the planning process is unceasing because of continual changes in the quantity and nature of resources, in production methods and in preferences. The digestion of this information and the actual decision-making process is enormously complex. Nor is the answer to be found in the use of computers. Complicated messages about preferences, product qualities and information on production processes simply cannot be coded on to a computer. Even if they could, it is doubtful if consumers could be articulate enough about their preferences. By contrast, the market mechanism is able to operate more efficiently because of the dispersal of decision-making—each bit of the economy, be it producer or consumer, only has to take account of a limited range of information in making its consumption or production decisions.

(b) Although the planners might set out with the intention of

[1] Not everyone, however, would regard this as an advantage. Thus Samuel Brittan writes that 'people will, in the last resort, accept a relatively low position in the pecking order if it is due to the luck of the impersonal market . . . they will recognize that no ultimate judgement has been pronounced. If, on the other hand, their low position seems to result from a moralistic evaluation of their merits made by their fellow citizens through some political process—whether by individual persons in the government or on boards appointed for the task—they will stop at nothing to get the judgements withdrawn. No one likes being consigned to the rubbish heap by a body of identifiable wise men appointed to express the supposed moral evaluations of society.' (From Samuel Brittan, *Participation Without Politics*, Institute of Economic Affairs, 1975, p. 85.)

taking the preferences of all consumers into account, the task would defy them and what would prevail would be the preferences of the planners. Thus what would be produced would not accord with the preferences of consumers.

(c) Physical rationing is inefficient in the sense that the consumer does not get that combination of goods and services which is in accordance with his tastes and preferences.

(d) Individual initiative and enterprise are stifled in such a system.

(e) Direction of labour, which is implied by the pure command economy, is inefficient (as well as being inhuman). This can best be seen by contrasting the situation with that of the market system. Under the market system, if more workers are required in a particular line of production the incentive to attract them is higher pay. Normally more workers will apply than are required so the managers will have the opportunity to select those whom they regard as most suitable for the post. It is unlikely that anyone essential in their present jobs would accept the new appointment because their old employers would in these circumstances offer them higher remuneration to stay where they were. Further, no one would apply to whom the move would involve personal hardship. Under direction of labour these conditions do not hold. Unless the selection has been very carefully made—and it would be made by others than the individual himself—there is a danger that the people selected would not be those most suitable for the post. Nor is there any guarantee that only those would be moved who would not face personal hardship as a result.

Advocates of a planned economy would maintain that these arguments overstate its inefficiencies because they exaggerate the genuineness of consumer difference. They would argue that consumers' wants are fairly standard and that it is the market system which generates and accentuates differences. Hence to override consumers' preferences is not a serious inefficiency. On the contrary, by so doing it becomes possible to reap economies of scale from standardization. It may well be that industrialization of an economically backward country, where wants are more basic and standard, can be more rapidly achieved by a centrally planned economy. But the more advanced the country, the wider the range of goods and services, the more difficult is the central planning of the economy.

2. *There is a lack of individual freedom.* In a command economy

there is a concentration of economic power and a concentration of political power. People have less freedom as consumers in their choice of products, as producers in their source of employment, and as participants in a political process. For example, direction of labour restricts personal freedom and can create serious human problems. Because the state is the universal employer, anyone who falls out with his employer may be deprived of all employment. With restricted scope for acquiring personal wealth, people are less independent and less able to resist oppression. The ownership of all the means of production distribution and exchange by the state means that all organs of communication and education are owned and run by the state, freedom of expression is seriously curtailed.

3. *In practice the goal of reducing inequalities is only imperfectly realized.* As David Lane writes, 'inequality is a characteristic of state-socialist society as it is of capitalist: there is inequality of control over wealth, inequality of political power, inequality of income and inequality of status'.[1] Moreover there is a particular form of unmerited remunerations which tends to characterize command economies with great planning bureaucracies, i.e. corruption, the giving and receiving of 'inducements' to oil the bureaucratic wheels.

In reality, just as there is no such thing as a complete laissez-faire economy, so also the complete command economy, without prices, does not exist. But some economies, e.g. the USSR, approach fairly closely to it.

SUMMARY AND CONCLUSIONS

State intervention in the economy to make good the limitations of the price system can take one or more of three forms: regulation, fiscal measures and provision. With publicly-provided goods there is no direct relationship between benefit and cost and an irreducible element of compulsion. The most convenient single measure of the size of the public sector is public expenditure expressed as a percentage of GNP—though the measure is imperfect and must be interpreted with caution. The twentieth century has witnessed an enormous growth of the public sector in the UK and major changes

[1] David Lane, *The End of Inequality*, Penguin Books, 1971. *See also*, David Bonavia, 'But some are still more equal than others', *The Times*, 21 April 1972.

in its content—more than 50 per cent of government spending is now on social services. The socialist command economy has attractions, particularly to those concerned about inequality, but it is characterized by inefficiency and lack of freedom.

6 The Social Balance

The Mixed Economy

In Chapter 4 we pointed out the inherent limitations and defects of the unregulated market mechanism of the extreme laissez-faire capitalist economy. Such an economy had a high potential for achieving freedom and efficiency but at the cost of considerable inequality. Moreover, in the absence of government intervention, the freedom includes freedom to starve and the efficiency is only imperfectly realized – for example, no allowance is made for divergencies between social and private cost. At the end of Chapter 5 we examined the opposite extreme. The socialist command economy has a high potential for reducing inequality, but at the cost of loss of freedom and inefficiency, and, in practice, the potential for equality is not necessarily realized. Thus, the course of wisdom would point to some sort of mixture of the two.

There is a sense in which all economies are mixed economies, because neither the capitalist laissez-faire economy nor the socialist command economy exists in their extreme form. But some economies approximate fairly closely to the extremes and it seems most useful to restrict the term 'mixed economy' to those where the private and the public sectors are both substantial and neither is overpowered or undermined by the other. In Chapter 5 we briefly traced the development of the United Kingdom public sector which marked, historically, a move during the nineteenth and twentieth centuries from an economy approximating to the capitalist laissez-faire model to a mixed economy with a large public sector alongside a private sector. To an important extent the public sector expanded in attempts to make good the deficiencies of the unregulated market system. In this chapter we examine the issue of the ideal relationship between the size of the public and the size of the private sectors. Professor J. K. Galbraith has coined the term 'the social balance', which he defines as 'a satisfactory relationship between the supply of privately-produced goods and services and those of the state'.[1] Thus

[1] J. K. Galbraith, *The Affluent Society*, Pelican, 1968, p. 209.

we are concerned in this chapter with the question 'Where does the social balance lie?'

It is possible to answer this question in abstract terms. For instance, we can say that the social balance is achieved with that combination of private and public sectors at which social utility is maximized. We might loosely interpret this, in a democracy, as being that combination of public and private sectors of the economy which is in accordance with the wishes of the majority of the community, assuming all its members to be perfectly knowledgeable, perfectly rational and imbued with a desire to further the common good. In practice this kind of statement does not take us far. It seems better to start by taking the United Kingdom economy, which is our particular interest, and to point to certain biases in the system which affect the size of the public sector and have an important bearing on the social balance.

The Bias Against the Public Sector

'Private opulence and public squalor'. This was the famous antithesis in which Professor J. K. Galbraith, in *The Affluent Society*, epitomized the social imbalance which he saw between the public and private sectors of consumer-oriented western economies. In his own inimitable prose he paints the contrast:

> The family which takes its mauve and cerise, air-conditioned, power-steered, and power-braked car out for a tour passes through cities that are badly paved, made hideous by litter, blighted buildings, billboards, and posts for wires that should long since have been put underground. They pass on into a countryside that has been rendered largely invisible by commercial art. They picnic on exquisitely packaged food from a portable icebox by a polluted stream and go on to spend the night at a park which is a menace to public health and morals. Just before dozing off on an air-mattress, beneath a nylon tent, amid the stench of decaying refuse, they may reflect vaguely on the curious unevenness of their blessings. Is this, indeed, the American genius?[1]

In Professor Galbraith's view social balance fails to be attained because the consumer-voter does not face an independent choice between public and private goods. He is subject to the forces of advertising and emulation (keeping up with the Jones's) by which

[1] J. K. Galbraith, *op. cit.*, pp. 207–8.

production creates its own demand. But advertising operates exclusively, and emulation mainly, on behalf of privately-produced goods and services. Thus publicly-provided goods have an inherent tendency to lag behind.

Although Professor Galbraith's illustration is drawn from the USA, it is clear from the nature of his explanation of the tendency of the public sector to lag behind the private that this generalization is intended to apply to all western mixed economies. Leaving out of account the nationalized industries (which do advertise), Table 5.1 (p. 64) showed public expenditure rising this century from a figure equal to 12 per cent of GNP in 1910 to 38 per cent in 1961; with a further unprecedented peace-time rise since then which has brought the figure to 50 per cent by 1975. If we include state spending on financial assets the 1975 figure would be 55 per cent. Whilst these figures do not disprove Galbraith's generalization—the public sector might still have lagged behind what was desirable—they certainly call it into question. Indeed, there are strong reasons for arguing that any effect which advertising and emulation exert in favour of private sector growth has been swamped by a variety of other influences in recent years, some affecting all western mixed economies, others applying only or particularly to the United Kingdom.

Some reasons for the growth of the public sector may be taken as a genuine reflection of widespread views within the community. For example, evidence of the growth of expenditure on education and health services in other countries supports the view that whether the provision is public or private, these services are 'income elastic' —that as a community's income increases, so it wishes to spend an increasing proportion of income on these services. In Britain, because they have come to be predominantly supplied by the state, growing public expenditure on these services can be regarded as reflecting the wishes of an increasingly affluent electorate. In other respects, however, the public sector may have grown not as a reflection of the rational views of well-informed electors, but from a complex of factors which have obscured or distorted the real choice for the citizen. In the next section we attempt to list such influences. Our list is tentative and a little speculative and it is not possible to assign a weight to the various influences. Further, one must add the caveat that not only are these factors inter-related, but often a widely-held argument for increased public spending may be linked with an institutional feature generating public spending. Thus, state expenditure to increase public sector employment in times of unemployment may be widely desired, but it is the nature of the public sector that this additional labour is often not released from public employment when unemployment has fallen and the private sector is seeking skilled manpower.

The Bias Towards the Public Sector

1. *The change in the nature of public goods.* The first and possibly the most fundamental reason for the growing bias in favour of the public sector is bound up with the complex relationship which exists between costs and benefits for public sector goods and the changing composition of the public sector. As we saw in Chapter 5, with public goods—unlike private goods—there is generally no direct relationship between cost and benefit. The costs of public goods, in the form of extra taxation, are divorced from expenditure both in the decision-making process and often in time. Nor do the beneficiaries of public expenditure normally pay in proportion to benefit received. Further, some forms of public spending, notably on pure public goods, carry benefits which are diffuse, indiscriminate and impersonal, whilst with quasi-public goods, such as social security transfer payments, the benefits are of a very personal and tangible kind see pp. 57-8).

The figures in Table 5.2 (p. 66) showed how public expenditure was defence-dominated in the eighteenth and nineteenth centuries. As late as 1910, a peace-time year, over 40 per cent of government expenditure went on administration and defence—services of the pure public good variety. For such goods the costs, in terms of taxation, were more real and personal to most citizens than the benefits. The nature of the public sector then supported the views, advanced by Professors Peacock and Wiseman, that in settled times notions of acceptable tax burdens were more influential than ideas about desirable increases in expenditure in determining the level of public spending. But as the century had progressed, and especially since the Second World War, the situation has changed. The proportion of public expenditure applied to pure public goods has diminished and that applied to quasi-public goods has increased (see above for the definition of these). Thus by 1974 defence and administration had dropped to under 20 per cent of public spending whilst social service expenditure (including education and housing) had risen to well over 50 per cent. For a growing proportion of the population the benefits of public expenditure have been assuming a more immediate and direct relevance than the cost. This tendency has been reinforced by demographic trends. Few benefits could be more direct and personal than state retirement pensions. The 1971 census showed that 16 per cent of the UK population were over retirement age (60 for women and 65 for men) nearly all of whom were receiving state retirement pensions. The corresponding age groups were only 12 per cent of the population in 1941 and a mere 7 per cent in 1911.

2. *The growth of public sector employment.* Besides the consumers of public services, some of whom have come to depend for much of their livelihood on public provision, the growth of the public sector has necessarily entailed a growth in the numbers of public sector employees whose income, employment and conditions of work depend on public spending. This growth was particularly marked during the 1960s and the early 1970s. Thus public sector employment, excluding the nationalized industries, grew by 928,000 between 1964 and 1973, despite a fall of over 60,000 in the numbers of HM forces. Civilian employment in central government employment rose by 19 per cent whilst local government employment rose by 35 per cent; there was a 47 per cent increase in teachers and a 64 per cent increase in support staff in education; and in the health services employment rose by 58 per cent.

The more people the public sector employs, the larger the proportion of the electorate whose personal interest is bound up with public sector spending. Nor are public employees only concerned with salaries and employment prospects, their concern extends also to conditions of work. Thus teachers' unions lobby for new schools and increased book allowances, and consultants press for better hospitals and research facilities within the NHS.

3. *Productivity lag.* The particularly large growth in public sector employment reflects the labour-intensive nature of public sector output, a large part of which consists of services as distinct from goods. It is this characteristic which gives rise to the phenomenon known as the 'relative price effect' or productivity lag. Where output consists of services, there is less scope for productivity increases than in the economy as a whole. Productivity increases tend to be most rapid in manufacturing industry or in agriculture and are usually associated with the introduction of new machines. With services, such as teaching or administration by local or central government officials, the opportunity for raising productivity is more limited. (Assuming the same quality of education, a productivity increase for a teacher would mean larger classes.) That being so, if wages and salaries in the public sector keep pace with those in the

private sector, public sector costs rise more than prices in general. In other words, even to retain the same proportion of total real output, the public sector input (i.e. the resources it uses) has to rise relatively to private sector input.

4. *Government commitment to full employment.* Following the work of Keynes in the 1930s, the war-time coalition government, with the approval of all the political parties, in a famous White Paper of 1944 accepted the responsibility for maintaining a 'high and stable' level of employment. This commitment to full employment has meant that, in times of recession, governments have sought to increase spending to stimulate demand or to shore up ailing firms. Although governments may also have attempted to reduce spending in times of excess demand, the rigidity of public spending makes for a one-sided process. Many forms of government spending, once embarked on, become commitments from which it is difficult to disengage and additional labour, once taken on, tends to remain within the public sector.

5. *Inherent characteristics of bureaucracy.* The terms 'bureaucracy' or 'bureaucrat' are not being used here in any pejorative sense. Following Niskanen,[1] we can define a 'bureau' as a non-profit organization financed, at least in part, from a periodic appropriation or grant (as distinct from the sale of its output). Such a definition may apply, for example, to research or service departments of firms, but clearly its most widespread application is to government departments. The term 'bureaucrat' can be used to describe any full-time employee of a bureau, but more specifically it denotes a senior official in a bureau with a separate budget.

What motivates bureaucrats? Among possible motives are salary level, perquisites of office, public reputation, power, patronage, and pride in the output of the bureau. The ease of making changes and of managing the bureau may also intrude. All these motives except the last two are a positive function of the total budget of the bureau and, although managing the bureau and making changes may be more difficult at higher budget levels than at lower, an increase in the budget will ease them both. Thus budget maximimization can reasonably be taken as a proxy for the motivations of bureaucrats.

This assumption is not necessarily based on a cynical view of bureaucrats. Many of them undoubtedly seek to serve what they perceive as the 'public interest'. But the bureaucrat will normally

[1] W. A. Niskanen, *Bureaucracy: Servant or Master*, IEA, 1973. The author acknowledges his debt to Niskanen for most of the ideas in this section.

work within a narrow field; he develops an expertise in that field, often generating a sense of dedication, and will naturally tend to equate that dedication with the public interest. Hence the most dedicated bureaucrats describe their objectives as increasing the budget for the *services* (such as defence, education or housing) which they provide. Moreover, even though a bureaucrat may accept that some of the funds he uses might, in principle, be 'better' used elsewhere, he may have no confidence that, if he forgoes them, they will be spent in this better way.

At the same time, bureaux are likely to be less concerned with economizing than profit-making organizations. If a bureaucrat reduces costs by 5 per cent he may have that much more to spend on other items. If the head of a profit-making organization, which previously had a 5 per cent difference between receipts and costs, saves 5 per cent on costs, profits rise 100 per cent. Moreover the bureaucrat does not face the economizing pressure exercised by competition, but in a tight situation the very survival of the profit-making organization may depend on such economies.

In short, there are powerful reasons for believing that the public sector will tend to expand because the natural inclination of bureaucrats is to increase their budgets, while at the same time they do not face market pressures making for economy in the use of resources.

6. *The proclivities of ministers.* The same attitudes to public spending which characterize bureaucrats can be found amongst the political heads of the spending departments and for similar reasons. A minister is highly unlikely to make his political reputation by cutting the expenditure of his department. He will fight hard in Cabinet for his departmental proposals for new expenditure programmes and if he accepts expenditure cuts he will be thought weak. Moreover, like the dedicated bureaucrat, a conscientious minister is immersed in the work of his department and is likely to equate spending on his service with the national interest.

7. *Executive control of public expenditure.* The executive, particularly the Treasury, might be expected to control the spending proclivities of departmental bureaucrats and ministers. To some extent this undoubtedly happens. Estimates are vetted by the Treasury and special cost-effectiveness studies conducted. In the last resort the Chancellor of the Exchequer can use the full weight of his office to secure reduction in estimates. However, there are reasons for believing that the methods of executive control of expenditure in

the United Kingdom have developed a built-in bias towards expansion. The Plowden Committee Report of 1961, *Control of Public Expenditure*,[1] recommended that instead of the somewhat *ad hoc* way in which many public expenditure decisions had hitherto been taken, regular surveys should be made of public expenditure as a whole for a period of years ahead and in the light of prospective resources. This recommendation led to the formation of the Public Expenditure Survey Committee (PESC) and, since 1969, five-year rolling surveys have been published in annual public expenditure white papers.

In practice the 'prospective resources' of the Plowden recommendation has been taken to be the expected growth of GNP. As a result the public sector (public expenditure measured as a percentage of GNP) has grown most rapidly when actual growth has fallen short of expected growth. This consequence has been accentuated by the short-term rigidities in public spending and by the lack of comprehensive management information consistent with the public expenditure five-year programmes to show whether the trend of programmes has been on course.[2]

In the past decade the two periods in which public expenditure has grown most as a percentage of GNP have been 1965–68 and 1974–75. The first period was associated with the National Plan, in which public expenditure was planned to rise at 4.25 per cent per annum against an expected growth rate of 3.8 per cent per annum. However, actual growth only attained 2.5 per cent per annum, so public expenditure as a percentage of GNP soared. In 1974–75 real GNP actually fell by around 2 per cent whilst public expenditure continued to grow in real terms, hence there was a large jump in the size of the public sector. Thus errors in medium-term economic forecasting have been partly responsible for an unintended growth of the public sector. But on the basis of past experience, and on what one would expect of the psychology of ministers, growth forecasts will always tend to err towards optimism. Hence, the PESC system carries a built-in bias towards public sector expansion.

8. *The failure of parliamentary control of expenditure.* Traditionally the House of Commons, which alone can authorize taxation, has been

---

[1] Cmnd. 1432.

[2] For further reasons why the PESC system has been particularly unsatisfactory in a period of rapid inflation, see First Report of the Expenditure Committee of the House of Commons, General Sub-Committee, 1975–6, *The Financing of Public Expenditure*, HC69. Since then, the introduction of cash limits and of monthly returns has improved Treasury control.

regarded as the guardian of the public purse. In practice, however, whilst MPs may generalize in debates about the need to cut public spending or reduce taxation, the *specific* pressures they exercise are almost all in the direction of demands for increased spending. Members wish to secure their re-election and so they wish to demonstrate their active concern for their constituents' interests. Hence they are to be found pressing for new hospitals, schools or roads, or urging ministers into action to deal with potential or actual unemployment in their constituencies. The attitude of the individual MP is conditioned by the same kind of relationship between cost and benefit to which we have already referred. The benefit of a new hospital, school or employment subsidy to his constituents is tangible, real, direct and concentrated; the cost is vague, uncertain and diffused throughout the entire community. The one exception to this generalization, which proves the rule, is that there are always MPs who will demand cuts in defence expenditure. Whilst these demands often have an ideological basis, it is not without significance that this is one form of public spending where the benefit is intangible and diffuse.

A small number of MPs have been seeking, notably through the Expenditure Committee of the House of Commons, to exercise some meaningful control over expenditure. The General Sub-Committee in particular has produced perceptive and telling reports. But work on the Expenditure Committee rarely catches the headlines and is not likely to impress constituents. Nor is committee work likely to bring a member to the attention of his leaders as effectively as speaking in the House. Members lack both time and research assistance, and committee work is onerous if done properly. With so little pay-off in terms of constituency interests and the prospect of office, it is little wonder that effective work is confined to a few enthusiasts. Moreover, it is typical of the atomistic approach of MPs to the issues raised by public expenditure that the various sub-committees of the Expenditure Committee have never accepted a coordinated programme. Parliamentary debates on the annual Public Expenditure White Papers have mostly flopped. Thus, despite innovations of recent years which give more opportunity to MPs to scrutinize and comment on public expenditure as a whole, it remains true that the pressures MPs exert are nearly all in the direction of increased expenditure.

9. *The weakening link between taxation and expenditure.* With public goods there is, as we have seen, no direct link between cost and

benefit. On top of this various factors have been at work in recent years to weaken still further, or at any rate disguise, the link between taxation and public expenditure in the United Kingdom. The growing complexity of government has tended to obscure the relationship. Keynesian economics taught that there was nothing particularly virtuous about a balanced budget. Further, some politicians have encouraged electors to think that 'the rich' could be made to pay for additional state spending. Perhaps most important, the British budgetary system has operated in the way which may both encourage expenditure and weaken in the citizen's mind the link between taxes and public spending. On the one hand the main expenditure decisions are taken separately from, and before, the decisions on taxation; then (subject to any deficit or surplus required for the management of the economy) taxes are raised to cover the expenditure. This may generate a greater willingness to accede to expenditure demands rather than if the reverse procedure applied. Further, expenditure decisions are presented to Parliament separately from the tax decisions and they are debated separately. The system seems almost designed to accentuate the separation between benefit and costs. It is perhaps no wonder that some citizens see no inconsistency in calling for more public spending and lower taxes.

Nowhere has the effects of the separation between benefit and cost been more evident in recent years than in local authority expenditure. If all local expenditure were locally financed there would still be no direct relationship between cost and benefit. In fact, the relationship has become more tenuous as local government spending has become increasingly financed from central government grants. It is no coincidence that, measured as a proportion of GNP, local authority spending rose by 43 per cent between 1964 and 1974 (compared with 31 per cent for central government) at a time when a major change was taking place in the source of local government finance. In the early 1960s rates and grants contributed in about equal proportions to local authority expenditure: in 1964 the ratio of rates to grants was 49:51; in 1968 it was 45:55; in 1974 it was 38:62; and in 1975, 33:67. There must be a strong presumption, borne out by the views both of the Royal Commission on Local Government Reform and the Committee on Local Government Finance[1] that,

[1] *Local Government Reform* (Redcliffe-Maude Report), Cmnd. 4039, June 1969 (see Shorter Version, p. 12). *Local Government Finance* (Layfield Report), Cmnd. 6453, May 1976 (see, for example, p. 40).

had local authorities been obliged to find the bulk of the revenue locally, their attitude to spending would have been very different. Local expenditure which mainly benefits local residents will almost always seem a good bargain to local councillors if two-thirds of the cost is met from outside the locality.

Where Does the Social Balance Lie?

We have analysed the biases which exist in the United Kingdom economy, some making for reduced and some for increased government expenditure. This approach is far from indicating what is the social balance—the optimum size of the public and private sectors—though it may give some hint on whether a particular economy has moved too much in one direction. Can we say more than this?

Even if we cannot be precise about the ideal 'mix', it may be possible to set certain limits beyond which the mixed economy ceases to exist. Thus, Mr Roy Jenkins, in January 1976, pointed out that public expenditure (on the definition including capital expenditure of nationalized industries) was currently running at about 60 per cent of national income, and went on to state:

> I do not think that you can push public expenditure significantly above 60 per cent and maintain the values of a plural society with adequate freedom of choice. We are here close to one of the frontiers of social democracy. Our short-term problems apart, there is no future in believing that we can let public expenditure as a proportion of the national income rise significantly further. If we do that either the taxation or the inflationary consequences will be unacceptable.[1]

To elaborate on Mr Jenkins' thesis, the higher the level of government expenditure, the greater is the concentration of economic and political power in the hands of the state, with its threat to personal freedom. Specifically, the higher the level of government expenditure with its correspondingly high level of taxation, the less the freedom of choice of the taxpayer. The less personal choice he has in spending his income, the more it is spent for him by the state.

Yet the attempt to specify a percentage of public expenditure to GNP or national income beyond which the mixed economy is undermined, is not wholly satisfactory. Much depends on the nature

[1] Quoted in *The Times*, 24 January 1976.

of that expenditure. If a rise in expenditure takes the form of transfer payments, where the recipient not the state determines what shall be purchased and produced, the increase in the state's economic power has been minimal. Putting the point in another way, although the freedom of the taxpayer has been reduced by the tax to finance the expenditure, the freedom of the recipient of the transfer income has been enlarged. Much more restrictive of freedom is government expenditure on goods and services; and, in an intermediate position is government expenditure on subsidies, where people only gain in real income if they buy the subsidized product (and they may be debarred from doing so, e.g. the family which wants a council house but is a long way down the council's waiting list). Again, a percentage of public expenditure to GNP or national income does not tell all. As we pointed out in Chapter 5 (p. 61), a government may exercise a totalitarian control over the economy by means of regulations even when the percentage of public expenditure is comparatively small.

Another consideration relating to the social balance is the efficiency of the private and public sectors. The larger the governmental machine the more likely are there to be inefficiencies arising from diseconomies of scale—bottlenecks, delays in decision making, lack of co-ordination. The larger the area of public sector provision the bigger are the problems of finding a rational basis for allocating resources to the various services and the more difficult it may be to secure value for money in public spending.

Finally, we must recognize that the social balance depends on value judgments. The individualist and the collectivist, whilst both may wish to maintain a genuine mixed economy, will differ in their approach and in their perception of the social balance. The individualist tends to favour market provision, stresses the responsibility of the individual and the family, believes there is moral value in freedom of choice and political value in dispersion of economic power. The collectivist, on the other hand, is more doubtful of the capacity of individuals to choose wisely and of the relevance of the family to modern life and seeks state provision in education and health services to provide a common badge of citizenship and reduce class differences. The individualist is more inclined to cash transfers to reduce inequalities, whilst the collectivist more often favours state provision of essentials like housing. Not all people fall neatly into one or other of these categories, but there is nonetheless a fundamental difference of philosophy, and those who incline to individualist values will perceive the social balance in a smaller public sector than those who incline to collectivist values.

SUMMARY AND CONCLUSIONS

How large should the public sector be? Where does the social balance lie? Professor Galbraith has argued that the public sector has an inherent tendency to lag because of the influence of advertising and emulation on demand for private goods. On the other hand, a variety of influences, including the increasing proportion of public expenditure yielding direct rather than diffuse benefits, the inherent characteristics of bureaucrats and ministers, and certain institutional features in the United Kingdom, create a bias in the opposite direction. To specify a percentage of public expenditure to GNP as constituting the social balance, or even as a limit to the mixed economy, is not really satisfactory. Much depends on the nature of the expenditure, the extent of regulation and the efficiency of the public sector. In the final analysis perceptions of the social balance are strongly influenced by personal value judgments.

Part II

THE POPULATION BACKGROUND

Introduction to Part II

Population is of vital relevance to social economics. Its size and rate of change have important consequences for living standards and the environmental quality of life. Likewise, the structure of population, in particular the ratio of working to dependent population, is clearly relevant to living standards.

Further, as the Select Committee on Science and Technology expressed it, 'The size and structure of the population are critical to the scale of the social and environmental services provided by the government'.[1] Thus, for example, changes in the birth rate affect a whole series of social policies: first, the provision of maternity beds; then places in nursery, primary and secondary schools and in further and higher education; places in colleges of education and universities for training the teachers for these children and young people; then the provision of houses and jobs; and finally pensions and places in geriatric hospitals.

In Chapter 7 we look at the history of population in Great Britain over the past two centuries and then at the present structure of the population. The history provides a perspective. It gives some indication of the likely economic and social effects of population change, and explains the present structure of the population. Then we move on to look at population future in Chapter 8. For this purpose we need to sharpen our statistical tools and use more precise measures of fertility and mortality. We look at population projections and, in particular, review the work of the Population Panel. Finally we pose the question, 'Does Britain need a Population Policy?'

---

[1] *First Report from the Select Committee on Science and Technology*, Session 1970–71, *Population of the United Kingdom*, HC 379, 1971, p. iv.

7 Population Past and Present

Growth of Population in Great Britain

British population statistics can easily confuse the student by their variations in coverage. The chief, but not the only difficulty, relates to geographical area. Before the first census in 1801 we have only isolated estimates relating to England and Wales or Scotland. The best of these for England and Wales was that by Gregory King at the end of the seventeenth century who estimated the population at $5\frac{1}{2}$ million. Later scholarship has confirmed the substantial accuracy of King's figure but suggested that he may have over-estimated by some 5 per cent. The first census in 1801 showed a population of 9 million for England and Wales, suggesting a population growth in the eighteenth century approaching 80 per cent. In the census England and Wales on the one hand and Scotland on the other were enumerated separately, but we can, of course, combine the figures, as in Table 7.1 which gives the population of Great Britain for

Table 7.1   Population of Great Britain, 1801–1971.

Year	Population (millions)
1801	10.9
1851	20.8
1901	37.0
1911	40.8
1921	42.8
1931	44.8
1941	46.9
1951	49.2
1961	51.5
1971	54.1
1975 (est.)	54.4

Notes: up to 1931, the census enumerated (i.e. the domestic) population; after 1941 the total population, including British armed forces overseas. The 1801 population is an adjusted figure to allow for under-enumeration in the 1801 census. No census was taken in 1941.

Source: Office of Population Censuses and Surveys.

selected census years. If we want figures for the United Kingdom we must remember that its definition has changed: up to 1922 it included the whole of Ireland and thereafter only Northern Ireland. For 1971 the Northern Ireland figure was 1.5 million, so the United Kingdom population in 1971 was 55.6 million.

In examining the population changes we can distinguish three phases: firstly, a period with a phenomenal rate of growth, which we can date very approximately 1780–1880; secondly, a period from 1880 to 1940 in which the rate of growth was very much slower; and thirdly the period from 1940 to the present in which growth continued but with such marked fluctuations in the birth rate that it deserves separate treatment.

Changes in population size, in a narrow statistical sense, depend on birth rate, death rate and net migration (i.e. the net balance of emigration and immigration). Crude birth and death rates, which simply express births and deaths as so many per 1000 of the total population, can be misleading, mainly because they depend so much on the age distribution of the population at any particular time. However, they will serve well enough for our purposes in this chapter. In the next chapter we shall introduce some more refined measures.

During the period 1780–1940, covering the first two phases we have distinguished, there was substantial net emigration except for the decade of the 1930s. Thus the causes of population growth and the change in rate of growth must be sought in 'natural' increase (i.e. the excess of births over deaths).

Figure 7.1 gives the crude birth and death rate figures from 1780. Civil registration of births and deaths only became effective in 1838 and the figures before that date are necessarily speculative. Consequently in Figure 7.1 an estimated average figure is given for each of the two periods 1781–1800 and 1801–30.[1]

Phase I, 1780–1880

During this phase the birth rate remained high throughout, at between 30 and 36 per 1000 population, whilst the death rate, with some fluctuations, fell substantially from around 28 per 1000 to below 20 per 1000.

Historians have concentrated their efforts on trying to explain the

[1] Following P. Deane and W. A. Cole, *British Economic Growth*, Cambridge University Press, 2nd edition, 1969.

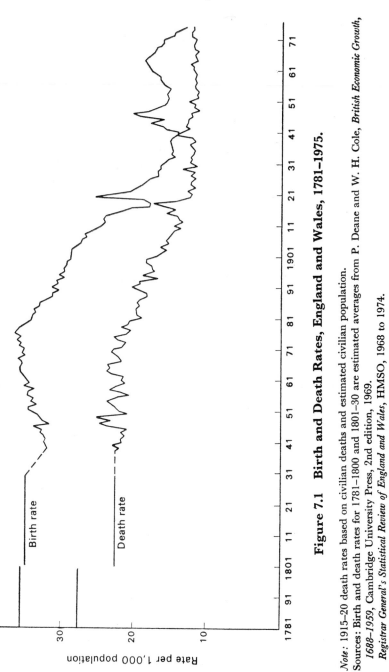

Figure 7.1 Birth and Death Rates, England and Wales, 1781–1975.

Note: 1915–20 death rates based on civilian deaths and estimated civilian population.

Sources: Birth and death rates for 1781–1800 and 1801–30 are estimated averages from P. Deane and W. H. Cole, *British Economic Growth, 1688–1959*, Cambridge University Press, 2nd edition, 1969.

Registrar General's Statistical Review of England and Wales, HMSO, 1968 to 1974.

acceleration in the rate of growth of population in the later eighteenth and early nineteenth centuries in an attempt to understand its relationship with industrialization. Did the growth of population generate industrialization? Did industrialization cause the population growth? Or were the two independent phenomena which happened to coincide?

There is a broad consensus that acceleration of the rate of population growth began around the middle decades of the eighteenth century. There is some, but not conclusive, evidence of an increase in the birth rate during the eighteenth century. It has been hazarded that the decline in apprenticeship and a decline in the practice of agricultural labourers 'living in' with their employers, together with the fact that a full adult wage could be earned early in occupations such as mining and factory work, may have stimulated earlier marriages and larger families. Further, it is possible that the demand for child labour and the Speenhamland system of poor relief on a rudimentary family allowance basis may have had some influence, but the case is not proven.

There is much wider agreement among historians that death rates were declining in the second half of the eighteenth century and then stabilized for much of the nineteenth century. Until recently medical improvements—including advances in vaccination, the development of inoculation and increased hospital facilities—were accepted as contributing to the fall in death rate. Also, a wide variety of other factors were believed to have reduced mortality: a decline in gin drinking following the gin legislation of the mid-century; improved food supply—fresh meat and milk and more vegetables—associated with the agricultural changes and helped by better transport; improvements in sanitation, water supply, refuse disposal and the burial of the dead; improved personal cleanliness associated with cotton instead of woollen goods and increased use of soap; the substitution of brick for timber and slate for thatch in housebuilding; and the removal of noxious manufacturing processes from the homes. Recent research has modified our views on some of these factors. The efficacy of the medical improvements has been seriously challenged by two medical historians,[1] although they may have

[1] T. McKeown and R. G. Brown, 'Medical evidence related to English population changes in the eighteenth century', *Population Studies*, vol. IX, No. 2, 1955, pp. 119–41. They pungently write, 'The chief indictment of hospital work in this period is not that it did no good, but that it positively did harm. . . . It was not until much later that hospital patients could be reasonably certain of dying from the disease with which they were admitted.'

overstated their case especially in the strictures on hospitals and their doubts about the value of inoculations. Few historians would now credit the gin legislation with much effect on death rates, or put much weight on improvements in living conditions in the towns. We are left with a variety of other possible influences, the quantitative contribution of which we cannot readily measure, and a further possible explanation, recently advanced, that the fall in death rate was mainly because the period saw a decline of endemic and epidemic deseases, most notably the plague, for reasons that are also obscure.

The explanation of the eighteenth-century population acceleration remains uncertain. The results of modern scholarship have been largely negative. As Professor M. W. Flinn writes, 'The really important advance in the scholarship of recent years is that for the first time in the study of Britain's population in the eighteenth century we recognize that we know so little.'[1]

Phase II, 1880–1940

In this phase the birth rate plummeted, a consistent downward trend being broken only by easily explicable fluctuations resulting from the First World War. From a figure of 36 per 1000 in the mid-1870s the birth rate fell to a nadir of 13.9 at the end of this period (1941). However the fall in birth rate was accompanied by a major reduction in death rate from an average of 19 per 1000 in the decade 1881–90 to 12 per 1000 in the decade 1931–40. In the earlier years of this period the rate of population increase was not much below that of the previous phase, but in the twentieth century the rate of natural increase slowed markedly.

Although, as compared with the previous period, the figures of birth and death rates are reliable, there remain obscurities about the reasons for the changes.

The fall in death rate can be put down, broadly, to improvements in medicine and living standards, with doubtless the beginning of the 'welfare state' (briefly described in Chapter 5) making its contribution. The fall in the birth rate, the crucial change, is more difficult to explain satisfactorily. Undoubtedly it was associated with the deliberate limitation of family size by the increasing use of methods of birth control; but this still leaves open the question why people wished to restrict the size of their families. It may be that

[1] M. W. Flinn, *British Population Growth, 1700–1850*, Macmillan, 1970, p. 50.

people had wished to before, but the means of birth control were less effective, dearer and did more violence to natural sensitivities.

That apart, a number of other possibilities have been suggested, mainly by the Royal Commission on Population which reported in 1949. The Commission suggested that a decline in the economic importance of the family may have contributed to the birth rate fall. In particular, with factory acts specifying minimum entry ages, and education made compulsory, children became more of a financial liability than an earning asset. A rather different argument is that many parents wished to give their children a better chance in life than they themselves had had, and rising standards of parental care made parenthood more costly. The Royal Commission suggested that industrialization may have intensified the struggle for security and social promotion, and in the enjoyment of the higher living standards which industrialization brought those with a family were at a disadvantage. It was even suggested that the choice in the 1930s was between a baby and a Baby Austin. People's outlook on life, too, was changing. Control of the size of family could be regarded as an aspect of the development of science, and the spread of education may have encouraged the use of birth control as may the decline of religious observance and the more tolerant attitude of some religious denominations to birth control. Social example also played a part, the restriction in family size starting with the 'upper class' and gradually moving down the social scale. The growing emancipation of women over the period may have stimulated a reaction against large families which hampered the career woman, and many women, with an increasing say in the ordering of these things, may have disliked the excessive pain and work associated with a large family. Finally, as the survival rate amongst infants rose, so the need for as many births to ensure a certain family size diminished. All these are plausible suggestions and they may all have played a part, but we can only treat them as tentative.

Some Economic and Social Consequences of the Population Growth 1780–1940

Some appreciation of the significance of the population growth can be gained from the realization that the increase was as great in the first thirty years of the nineteenth century as in the previous 300 years. These population changes pervaded almost all areas of economic and social life of which we shall examine four main aspects.

1. *Living standards.* The growth of the population towards the end of the eighteenth century was a matter of concern to many contemporaries. They were aware that population was expanding, but they did not know how fast. The first census of population in 1801 was taken as a response to this concern.

No one was more alarmed by the population growth than the Rev. T. R. Malthus, who wrote his first and famous *Essay on the Principles of Population* in 1798. He argued that population would always tend to outgrow the means of subsistence. As living standards fell in consequence of population growth, the growth itself would be checked by 'vice' (abortion), 'misery' (starvation and emigration) and he later added, 'moral restraint' (by which he meant later marriages).

The basis of his fear was that, as population expanded, the other factors of production would not expand in proportion. Whilst he recognized that 'with every mouth there came a pair of hands' (after a time-lag which was not very lengthy in his day) output per head and therefore income per head would fall if increases in labour as a factor of production were not accompanied by increases in the other factors with which labour worked. The big difficulty was land which, broadly speaking, was fixed in extent. As population grew it would be necessary both to farm land more intensively and to farm more extensively. But it was thought that, after a while, intensive cultivation would yield diminishing returns whilst extensive cultivation would involve bringing less and less fertile (or conveniently situated) land into cultivation. Either way additional food could only be obtained from the land at increasing cost.

A particular feature of the decline in the death rate was the decline in the infant mortality rate. At the end of the eighteenth and during the early nineteenth century the problem was how to feed and clothe children far outnumbering those of earlier generations.

In fact the Malthusian Devil was avoided in England (though not in Ireland) and population growth was shown to be compatible with rising living standards. The gloomy predictions of Malthus were not fulfilled for three main reasons. Firstly, agricultural improvements, from crop rotation and better stock-breeding to the development of artificial fertilizers, kept raising the productivity of land. The law of diminishing returns still held but higher levels of output could be obtained before diminishing returns set in. Secondly, industrialization and improvements in transport together enabled Britain to exchange manufactured goods for agricultural products on the world markets and thus to draw on the land of other countries. In effect this involved a substitution of capital for land, via industrialization. Thirdly, as we have seen, the birth rate ultimately (from the third quarter of the nineteenth century) fell; without that fall the Malthusian pressures would have mounted.

If the predictions of Malthus proved false for Great Britain, and population growth was shown to be compatible with rising living standards, the effect may nonetheless have been to slow up the benefits of industrialization to the working classes.

2. *Industrialization.* We said that industrialization was one of the main ways by which the Malthusian forecast of misery from population growth was avoided. But the population growth was itself a factor promoting industrialization. And, as we have already seen, in various ways industrialization may have promoted the rise in population. In short, there is a complex inter-relationship between population, industrialization and living standards.

Population growth in late eighteenth- and nineteenth-century Britain probably promoted industrialization both from its effects on the supply of the factors of production and its effects on the demand for goods.

The growth in population increased the supply of labour, and more especially it provided a particularly mobile and adaptable labour force. The mobility came from the inflow of new recruits and the low average age of population, particularly connected with the decline in infant mortality which was such a marked feature of the fall in death rates.

At the same time the growth of population helped to provide a rapidly expanding home market which acted as a stimulus to industrialists to invest and made possible increased specialization and economies of scale.

Nevertheless, we must be very cautious in our generalizations. A growth of population by itself does not secure industrialization, as Ireland in the nineteenth century and many developing countries today bear witness. If it is to generate industrialization, population growth needs to be supported by other favourable factors such as adequate supplies of raw materials, a supply of savings and people with the enterprise to take advantage of the opportunities. Given these factors a growth in population is likely to be accompanied by a growth in demand with the benefits of increased specialization, a high level of business confidence and possibly a higher level of technological innovation. A growing economy, too, is one in which adjustments can most painlessly be made, for example changes in demand for products are not as disruptive: with a rapidly growing population a gradual decline in individual demand for a product may mean little total reduction in demand for it, so that the reduction in the labour force employed in that industry may be brought about by retirements which are not balanced by recruitment, rather than by unemployment.

3. *Social amenities.* The period of most rapid population growth, coinciding as it did with urbanization, intensified problems of housing people in towns in the late eighteenth and early nineteenth centuries and providing them with civilized amenities, paving, lighting, waste removal and disposal, water supply and so on. Also the population growth and industrialization together scarred the physical environment.

4. *Emigration.* The vast natural increase in population provided the basis for the emigration of the nineteenth and early twentieth centuries. Much of the emigration was from Ireland and Scotland rather than England and Wales, but taking it together, the effect was to people large parts of the globe with British stock (USA, Canada, Australia, New Zealand, southern Africa). Besides its immense political consequences this had important economic results: it provided markets for British exports and opportunities for British overseas investment. At the same time it opened up 'New Worlds' to provide the foodstuffs for the population growing so rapidly at home.

Population Changes Since 1940

Figure 7.2 reproduces on a larger scale than Figure 7.1 the birth and death rates since 1940 to help us in examining the last 30–40 years in more detail. Let us start with mortality, then consider emigration and immigration, which have some effect both on mortality and fertility rates, and finally concentrate on the crucial factor of birth rate changes.

Death Rates

Whilst the death rates at each age group (known as the age-specific mortality rates) have generally continued to fall, the crude death

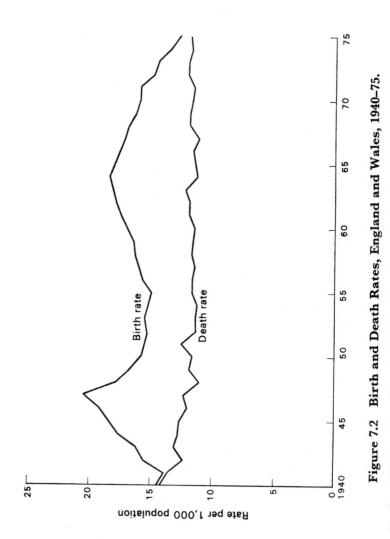

Figure 7.2   Birth and Death Rates, England and Wales, 1940–75.

rate has largely stopped falling because of the increase in the proportion of older people in the population. Since 1941 the overall death rate has been more or less constant at around 11–12 per 1000 population.

Emigration and Immigration

Whilst the statistics are far from perfect, it appears that in the late 1950s and early 1960s there was a *net* immigration which in the years 1956–61 averaged 43,000 per annum. That period apart, the net post-war movement has been outward. The numbers involved in the net migration over the period have not been such as to have a significant direct effect on population change, but the differences in characteristics of the immigrants and emigrants is important.

The immigrants have been mainly from the New Commonwealth (though also some from the Republic of Ireland), and they have been largely young adults. Adult emigrants, on the other hand, have tended to be slightly older, often moving in family groups with children. The immigrants have been responsible for a relatively high number of births partly because of their age but also because immigrants from the New Commonwealth (and the Irish Republic) tend to have larger families than average. Because of the high proportion of young people amongst immigrants, deaths among them have been relatively low.

The Population Panel[1] suggested that there were about 1 million coloured people in Britain in 1971 (about 2 per cent of the population) most of whom had arrived in the previous 15 years.[2] About 40,000 births a year, 5 per cent of all births, are to parents both of whom are coloured and some 10,000 are to mixed marriages. Deaths of coloured people are only 3000–4000, or half a per cent of all deaths. Although we cannot make equivalent calculations of the births amongst the emigrants, there is a reasonable presumption that over recent years the reduction in Britain's natural increase from emigration has been smaller than the addition to natural increase from immigration.

Experience of migrant fertility in other countries suggests that it is likely to move towards the national average; so the higher level of fertility amongst the immigrants may not be maintained.

[1] See p. 116.
[2] *Report of the Population Panel*, Cmnd. 5258, 1973.

Birth Rates

Changes in birth rates have been the most important determinant of fluctuations in the rate of population growth since 1940. From its low of 13.9 in 1941 the birth rate for England and Wales rose fairly steadily to a peak of 20.5 in 1947. Thereafter it fell to 15.8 in 1950, remaining fairly stable until a rise towards the end of the 1950s, which continued to 1964 (18.5). Since then a steady fall has set in which brought the rate down to 12.8 by 1975.

It is by no means easy to account for these changes. The Report of the Royal Commission in 1949[1] attributed the war-time and post-war increase to earlier marriages and consequent earlier families—'a borrowing of babies from the future'—rather than an increase in family size. But after 1947 the birth rate did not fall as rapidly as the Royal Commission expected and the rise in the late 1950s and early 1960s was by no means anticipated. This rise certainly suggested a move towards larger families. The prolonged fall in birth rate since 1964 is equally difficult to account for, occurring at a time when a rise might have been expected as those born in the high birth rate period of the middle and late 1940s began to start their own families. Clearly the birth rate fall owes something to further improvements in methods of contraception, most notably 'the pill', to increased dissemination of birth control information and also to the legalization of abortion. But these developments do not provide the whole answer. The recent reduction in the birth rate is characterized by a fall in births in the early years of marriage, but it is not yet clear how far this reflects a change in the timing of families and how far a fall in the completed size of family. Our examination, in the next chapter, of some more sophisticated measures of fertility will throw a little more light on the situation.

An economic explanation of the recent fall in the birth rate would be that the increased employment prospects for women and the relative rise in women's wages have increased the opportunity cost of having children. But as a falling birth rate has been experienced in recent years by nearly all the countries of Western Europe and North America perhaps the explanation should be sought less in the circumstances of a particular country than in widely-held changes in attitudes towards the role of women in society or towards population growth in a world of shrinking resources.

[1] Cmd. 7695.

The Population Structure

The importance of the recent population changes is to be found more in its effect on the structure of the population than on its size. There are two main aspects to changes in the population structure: the special nature of the immigration in this period, and the age and sex composition.

The nature and characteristics of the immigrant population raises economic and social issues. For example, it has affected particular occupations: many immigrants have been unskilled West Indians who have tended to move into occupations such as portering or unskilled jobs with London Transport. Other immigrants have been Africans and Asians with commercial skills; yet others have been doctors. Because they have concentrated in particular geographical areas the immigrants have had disproportionate effects on problems of housing and school provision. However, such economic effects, though important, are linked with and dwarfed by, the racial issues—which it would be outside the scope of this volume to consider. We shall therefore concentrate on the changes in age and sex composition.

Sex Ratios and Life Expectations

Each year a slightly higher proportion of male babies is born than of females (currently about 106–107 males for every 100 females). But mortality rates are higher for males than for females—nowadays the expectation of life of a female at birth is about six years more than that of a male. Expectation of life is a measure calculated by taking 1000 (hypothetical) males (or females), projecting them through the age groups allowing for current mortality rates at each group, then aggregating the years they would live and dividing by 1000. Table 7.2 shows how the calculation is done. By the same method the expectation of life can be calculated for ages other than age 0. It should be stressed that the method uses current mortality rates, but in fact we should expect babies born today to live longer, on average, than the current figures of life expectation, because we should expect death rates to fall farther during the course of their lives; but the figures of expectation of life are based, very properly, on current mortality rates for the year in question, not on hypothetical rates for all the future years which the population under consideration is likely to live.

Table 7.3 shows changes in the expectation of life in the period

Table 7.2 Hypothetical Example of the Calculation of Expectation of Life.

Age	Number of deaths	Aggregate years
0–1	20	10
1–2	5	8
. . .	. . .	. . .
40–41	10	405
. . .	. . .	. . .
70–71	100	7050
. . .	..	. . .
99–100	1	100
Totals	1000	75,000

$$\text{Expectation of life (at age 0)} = \frac{75{,}000}{1000} = 75$$

Note: the dots in the table indicate all the intervening age groups, deaths and aggregate years per age group. It would be tedious and space-consuming to set the data out in full.

Table 7.3 Expectation of Life in Great Britain, 1851–1971.

	Expectation of Life (in years)							
	1851	1901	1911	1921	1931	1951	1961	1971
At birth								
Males	40	46	51.4	55.4	58.4	66.2	67.9	68.6
Females	42	49	55.2	59.3	62.5	71.2	73.8	74.9
At age 5								
Males	50	55	57.0	58.3	60.0	63.9	65.0	65.2
Females	50	57	59.7	61.1	63.0	68.5	70.5	71.2

Source: Office of Population Censuses and Surveys.

1851–1971, at birth and at age 5. Apart from the continuing and substantial improvements in life expectancy over the period, two points of particular interest emerge. First, the vertical comparison: because of high mortality in the early years of life (especially the first year) the average age one could expect to reach (at current mortality rates) is higher at age 5 than at birth. Thus, in 1971, expectation of life for a male at birth was 68.6 years; but males who survived to age 5 had a *further* life expectation of 65.2 years (i.e. they could expect to live to be over seventy). This feature is most marked in the early years referred to in the table. Thus a male born in 1851 had a life expectancy of only 40 at birth. But if he survived the heavy mortality of the early years of life, his further life expectancy at age 5 was ten years more than at birth. The second feature is the one we have already referred to—the higher expectation of life of women than of men. Since the middle of the nineteenth century, the expectation of life of both men and women has been rising, but that of women has risen much more than that of men. In fact, at age 65 the life expectation of men has risen very little over the past century (only about one year) whilst that of women has risen much more (about four years).

Because of these differences in life expectation (but also because of past wars which affected male mortality much more than female) in the 1975 population of England and Wales there are over one-and-a-half times as many women as men over 65 and more than two-and-a-half times as many female octogenarians as male octogenarians.

These facts raise certain questions of social and economic importance. With the increase in life expectation of both men and women, would it be sensible to raise the ages for the receipt of the state retirement pension? Still more potently, what is the logic behind the present retirement ages (eligibility for state retirement pensions) of 60 for women and 65 for men? If there should be a difference between the sexes, demographic logic would point to a lower retirement age for men than for women to make more nearly equal the time during which retirement might be enjoyed. Some other countries with higher living standards than the United Kingdom have higher retirement ages and do not discriminate in favour of women; thus in Sweden the retirement age is 67 for both sexes.

Age Distribution and Dependency Ratios

When we turn to age distribution, the most important breakdown is that distinguishing population in the working age-groups from that in the school and in the retirement ages. Table 7.4 gives a breakdown on these lines for (a) the United Kingdom in 1911, 1941 and 1971; and (b) a slightly more detailed breakdown of the most recent figures for England and Wales, enabling us to see the broad age division within the working population.

Table 7.4   Age Distribution of Population.

(a) *United Kingdom, 1911, 1941 and 1971.*

	Percentages		
Age Group	1911	1941	1971
Under 15	30.8	21.0	24.2
15–64/59*	62.3	67.2	59.8
65/60 and over**	6.8	11.8	16.0

(b) *England and Wales, mid 1975.*

Age group	*Percentage*
Under 15	23.0
15–44	39.4
45–64/59*	20.4
65/60 and over**	17.1

*   64 for males; 59 for females.

** 65 and over for males; 60 and over for females.

Note: columns do not always add exactly to 100 because of rounding.
Source: Office of Population Censuses and Surveys.

The table shows the fall in the proportion of child dependents from 1901 to 1941 and its subsequent rise to 1971, a rise now being reversed. It also shows the substantial and continuing increase in the proportion of the population of retirement age. The same data can be expressed in the form of dependency ratios (Table 7.5). An increase in the dependency ratios, other things remaining the same, means a larger ratio of consumers to producers in the population.

Table 7.5 Dependency Ratios per Thousand Population of Working Ages.

| | United Kingdom | | | England and Wales |
	1911	1941	1971	1975
Child	494	313	406	385
Retirement ages	110	175	267	287
Overall dependency ratio	604	488	673	672

Even if state pension rates remain the same in real terms (and the higher the proportion of the electorate who are retired, the more the political pressure for higher pensions), a rise in the proportion of the old increases the total cost of state retirement pensions, which must be met, at least in part, from higher taxes and national insurance contributions from the working population. A rise in the proportion of the old also tends to increase the costs of the National Health Service because they (and the very young) need more medical attention. Also, it can be argued that a higher proportion of the old makes for less investment, for the old tend to be dissavers rather than savers.

Whilst the rise in the proportion of the population of retirement age is economically important the effects should not be exaggerated:

1. The higher retirement dependency ratio may be partly offset by a fall in the child dependency ratio (as has happened since 1911).
2. The additional annual cost to the community from the worsening of the retirement dependency ratio is only a small proportion of the average annual increases in GNP which has been achieved since the Second World War.
3. Dependency ratios are formalized relationships between particular age groups, rather than the actual ratios of dependents to workers. If we look at the actual relationship the position is significantly different. On the one hand there have been more 'child' dependents in recent years than the ratio indicates because of the raising of the school leaving age, the increased

proportion of children staying on at school beyond the leaving age and the rise in the numbers in full-time further and higher education. On the other hand the proportion of people of working age who have actually been working (known as the activity rate) has been much higher in the past thirty years than earlier in the century largely because of the much larger proportion of married women in employment. Finally, people do not always retire from employment at the 'official' retirement ages and these ages are themselves a matter of policy; rising expectation of life, as we have seen, provides an argument for extending the length of working life if we are concerned about the increasing burden of dependency.

Is the Malthusian Devil Dead or Alive?

Malthus was concerned at the consequences of an increasing population on living standards when the amount of land was more or less fixed. It should be remembered that 'land' in economics is an umbrella label for those factors of production which are not manmade. In answering this question it would therefore be entirely proper to include, for example, the consequences of population growth on exhaustible mineral deposits and we shall be looking at this issue in our final chapter. Malthus himself, however, concentrated on the effects of population growth on food supplies, so let us do the same at this point.

In considering this question we need to examine both the position of Great Britain and of the world as a whole.

Great Britain

We saw earlier in the chapter that the predictions of Malthus were not fulfilled in Britain. Because of agricultural improvements, industrial and transport developments and the ultimate fall in the birth rate, population growth proved to be compatible with big rises in living standards. Can it then be said that, for Great Britain, with a population growing only very slowly and with little likelihood of further rapid growth (see Chapter 8) the Malthusian Devil is dead?

The question is not as simple as it seems. Britain overcame the Malthusian Devil by importing a large proportion of its foodstuffs and exporting manufactured products in exchange. It thus became heavily dependent on foreign trade. As a result Britain was left with certain hostages to fortune—especially the possibility of an adverse movement in its terms of trade (the ratio of export to import prices) which could cut deeply into living standards. Just such a movement took place between 1972 and 1974 when world food prices soared and this alone caused a big deterioration in the terms of trade. The position was made worse by the rise in commodity prices of all kinds and the considerable increase in the price of oil provided by countries in OPEC (the Organization of Petroleum Exporting Countries). One of the advantages of EEC membership for Britain is a reduced dependence on the supply of foodstuffs from the rest of the world. But, clearly, though the Malthusian Devil in Britain may have been largely tamed, he still has a sharp horn or two.

The World

When we turn to the world as a whole, the ugly head of the Malthusian Devil is very much in evidence. World population is growing at a phenomenal rate. In 1800 world population was probably under 1000 million; in 1950 it was about 2500 millions; in 1970 it was some 3600 millions; and the United Nations medium fertility estimate is of 6500 million by the year 2000. Mass starvation is not uncommon in parts of the globe and malnutrition is endemic.

Can we learn anything from the British experience of the way to control the Malthusian Devil? One of the main ways in which Britain held the Devil at bay was by importing much of its food, i.e. by drawing on the land of other countries. Whilst there remain areas of the world which could be brought into cultivation, for the world as a whole to draw on land from elsewhere is not open, save in the unlikely event that it becomes possible to draw on other planets. The solution therefore seems to lie in agricultural improvements and a reduction in birth rates by the adoption of methods of birth control. There is immense scope for both, but the difficulties are manifold and also immense. Most of the expected population growth is in the developing countries and the rate of increase in their population— with birth rates around 40 per 1000 and death rates around 16 per 1000—is much more rapid than Britain ever experienced. The Malthusian Devil is very much alive.

SUMMARY AND CONCLUSIONS

Population growth in Britain accelerated in the latter half of the eighteenth century. From then three phases of population change can be distinguished:

1. 1780–1880: a period of very rapid growth, probably mainly due to a fall in death rate;
2. 1880–1940: a period of slower growth in which the death rate continued to fall but the birth rate fell more rapidly;
3. 1940–75: a period notable for immigration and birth rate fluctuations.

During the period of most rapid growth, the increasing population size was closely connected with industrialization, accentuated the social problems of urbanization and provided the basis for a large net emigration. During the last 100 years the expectation of life has increased markedly, but more for women than men. This raises questions about the appropriateness of present policies on retirement ages, especially in view of rising retirement dependency ratios.

In Britain the worst Malthusian horrors of over-population were avoided by agricultural improvements, trading industrial goods for foodstuffs and ultimately by a reduction in the birth rate by the use of birth control. Solving the problems raised by the rapidly growing population of the world as a whole will be more difficult.

8 Population Future

Measures of Births and Deaths

Any serious attempt to evolve a policy for total population, or to provide realistic social policies in the fields of education, health and housing, which are heavily dependent on the age structure of the population, requires a population analysis based on more sophisticated measures than crude birth and death rates. These rates may fluctuate because of changes in the age and sex composition of the population without any change in underlying fertility or mortality, and the crude birth rate could change because of changes in the timing of families, even though the completed size of families remained the same. In remedying some of the deficiencies of the crude birth and death rates, specific mortality and fertility rates are very useful. The age-specific mortality rate gives the number of deaths per 1000 population for specific age/sex groups, and the age-specific fertility rate gives the number of births per 1000 women of a particular age.

Attempts have been made to devise a measure which sums up the population trend in one convenient figure: the reproduction rate. Reproduction rates (or, more accurately, female reproduction rates) give the average number of girls a woman may be expected to bear on the basis of current age-specific fertility rates. The measure is calculated by taking 1000 girls assumed to be born this year, projecting them through the child-bearing ages to see how many girls they may be expected to bear at current age-specific fertility rates and then dividing this total by 1000. There are three measures of reproduction calculated in this way. The Gross Reproduction Rate, is exactly as described above, with no allowance for mortality. The Net Reproduction Rate (NRR) incorporates current specific mortality rates into the measure, allowing for the fact that some of the 1000 women will die before they reach the child-bearing ages and as they pass through them. The Effective Reproduction Rate is similar to the Net Reproduction Rate except that the mortality rates used are expected rates rather than current rates. Of these measures, the Net Reproduction Rate is the one most frequently used. If, over a long period of time, the NRR remains below unity, then, assuming no net immigration, the population would at some point start to decline. Similarly an NRR of unity, if continued indefinitely, in the absence of net migration, would in the long run mean a stationary population and could therefore be taken as replacement fertility.

In the short term, however, these measures are defective because they are based on the fertility experience of a single year and take no account of the changes in the *timing* of families. Thus, for example, a trend to earlier marriages and earlier families makes the figures misleading. Over the past twenty years the figures of NRR for Great Britain have fluctuated very considerably as Table 8.1 shows. The provisional figure (at the time of writing) for 1975 is 0.84, whereas ten years earlier it was 1.34.

Table 8.1   Net Reproduction Rates, Great Britain.

1955	1.05	1971	1.13
1960	1.26	1972	1.04
1965	1.34	1973	0.96
1970	1.13	1974	0.90

A more recent demographic technique which obviates the disadvantages of the NRR is that of *cohort analysis*. The objective is to follow through the fertility experience of a given group of women and to study the time-pattern of their family building, e.g. women born in 1940 form a birth cohort; those married in 1960 form a marriage cohort, and so on. The experience of different cohorts can be compared. By following a cohort through the child-bearing ages one can see the average number of children born and the different ages at which the mothers had children. Variations in the timing of their families do not, then, create misleading impressions. In short, as the Report of the Population Panel expressed it, 'It is the average number of births which women will have that is the important determinant for longer-term population trends, and the timing of those births is a secondary factor. Yet it is changes in timing which can be the major determinants of shorter-term trends in current fertility measures.' This means that cohort analysis suffers from the big disadvantage that it only fully reveals what has happened some fifteen years after the event. Even then, in common with other fertility measures, it does not explain why it has happened.

Population Projections

In making forecasts or projections of the population we have to allow for births, deaths and any net migration (the excess of immigration over emigration or vice versa). If we leave out of account net migration as a factor largely dependent on political decisions then we are left with births and deaths. Three main stages are involved.

1. *The existing age structure.* The starting point of a population projection is an examination of the existing population assembled in age groups. A stationary population which had been exactly reproducing itself for many years would have a beehive shape, with each age group being smaller than the one below it and larger than the

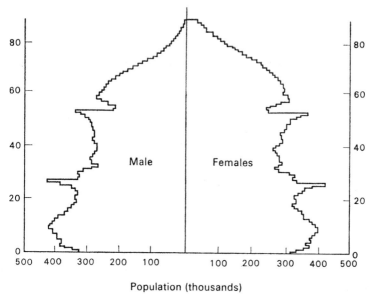

Population (thousands)

Figure 8.1   Age and Sex Structure of England and Wales, mid-1974.

one above it. An actual population will not have the same regularity of pattern, as the age groupings will reflect earlier fluctuations in the birth and death rates. Figure 8.1 shows the population of England and Wales in 1974. In the age-groups 0–10 the younger the group the smaller its size because of the continued decline in the birth rate over the previous ten years. The relatively large groups around ages 10–14 and 25–30 reflect the birth rate peaks around 1964 and 1947 respectively.

2. *Mortality assumptions.* Having assembled our population in age groups we project it into the future, making assumptions about mortality rates at each age group. Barring major catastrophes, these assumptions are not likely to prove wide of the mark. Specific mortality rates have shown a fairly consistent trend in the past, and the experience of other countries with lower mortality rates (e.g. Sweden, New Zealand) gives confidence that the trend will continue, though possibly the rate of fall will be less.

3. *Fertility assumptions.* As we project the population into the future, so we add in the births at the bottom on the age-table. The number added in depends primarily on assumptions about the number of married couples and the marital fertility rate (the average size of family). Assumptions about the number of couples are derived from knowledge about the numbers of people in each age group and assumptions about the age of marriage. The marital fertility rate is based on assumptions about current rates. This is where most of the difficulties arise. As we have seen, changes in the timing of families may make the current specific fertility rates misleading, and the information from cohort analysis is always, necessarily, behind the times. But even if we could assess with complete accuracy the current marital fertility rate, there is no guarantee that future marital fertility rates would be similar. Marital fertility rates appear to have varied considerably in ways which defy explanation.

According to the assumptions made, so will the projections differ. The longer ahead the period of the forecast the more the likelihood of errors, which tend to be cumulative. For instance, if the number of babies is over-estimated in the present generation then the number of parents is over-estimated for the next generation. Conversely, the shorter the period of the forecast the less the likelihood of error: the survivors of the existing, known, population will comprise the bulk of the predicted population. For particular projections over limited periods all the relevant people are alive today, e.g. the numbers in the working population over the next sixteen years, or the numbers from whom the university populations will be drawn over the next eighteen years. However, the proportion that these age groups bear to the total population is more uncertain.

One such limited forecast for Great Britain—which because it is not heavily dependent on fertility changes has a high degree of reliability—is encouraging: the medium-term forecast of dependency ratios. We saw, in the previous chapter, that the overall dependency ratio had been worsening for decades. Whilst into the early 1980s there will continue to be an increase in the proportion of the population over the official retirement ages, at any level of fertility considered at all likely it will be more than compensated for by the fall in child dependency resulting from the decline in births during the past decade. The overall dependency ratio in 1974 was not only the highest of the past 45 years but is also likely to be the highest of the next 35 years. Thus the prospect in the medium term is a relatively larger proportion of the population at work.

When we turn to predictions of the total population, the outcome is highly uncertain.

The Numbers Game

All forecasts of the total population over anything more than a relatively few years should be regarded with extreme caution. Past forecasts of the population of Great Britain make a very poor showing. Malthus' gloomy predictions at the end of the eighteenth century went badly awry. In the 1930s a series of studies were published[1] all of which predicted a massive fall in the size of the British population in the second half of the twentieth century. Within ten to fifteen years the assumptions on which these studies were based were looking utterly unrealistic.

Recent predictions have faired no better. Reporting in 1949 the *Royal Commission on Population* modified the 1930s' views on population decline but did not wholly reverse them. On what the Commission regarded as the most likely set of assumptions the population was expected to increase slightly up to about 1977 after which a slow decline would commence. Within three years of the publication of the Report its assumptions about births had already proved to be nearly five per cent too low.

There followed something of a panic about the possibility of 'overpopulation'. In 1965 the Registrar-General, on what seemed

[1] A study by P.E.P. in 1934; Enid Charles, *The Menace of Under-Population*, Watts and Co., 1936; G. F. McLeary, *The Menace of British Depopulation*, Allen and Unwin, 1937.

the most reasonable assumptions at the time, was forecasting a population for the United Kingdom of 75 millions by the year 2001. Although, subsequently, the Registrar-General's annual projections showed reductions on this figure, as late as 1971 a House of Commons Select Committee reporting on population reached the conclusion that 'The Government must act to prevent the consequences of population growth becoming intolerable for the every day conditions of life.'[1]

Report of The Population Panel

The Population Panel was set up in November 1971 in response to the Select Committee's Report with terms of reference 'To assess the available evidence about the significance of population growth for both public affairs and private life in this country at present and in prospect: to make recommendations about further work required, and how it should be conducted: and to report within one year.' The Panel submitted its recommendations and conclusions in November 1972 and a more detailed report was submitted in February 1973 and published in March 1973.

The Panel expected the population of Great Britain to go on rising until at least the end of the century. It expected an increase in births because of an increase in the number of women of child-bearing ages; and it took the view that average family size was above replacement level and was likely to remain so. It held that the main reason for the recent fluctuations in the birth rate—the peak of 1964 followed by the fall—was one of timing (the present 30–40 year-olds having their families earlier, the present 20–30 year-olds having theirs later). It anticipated that the birth rate would pick up again in the early or mid-1970s.

The Panel made population projections on the basis of three growth models. From a population for Great Britain of 54 millions in 1971 its 'low growth' projection was of 61 millions in 2011; its 'medium growth' was of 66 millions; and its 'high growth' of 74 millions.

The Panel examined the effect of these rates of growth on living standards, on land use, on problems such as urban congestion, pollution and noise levels. The Panel did not see growth at any of the projected levels as posing a serious threat to living standards or making any serious difference to the other issues, though it held that

[1] *First Report from the Select Committee on Science and Technology*, Session 1970–71, *Population of the United Kingdom*, HC 379, 1971, p. x.

there were some advantages in the lower rate as compared with the higher.

The Latest Situation

Since then the Population Panel's expectation of a rise in births in the early 1970s has not been fulfilled and even its 'low growth' projection is looking too high. The latest population projection[1] from the Office of Population Censuses and Surveys puts the population of Great Britain at 57½ million in 2011. On the basis of data from interview surveys about intended size of families the projection assumes some recovery from the low fertility levels of 1975 to an average size of completed family of 2.1 children (just about replacement level).

Some unofficial voices are now being raised to suggest that this is still an over-estimation and that Britain faces the prospect of a long-term decline in its population. And, to quote from a recent publication, 'It is not too far-fetched, in our view, to suggest that positive pro-natalist policies may come firmly on to the political agenda in the 1980s'.[2]

Should Britain Have a Population Policy?
It all depends what is meant by a population policy.

1. 'A Policeman Under Every Bed'

The most thorough-going policy would require: (1) the calculation of an optimum population size; (2) setting a date to achieve that size; (3) devising effective and acceptable means for (a) attaining the optimum and (b) maintaining the optimum.

There are insuperable difficulties associated with each stage of such an undertaking. Firstly, what is the optimum? An economist would define it as that level of population at which output per head was at a maximum. But this depends on all sorts of conditions, such as the state of technology and the terms of trade, which change and are themselves almost impossible to predict. Moreover, the economist's optimum is not the only one. There are other conflicting

---

[1] OPCS Monitor, *Population Projections: mid-1975-based*, August 1976, Office of Population Censuses and Surveys.

[2] M. Buxton and E. Craven, eds., *Demographic Change and Social Policy: The Uncertain Future*, Centre for Studies in Social Policy, 1976, p. 85.

optima, such as environmental optima, which, whilst important, are still less susceptible of objective measurement than the economist's.

Secondly, to attain this optimum by a certain date it would be necessary to predict accurately the current trend in population to see how far, in the absence of special action, the population would differ from the required population by the target date. Then it would be necessary to estimate the modification required to births, deaths and migration to achieve the target. But virtually every major forecast for Great Britain has turned out to be wildly inaccurate because of the difficulty of accurately predicting fertility. Currently there is not even agreement amongst the demographers on whether population is most likely to rise or fall. If action were started on the basis of inaccurate forecasts problems could be accentuated or new ones created, e.g. if measures were taken to restrict births to stablize a population which was incorrectly believed to be on an upward trend, a rapid decline might set in and at some stage the age distribution would then give rise to serious problems.

Thirdly, it is very doubtful how far 'effective' and 'acceptable' methods exist. Fiscal measure to alter fertility rates, such as trying to increase (or reduce) births by raising (or lowering) family allowances, are of doubtful effectiveness and could easily conflict with welfare policies. Various policies—relating to contraception, abortion and sterilization—could be devised to interfere with conceptions and pregnancies. The theoretical possibilities are numerous, but, in varying degrees, policies on these matters meet deep-felt opposition, and anything *compulsory* would be regarded as an intolerable infringement on personal freedom. Emigration/immigration policies might conflict with basic human freedoms (e.g. to emigrate) or with welfare policies (e.g. prohibiting the families of immigrants from entering a country).

In view of the Report of the Population Panel and the subsequent information on the trend of population, no policy of this kind is remotely justifiable and, if attempted in our present state of ignorance, could easily create more problems than it solved.

2. *Careful Monitoring*

An alternative meaning to a population policy is that there should be continual government review—monitoring carefully what is happening in view of the importance of population. This was the approach suggested by the Population Panel. They recommended that work should be undertaken to improve knowledge of population trends and to improve forecasting methods; that information on population should be made widely available; and that action should be taken to reduce unwanted births (e.g. by making oral contraceptives freely available under the NHS)—but on welfare rather than on population grounds.

3. *Responding to Demographic Change*

A very different approach to the thorough-going population policy, outlined under (1) above, but entirely compatible with (2), is a policy which seeks not to alter population trends but to respond to them. In a sense this is what Britain has always done, but it could be done much more deliberately. Where there is so much uncertainty about fertility trends, likely numbers of births and future patterns of family size, one general strategy is that of flexibility. For example, after a long period of expansion the number of children in full-time compulsory education in Great Britain must fall for the next seven or eight years at least; thereafter it might turn sharply upwards. In these circumstances school buildings need to be retained but adapted for other uses; teachers should be trained to move more easily between the main educational sectors—nursery, primary and secondary; further, there might be more common ground in the training of professions so that, for example, teachers might double with social workers. Similar flexibilities might be introduced into hospital or housing policies. Such flexibility is not costless, but it might prove the most economic response to Britain's demographic uncertainties.[1]

Finally, before we leave this issue, we must briefly examine one argument sometimes used to support the idea of a policy aimed at reducing Britain's population. Although it is acknowledged that population growth is much more rapid in the so-called 'developing' countries than in the developed countries, it is sometimes argued that, in the world interest, it is more important to restrict population in the developed countries because every child born into a developed country, like Britain, consumes many times the amount of resources of the child born into an undeveloped country. This is

[1] For further illustrations and discussion of this approach, see M. Buxton and E. Craven, *ibid*.

true, but it is not a valid argument for giving priority to reducing population growth in the developed countries because it looks only at the 'demand' side of the problem and ignores the 'supply' side. As we shall see in our final chapter, the issue of a world eco-catastrophe rests, to an important extent, on the outcome of a race between the demand on resources on the one hand and technological progress on the other. If the population of the developed countries make the biggest *per capita* demands on resources they also contribute the most to technological innovations.

SUMMARY AND CONCLUSIONS

Age-specific fertility and mortality rates, reproduction rates and cohort analysis all help our understanding of demographic trends, but all have their limitations. Population projections are essential for certain social policies and some limited projections, not heavily dependent on fertility assumptions, have a high degree of reliability. But forecasting the total population of Great Britain over a lengthy period is hazardous in the extreme. Currently it is far from clear whether the population is most likely to grow or decline over the next thirty or forty years. Any 'thorough-going' population policy in such circumstances makes no sense, but careful monitoring of population trends and improvements in methods of forecasting should be encouraged and can be used in conjunction with social policies based on flexible response to demographic change, rather than on attempts to alter it.

Part III

INEQUALITY AND POVERTY

Introduction to Part III

In Part III we shall examine inequalities in the distribution of income and of wealth and the problem of poverty in the United Kingdom. All three topics are closely interconnected and we must say something about these inter-relationships.

Before we do that, a word on the meaning of 'inequality' is called for. The use of the word 'inequality' is not intended to imply any judgment. It might, indeed, be better, to use the word 'differences', because 'inequality' may be thought to be pejorative—to carry the implication of injustice. Whilst particular inequalities or differences in income or wealth may be regarded as unjust, which is very much a value judgment, it is far from clear that all should be so regarded. Indeed, 'equality' in certain cases would be regarded as unjust; for example, if two men of equal ability and physical strength were paid the same wage when, with equal opportunities for work, one had worked twice as hard or as long as the other, this treatment would widely be regarded as unjust. We continue to use the term 'inequality' because it is customary to do so when speaking of differences in income and in wealth, but we are not thereby intending to offer a judgment.

Now let us look at the terms 'income' and 'wealth'. Income we met in Chapter 3 in the context of the national income and output. Money income is the receipt of money per period of time usually in return for services rendered (for labour services or for lending property). Real income is the flow of goods and services which a person can enjoy in a period of time without having to dispose of his assets or capital. In other words real income is what money income can buy. We shall need to amplify that later in Chapter 9, but it will suffice for the moment as a definition to enable us to distinguish income from wealth.

Wealth is a word which is used very loosely in everyday speech. If we say that a man is wealthy we may mean that he has a high

income or a large stock of property or both. In economics we confine
the term wealth to a stock of assets. Basically these are goods of all
kinds and wealth can be taken as synonymous with capital (see
Chapter 3), a stock of goods of all kinds existing at a particular point
of time. The difference between wealth and capital is only one of
approach; when we talk of capital we tend to think of goods to be
used for future production, whilst when we talk of wealth we think
of (the same) goods as a store to be drawn on for future consumption.
A person's wealth would fall into three categories: (1) Various goods
in his possession, such as a house, car, furniture, clothes, jewellery
and so on; if he was the individual owner of a business it would
include his business—the value of the premises, machinery and stock.
(2) Financial assets such as shares in a business (which are a title to
so much physical capital or wealth) or government stocks (which
can be sold and exchanged for goods). (3) Money, as cash or bank
deposits, which derive their value because they can be exchanged
for goods. Again, we shall need to amplify this definition later because there are some difficult borderline cases. But, for the moment,
we can say that personal wealth constitutes a stock of assets (less
liabilities) which a person possesses at a particular point of time.
Income (like output) has meaning only in relation to a period of
time, whilst wealth necessarily refers to a point of time.

Inequality in the distribution of income and of wealth is related,
but the two are different. The higher a person's income the greater
his scope for saving, i.e. accumulating wealth. The more wealth a
man has, the more income that wealth is likely to generate. This
inter-relationship should be borne in mind in the following chapters.
Thus, measures which reduce inequalities in the distribution of
income are also likely to have some effect in reducing inequalities in
the distribution of wealth and vice versa.

Finally we must distinguish between inequality in income distribution and poverty. We shall need to spend some time looking more
closely at the meaning of poverty in Chapter 10. Big differences in
income distribution in a country do not necessarily mean the
existence of poverty though, for any given GNP, the bigger the
dispersion of incomes around the mean the more likely it is that
there are people in poverty. By those in poverty we mean those
whose income falls below a specified level which takes account of
their family needs. The problem of poverty is therefore primarily
one of income maintenance. But the 'poverty level' itself cannot be
treated as independent of the incomes of the rest of the society.

One of our particular concerns in this part of the book will be to examine how far the state can reduce the inequalities of income and wealth generated by the market mechanism without at the same time destroying the advantages of efficiency and freedom which the market offers.

9 Inequality and the Distribution of Income

Causes of Differences in Income Distribution

In examining the ways in which differences in income arise we need to distinguish between 'earned' income, i.e. income from work, and investment income, i.e. income from property.

Earned Income

Differences in earned income may perhaps best be explained in terms of differences in 'productive capacity' and such differences in turn depend on a variety of factors such as education and training, ability of various kinds, including what is sometimes known as the 'D' factor standing for drive, doggedness and determination, on-the-job training or experience, degree of responsibility and a range of other factors not excluding luck.

We can put the same points in a different way by saying that some differences in earnings arise out of the amount and nature of the work and such differences would exist even if all people had equal abilities and equal opportunities and there was perfect knowledge and perfect mobility between occupations. These include differences in earnings because some people choose to work longer or more intensively than others, or are prepared to take on more arduous, dangerous or responsible work or receive higher pay in the present because they have sacrificed earnings and/or leisure in the past in order to acquire training which a particular job requires.

Other differences in earnings arising because of differences in the supply of different types of labour in relation to the demand for it. These supply factors recognize that people do not all have equal abilities and have not all had equal opportunities, including opportunities for education. To give some extreme examples, a person may have very scarce innate abilities, which are very much in demand, like the abilities of a pop star or footballer. While they may improve these abilities by training or experience, essentially their very high earnings rest on the existence of innate ability. On the demand side, earnings may fall very low in an occupation because changes in technology or tastes may reduce the demand for a particular kind of labour. A worker with a particular skill, which may have required a lengthy training, may find himself redundant because of a change in technology or in tastes and be forced to accept a much lower wage in alternative employment. Conversely another worker may find his skills suddenly in demand and enjoy a gratuitous rise in income when the price of the kind of labour he offers is increased to attract new workers into that line of production. The demand-generated differences in earnings are likely to be more short-lived than the supply-generated differences, but they may nonetheless be very significant for the persons affected.

Such differences in earnings help to ensure that labour of various kinds is used in ways which most accord with the wishes of society expressed through markets. The differences are necessary to the efficiency of the economic system, but they have little or no justification in equity.

Putting the point in another way, in Chapter 4 we examined the market mechanism, and saw that prices acted as the signal of changes required in production and as the mechanism by which resources could be transferred from one use to another to meet the demands of consumers. The prices of the factors of production served also as a guide to the organization of production, helping to secure the most economic use of scarce resources. But a wage is both a price and an income. Variations in price to secure an efficient use of resources generate changes in earned income which have no moral justification. Efficiency and equity considerations may conflict.

In practice, quite apart from government intervention, the forces of supply and demand are muted by ignorance and immobility, including various restrictions imposed by trade unions and professional bodies to limit entry to particular occupations. Nonetheless, efficiency considerations remain of considerable importance in bringing about changes in the price of particular kinds of labour and hence in earned incomes.

Investment Income

The major cause of differences in investment income is differences in the amount of wealth owned—a subject we consider in Chapter 11. But differences in the yield on investments (including capital appreciation) are also important and tend to accentuate the effects of differring amounts of wealth because, in general, the wealthy are in a position to afford the best advice and to spread their investments and hence to get a higher return on their assets.

Measurement of Inequality in the Distribution of Incomes

The difficulties can be divided into the conceptual and the statistical.

Conceptual Problems

Even if we were able to obtain perfect statistics we should still face a number of problems in deciding how best to measure inequality in the distribution of income.

What is Income? There are some difficult borderline cases in deciding what should be regarded as income. Clearly any fringe benefits and income in kind should be included. One major problem we have already met in Chapter 3 when we were considering national income and output: should consumers' durable-use goods be regarded as contributing to output (and income) throughout their life or only when they are first produced and purchased? In practice the answer taken is to regard all such goods as constituting output and (real) income when purchased, with the exception of houses, which are regarded as providing an 'output of house-room' during their life. The best we can do in examining income distribution is to take the same approach. Where a person owns a house which he lets to someone else he receives a money income from it; where he occupies his own house we need to impute an income to the house equivalent to the value of the house-room (or what the owner would have had to pay in rent if he had not been an owner). In theory there might be a good case for imputing an income also to the satisfaction (sometimes referred to as psychic income) which owners get from the most durable of other consumer durable-use goods, such as jewellery and pictures, which are also likely to be an investment with a good return in the form of capital appreciation; but in practice it would be very difficult to impute such an income.

Reference to the capital gain on assets raises another problem. In Chapter 3 we defined national income as the flow of goods and services available to the members of a community over a period of time *whilst maintaining capital intact*. If a capital gain is a real gain, not just an appreciation in line with prices in general, there is a strong case for arguing that it should be treated as income to the beneficiary. He could, for instance, realize part of the gain, consume the proceeds, and still be as well off as before the gain occurred. Conversely, of course, a capital depreciation should be regarded as a reduction in income.

Another problem is the correct treatment of employers' contributions to national insurance and superannuation schemes for their employees; it could be argued that these really constitute a part of the employee's wage and therefore should count as income of the employee.

These are some of the main, but not the only problems which arise in seeking to determine precisely what should be regarded as constituting income in general.

There are further problems when we look at personal incomes. Our concern is often not with some gross figure before tax and insurance contributions, but rather with 'disposable income'. This is the income available to the individual after allowance for contributions and tax. Similarly, we are concerned with how much disposable income is subsequently taken in taxes on the goods an individual buys, and with what direct benefits he obtains from government expenditure (the so-called 'social wage'). In examining the distribution of personal incomes we need to consider each stage, and at each stage there are conceptual problems which we shall briefly touch on at the time.

What income unit? What is the most appropriate unit to use in analysing income distribution? There is much to be said for using a household unit rather than the individual, defining a household as those engaged in common housekeeping. On the other hand, if we do this we must recognize that households vary very much in size and composition.

The snapshot problem: variations in life-time income. The figures of personal income distribution which we shall be examining relate to single years. In many ways a more meaningful comparison would be lifetime income. For most people earnings start low and rise to a maximum which is generally reached by unskilled workers in their thirties, by skilled workers in their forties and by managerial and professional workers in their fifties. After the maximum has been reached earnings may stay on a plateau or, especially with manual workers, may decline somewhat until retirement, when earnings are wholly or largely replaced by pensions, and income slumps. Income from savings or investments tends to grow with age up to retirement (especially the net imputed income from owner-occupied houses as mortgages are paid off); thereafter some spending from capital may take place and investment income as well as earned income is likely to fall. To illustrate the point: university students regard themselves as amongst today's poor, and they would appear as such in comprehensive statistics giving the snapshot position of a single year; but the lifetime income of present students would put nearly all of them in the top 10 per cent of income receivers.

It follows that comparisons of the distribution of income in single years might give the impression of an increase (or reduction) in inequality of incomes when the changes were simply a reflection of the changing age-distribution of the population. As our chapters on population show, during the past decade the proportion both of young earners and of the retired in the population has increased. One would expect this to bias comparisons between the early 1960s and early 1970s, so as to suggest an increase in inequality.

Measuring inequality. There are a number of possible measures of inequality but none is ideal. One of the most common and convenient ways to present data on personal income distribution is in the form of cumulative percentage shares, e.g. the top 5 per cent of income receivers receive 14 per cent of income; the top 10 per cent receive 24 per cent, and so on. The same data can also be conveniently expressed graphically in a Lorenz curve (by way of illustration, see Figure 9.1 which shows the income distribution for the UK in 1971–72). The percentage of the relevant 'population' is plotted on the horizontal axis and the percentage of total personal income on the vertical axis. If income was exactly equally distributed 25 per cent of the population would receive 25 per cent of the income, 50 per cent of the population would receive 50 per cent of the income, and so on, thus the 'curve' of equal distribution would be a straight line. The difference between an actual income distribution and the line of complete equality can be taken as a measure of the degree of inequality (the shaded area in Figure 9.1).[1]

If one Lorenz curve is nearer to the line of complete equality than another, this can be regarded unambiguously as constituting a reduction in inequality. But we might have a situation in which

---

[1] The ratio of the shaded area to that of the whole triangle is a measure of inequality known as the Gini coefficient, which can vary between 0 (complete equality of income) and 1 (the theoretical position where all income is received by one person and the Lorenz curve follows the axes). The lower the Gini coefficient, the less the degree of inequality.

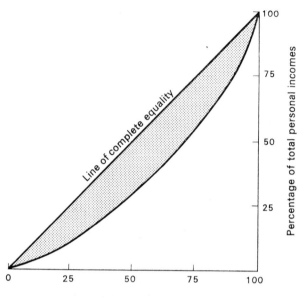

Percentage of population

Figure 9.1   Cumulative Shares of Total Income Before Tax in the United Kingdom, 1971–72.

Lorenz curves crossed—then (assuming a desire to reduce inequality) the preferred distribution becomes a matter of value judgment. Such a situation would arise where the distribution had been made less unequal at one end but more unequal at the other, as with the hypothetical figures opposite.[1]

Statistical Inadequacies

As always what we can measure in practice is constrained by the statistics available which are largely collected as a by-product of administration and are not designed for the purposes of the social scientist. The data on personal income distribution is derived from two main sources: Inland Revenue statistics which form the basis

[1] The Gini coefficient is similarly ambiguous. The same Gini coefficient is compatible with two very different income distributions; indeed, one egalitarian might actually prefer a distribution with a higher Gini coefficient than one with a lower if that meant a more even distribution at the lower end of the scale (implying less extreme poverty).

	Situation A		Situation B	
	% of population	% of income	% of population	% of income
Top	5	20	5	10
	10	30	10	25
	50	65	50	65
	80	90	80	92
Bottom	20	10	20	8

of an annual Survey of Personal Incomes (SPI), and data from the Family Expenditure Survey (FES). Data from these two sources is to some extent combined in the figures of income distribution published in the National Income and Expenditure Blue Books. A word about each of these sources is necessary.

Inland Revenue Data (SPI). The Inland Revenue data is compiled from the administration of income tax. The unit used is therefore the income tax unit, whereby husband and wife are treated as one. The coverage is national, but omits income which, for one reason or another, is not subject to income tax. Besides those with incomes so low as not to come within the income tax authorities' orbit, a range of untaxed social security benefits are omitted, such as sickness benefits and unemployment pay, and also scholarships and educational grants. Certain fringe benefits such as luncheon vouchers and miners' concessionary coal are omitted, whilst other benefits, such as the use of the company car, are probably included at less than their real value. There is no imputation of rent to owner-occupiers, but mortgage interest payments are deducted from taxable income. Capital gains, superannuation contributions by employees and the self-employed, employers' national insurance and superannuation contributions, are all excluded. Any income not disclosed, so that the receiver can evade tax, is necessarily left out of account. Also the Inland Revenue believe that both investment income and the part-time earnings of wives whose income does not reach the effective exemption limit is understated. There is a further complication in comparing different years because changes in allowances and the tax laws alter the coverage somewhat.

Family Expenditure Survey Data. The FES is a voluntary survey of a sample of some 7000 households undertaken annually. The degree of accuracy is less than the Inland Revenue data: there is some non-response and the information is particularly unreliable for the higher income groups, where the numbers in the sample are very small, and for expenditure on drink and tobacco, which is very much under-stated. The unit taken is the household, which consists of one person living alone, or a group of people living at the same address having meals prepared together and with common housekeeping. Although data is collected about the individual income of members of the household it is presented in the form of combined household incomes. On average, household income comes out at about $12\frac{1}{2}$ per cent higher than 'tax unit' income. The biggest advantage of the FES data is that it includes low incomes which are below the tax threshold and also incomes such as national insurance benefits which are not subject to tax.

The SPI and FES data are the sources of our main tables on personal income distribution. In addition we have drawn on the national income figures for the distribution of income by category: factor shares (the proportions going to the factors of production) and transfers. The *New Earnings Survey* of the Department of Employment provides data on the differentials between employees in different occupations.

In August 1974 the Labour Government set up a Royal Commission (chaired by Lord Diamond and hence referred to as the Diamond Commission) charged with the responsibility for analysing the distribution of income and wealth, including past trends. Its reports are a very useful source. The early reports have mainly brought together, in convenient form, known information, but the Commission is also engaged in improving and enlarging the statistics on the distribution of income and of wealth.

Income Distribution in the United Kingdom

Distribution of Income by Factor Shares and Transfers

We start our survey of income distribution in the United Kingdom by looking first at the broad division between earned income, investment income and transfer income (Table 9.1).

Perhaps the most notable point from a vertical comparison is the very small proportion of investment income. Two caveats can be made about the figures. It is the practice to treat all the income of the self-employed from unincorporated businesses (including owner-

Table 9.1   Division of Income pre-Tax, by Factor Shares and Transfers, UK.

	1955 %	1965 %	1975 %	£m
Earned income				
Income from employment	72.9	70.8	71.3	68,181
Income from self-employment	10.7	8.3	9.1	8,705
Investment income				
Rent, dividends and net interest (including imputed rent of owner-occupiers)	9.6	12.2	9.0	8,564
Transfer income				
National insurance and other cash benefits from public authorities	6.7	8.6	10.7	10,208
	100	100	100	95,658

Note: percentage columns do not exactly add up because of rounding.
Source: *National Income and Expenditure, 1965–75*, HMSO, 1976, Table 1.2.

occupiers in agriculture) as earned income, although strictly some of it should count as investment income. Secondly, the official figures of imputed rent, based on rateable values adjusted for changes in rents, are very much an understatement. Even so, the point remains valid: investment income represents a very small proportion of the total, with earned income the predominating source, constituting around 80 per cent of the total in each of the three years examined.

Other points of interest emerge from a horizontal comparison. The most marked change has been the rise in transfer incomes, which, as a proportion of total incomes, were some 60 per cent more in 1975 than in 1955. 1975 was a bad year for profits and, of the three years shown, the 1975 investment income was lowest. Finally the changes in income from self-employment call for comment. While the 1975 figures suggest the reversal since 1965 of an earlier downward trend, this may be misleading. The numbers of self-employed in agriculture and distribution declined over the past decade, but the numbers of self-employed in the construction industry more than doubled. However, this almost certainly represented a move by building workers to adopt self-employed status because of tax advantages with Selective Employment Tax (now defunct) and also with income tax.

Earnings Differences Between Occupations

One indication of the degree of inequality in *earned* incomes is the differentials between occupations. Some light is thrown on this topic by the *New Earnings Survey*, undertaken annually by the Department of Employment. The latest was carried out in April 1975—a 1 per cent random sample survey of full-time adult-employees in all occupations in all types and sizes of businesses in all industries in Great Britain. The information was provided by employers who were required to give total gross earnings for one pay period for each of the employees included in the sample. Abnormal payments (for example, arrears of pay or sick pay) were excluded and generally no account was taken of payments in kind. Average weekly earnings of employees in a particular occupation were calculated by dividing the sum of their individual weekly earnings by the number of employees. This information, for male workers, is presented in column 1 of Table 9.2 for a selection of occupations. In column 2 an index has been calculated to facilitate comparison, the occupation with the lowest gross weekly earnings (general farm workers) being taken as 1.00 and the others related to it, for example site managers and clerks of works at 1.90 receive gross earnings which are 90 per cent higher than general farm workers. Column 3 shows the relative position of the selected occupations after allowance for national insurance contributions and income tax on the assumption that each employee, on average, paid tax after deduction of allowances equivalent to that of a married man with two children under eleven. This assumption is arbitrary, but does give some general indication of the effect of tax on earnings differentials.

The table shows earnings from the occupation with the highest earnings coming out at about two-and-a-half times that from the occupation with the lowest earnings when no allowance is made for tax, and at about twice the lowest when tax is deducted. Before too much is read into this conclusion we should remember the basis on which the survey is compiled. It is a sample survey and there are liable to be sampling errors. The data in the survey is derived from one pay-period only. It could be, therefore, that one of the groups

Table 9.2   Differentials of Adult Male Workers, GB, 1975 (Selected Occupations from the New Earnings Survey).

Occupation	(1) Average gross weekly earnings (£)	(2) Indices Before tax	(3) Indices After tax
General farm workers	37.1	1.00	1.00
General clerks	45.2	1.22	1.15
General labourers	45.3	1.22	1.16
Painters and decorators	51.4	1.39	1.27
Bus conductors	55.1	1.49	1.34
Carpenters and joiners	55.9	1.51	1.36
Clerical supervisors	60.0	1.62	1.43
Site managers/clerks of works	70.6	1.90	1.64
Police sergeants/security supervisors	75.8	2.04	1.73
Electrical and electronic engineers	82.5	2.22	1.86
Marketing and sales managers	84.7	2.28	1.90
Coalmining deputies	86.2	2.32	1.93
Teachers in further education	86.9	2.34	1.94
Civil servants (administration and executive)	91.6	2.47	2.03

had just received a pay increase whilst another was just about to have one. To try to ensure the reliability of the information, average gross earnings are only given in the survey for those occupations where more than one hundred men appear in the sample, but this may tend to exclude occupations with the highest earnings where the numbers may be fewer. It should be re-emphasized that it is a survey of employees only. So, for example, self-employed professional people, such as accountants and solicitors in private practices, are excluded. Further, the assumption we have used for allowing for income tax may (relatively) overstate the tax paid by the better off, who are likely to be benefiting from tax concessions on high mortgages. Finally, averaging within an occupation helps to iron out differences—but this probably makes for a fairer picture because it partly deals with the 'snapshot' problem of variations of life-time income—the sample for an occupation will include people of all ages. The significance of age in high earnings was brought out by a recent report of the Royal Commission, drawing on data from the *New Earnings Survey* for 1974. They found 'that a markedly larger proportion of high earners compared with all full-time men are in the 40–60 age group, i.e. 70 per cent compared with 45 per cent; and that above £12,000 the proportion in the 50–59 age group is more than double that among all full-time men, i.e. 47 per cent compared with 22 per cent.'[1] (In the Royal Commission's study a higher earner was defined as someone receiving £8,000 and over.)

International comparisons can be made rather more reliably for earnings than for other types of income (or the distribution of wealth) and Professor Lydall has summarized some of the most interesting features of these comparisons:

> First, . . . differences between earnings are much greater in poor countries than in rich ones. Secondly, such differences are relatively small in some of the communist countries of Eastern Europe —although probably not in the USSR itself—and also in Australia and New Zealand. Thirdly, the differences between pre-tax earnings in this country are at the low end of the range for Western Europe and North America, and less than in some communist countries, such as Poland and Yugoslavia. After tax, the range of earnings in Britain is almost certainly amongst the most narrow in the world.[2]

Now let us turn to the distribution of personal income.

Distribution of Personal Income Before and after Income Tax

Table 9.3 shows the distribution of income before and after income tax in 1973–74. It is based on Inland Revenue data (the SPI) with some supplementation, especially on the lowest incomes and on untaxed social security benefits, from the FES. The unit is the tax unit, not the individual or the household and, because of the way the data is compiled, some 18 per cent of income cannot be allocated to income ranges: the biggest items not allocated consist of employers' national insurance contributions, imputed rent of owner-occupied dwellings and an item of income from self-employment arising from a timing adjustment (accounts from the self-employed, determining their taxable income, are necessarily submitted after the end of the

---

[1] Royal Commission on the Distribution of Income and Wealth, *Report No. 3, Higher Incomes from Employment*, Cmnd. 6383, 1976, p. 35.

[2] Harold Lydall, 'The economics of inequality', *Lloyds Bank Review*, July 1975, p. 37.

tax year and it may be a long time afterwards before they are finally agreed). In the table we need to include a classification by income ranges both before and after tax because the effect of income tax is to move some income receivers from one income range to another. Table 9.3 shows us, for example, that in 1973–74 there were 136,000 'tax units' with incomes over £10,000, receiving an aggregate income of £2183 million; of this total £1056 million, or nearly 50 per cent, went in income tax. As a result, the number with incomes over £10,000 after tax was reduced to 21,000.

Using data from much the same basic sources, the Royal Commission has calculated shares for various years from 1949 to 1973–74, reproduced in Table 9.4. The statistics reveal a marked decline in the pre-tax income of the top 1 per cent of income receivers over the period and a distinct fall in that of the top 2–5 per cent, but the top 6–10 per cent has maintained its position. Most of the benefit from the reduced concentration at the very top seems to have gone to those in the income ranges 10 to 50 per cent and rather less to the bottom half of the income distribution; but in assessing these changes over time the limitations of the 'snapshot' approach must be borne in mind. The period saw an increasing proportion of retired people in the population and for much of the period a growing number of young workers. There is a particular quirk in the statistics associated with school leavers. The bottom 20 per cent of income receivers includes a large number of 'part-year tax units'—people working for part of the year only—and variations in their number affect the proportion of income going to the bottom 20 per cent. In particular about one-eighth of the increase in the share of the bottom 20 per cent in 1973–74 resulted from the raising of the school leaving age during 1973, which reduced the number of low, mostly part-year incomes by about a quarter of a million in that financial year.[1]

Income tax reduces the top 5 per cent in each of the years examined and the bottom 50 per cent emerges with a rather larger proportion of post-tax income. But it is notable that the shares of the top 6–10 per cent or the top 10–20 per cent are very much the same before and after income tax. This possibly reflects the limited progression of the United Kingdom income tax at levels below the start of higher rate tax (or surtax, as it then was).

Pre-war, the figures are less reliable, but unadjusted Inland Revenue data for 1938–39 gives a pre-tax figure of 17 per cent owned

[1] Royal Commission on the Distribution of Income and Wealth, *Report No. 4, Second Report on the Standing Reference*, Cmnd. 6626, October 1976, p. 11.

Table 9.3   Distribution of Incomes Before and After Income Tax in United Kingdom, 1973–74.

| Range of incomes | | Before tax | | | | After tax | | | |
From and including	To but not including	No. of tax units	Income before tax	Taxes on income	Income after tax	No. of tax units	Income before tax	Taxes on income	Income after tax
		Thousands	*£ million*	*£ million*	*£ million*	*Thousands*	*£ million*	*£ million*	*£ million*
—	595	3579	1800	2	1798	3589	1808	5	1803
595 —	1000	5499	4513	117	4396	6328	5397	224	5173
1000 —	2000	8708	12,921	1481	11,440	10,579	17,967	2349	15,618
2000 —	3000	6564	16,043	2412	13,631	5790	16,488	2579	13,909
3000 —	4000	2415	8209	1437	6772	1229	5201	1020	4181
4000 —	5000	699	3102	637	2465	288	1688	408	1280
5000 —	6000	234	1279	296	983	133	1029	303	726
6000 —	8000	204	1409	370	1039	125	1344	486	858
8000 —	10,000	85	760	239	521	41	667	302	365
10,000 —	15,000	87	1035	404	631	18	472	263	209
15,000 —	20,000	27	456	214	242	2	90	58	32
20,000 and over		22	692	438	254	1	68	50	18
Total		28,123	52,219	8047	44,172	28,123	52,219	8047	44,172
Income not included in classification by ranges			11,156				11,156		
Total income of households			63,375				63,375		

Table 9.4 Distribution of Personal Incomes in the United Kingdom: Percentage Shares of Income, Before and After Income Tax, 1949–1973/74.

	Before income tax					After income tax				
	1949	1959	1967	1972–73	1973–74	1949	1959	1967	1972–73	1973–74
	%	%	%	%	%	%	%	%	%	%
Top 1 per cent	11.2	8.4	7.4	6.4	6.5	6.4	5.3	4.9	4.4	4.5
2–5 ,, ,,	12.6	11.5	11.0	10.8	10.6	11.3	10.5	9.9	9.8	9.8
6–10 ,, ,,	9.4	9.5	9.6	9.7	9.7	9.4	9.4	9.5	9.4	9.3
Top 10 per cent	33.2	29.4	28.0	26.9	26.8	27.1	25.2	24.3	23.6	23.6
11–20 ,, ,,	14.1	15.1	15.2	15.8	15.6	14.5	15.7	15.2	15.8	15.5
21–30 ,, ,,	11.2	12.6	12.6	13.1	12.9	11.9	12.9	13.0	13.2	13.2
31–40 ,, ,,	9.6	10.7	11.1	11.0	11.2	10.5	11.2	11.0	11.2	11.2
41–50 ,, ,,	8.2	9.1	9.1	9.2	9.3	9.5	9.9	9.7	9.5	9.5
51–60 ,, ,,	23.7	7.5	7.7	7.5	7.5	26.5	7.2	7.7	8.0	7.8
61–70 ,, ,,		5.9	6.0	5.9	5.8		6.6	7.1	6.5	6.4
71–80 ,, ,,		4.4	4.8	4.8	4.7		5.2	4.9	5.5	5.4
81–100 ,, ,,		5.3	5.6	5.8	6.2		6.0	7.1	6.8	7.4

Notes: columns do not always add up exactly to 100 because of rounding.
    income unit: tax unit.
Source: Royal Commission on the Distribution of Income and Wealth, *Report No. 1*, Cmnd. 6171, Table 15; *Report No. 4*, Cmnd. 6626, Table 4.

by the top 1 per cent of income receivers, reduced to 12 per cent post-tax; the corresponding figures for the top 10 per cent were 40 per cent and 35 per cent. The post-war situation thus shows a large reduction in the concentration of income at the top of the scale.

Professor Lydall, drawing on a recent study, again provides us with a convenient summary of the most significant features of international comparisons of income distribution:

> In the poor countries the typical share of pre-tax income received by the top 5 per cent of households is about 30 per cent. This implies that the average household in the top 5 per cent of the distribution has a pre-tax income about six times as large as the average for the country as a whole . . . the degree of inequality tends to diminish as income rises. Among the countries of Western Europe, other than Scandinavia, the typical share of pre-tax income received by the top 5 per cent is about 20 per cent, while in the United States, Australia and Scandinavia it is nearer to 15 per cent. . . . If incomes were estimated after direct taxes, the lesser inequality among the richer countries would be even more conspicuous.

Professor Lydall recognizes the limitations of statistics derived from voluntary household surveys in which the incomes of the richer households are usually understated, but he maintains, 'There can be little doubt that they reflect real differences in inequality.' He concludes 'There is no general support for the cliché that economic growth causes "the rich to become richer and the poor to become poorer".'[1]

Distribution of Personal Income After All Taxes and Benefits

The picture we have so far presented for the United Kingdom takes no account of taxes other than income tax and only allows for those state benefits which, like retirement pensions, enter taxable income. To try to allow for all allocable taxes and benefits we must use FES data. We have already discussed the general characteristics and limitations of the FES data, but there are some particular features which need to be mentioned when it is used for this purpose.

The starting point of the compilation is *original income* which is the

[1] *Ibid.*, pp. 34–5.

ncome in cash and kind of all members of the household before the deduction of taxes or the addition of any state benefits. Income in cash includes earned income, income from investment and private pensions. Income in kind includes an imputed rent to owner-occupiers and the value of concessions on items such as miners' coal.

The next stage is to add state benefits in cash, family allowances, retirement pensions, unemployment benefit and other social security benefits to give *original income plus cash benefits*. Such benefits, as Table 9.5 shows, are very markedly redistributive, those with the lowest incomes benefiting most.

Then income tax and the employees' national insurance contributions actually paid by the households are deducted to reach a figure of *disposable income*, which is less unequally distributed than original income plus cash benefits.

The next stage is to deduct indirect taxes and add subsidies on the goods and services purchased by the household to obtain *income after all taxes and transfers*. The items covered are local rates, taxes on alcoholic drinks, tobacco and oil, VAT, import duties and other miscellaneous taxes, together with the element of tax on intermediate products, and subsidies on food and housing. The attribution of tax and subsidies to households raises difficult issues—subsidies and taxes affect the amount of these goods purchased, which in turn affects the incomes of the suppliers. Such secondary consequences, however, are ignored. It is assumed that the whole of the tax is paid by the consumer and that the subsidy benefits him to an extent equal to the cost to the government. The outcome on the distribution of incomes is somewhat complicated. Indirect taxes as a whole are roughly proportional in their incidence over most of the income range, declining as a proportion of income at the upper end of household incomes. On the other hand, subsidies are progressive in their effect (i.e. they represent higher percentages of the incomes of less well-off households) and also lead to a redistribution between household types at each income level, e.g. households with three or four children receive above average subsidies.

The final stage is to add on an allowance for certain benefits in kind to obtain *income after all taxes and benefits* or *final income*. The items covered are education, health and welfare foods. The benefit to the recipient is assumed to be equal to the average cost of the service to the state, and the allocation of education and health benefits is on a standardized basis. Thus the costs of each education (primary, secondary, etc.) sector are allocated to those households with children

Table 9.5   Average Incomes Before and After Taxes and Benefits, All Households in FES, United Kingdom, 1974.

Range of original income (£ per year)	Under 381	381–461	461–557	557–674	674–816	816–987	987–1194	1194–1446	1446–1749	1749–2116	2116–2561	2561–3099	3099–3750	3750–4531	4531–5490	5490+	Average overall
Number of households	1116	91	86	101	112	109	153	207	295	475	637	774	806	680	498	555	6695
(a) Original income	104	422	505	612	739	903	1088	1319	1606	1946	2346	2816	3411	4108	4956	7639	2719
(+cash benefits, i.e. transfers)																	
(b) Original income and cash benefits	833	1118	1229	1225	1353	1493	1583	1752	1868	2174	2505	2977	3538	4222	5044	7752	3017
(−income tax and employees N.I. contributions)																	
(c) Disposable income	828	1101	1203	1176	1284	1389	1462	1591	1636	1869	2104	2492	2907	3433	4054	6071	2509
(+subsidies−indirect taxes)																	
(d) Income after all taxes and transfers	750	933	1017	984	1084	1156	1206	1338	1334	1515	1704	2022	2358	2808	3341	5101	2074
(+direct benefits in kind)																	
(e) Income after all taxes and benefits	981	1207	1199	1219	1344	1450	1480	1680	1671	1859	2111	2437	2802	3264	3752	5627	2448
(f) Net change (e)−(a)	+877	+785	+694	+607	+605	+547	+392	+361	+65	−87	−235	−379	−609	−844	−1204	−2012	−271

or young persons of the relevant age recorded in the FES as receiving
state education. The current costs of the National Health Service
are apportioned according to the average use by persons of each age
and sex (thus, for example, the highest benefits accrue to the very
old and the very young) and are allocated to households according
to the age and sex of each member whether or not they have used
the facilities of the Health Service during the year. The cost of
maternity services is allocated to those households recording a birth
during the year. The allocation of benefits in kind depends far more
on the composition of a household than its income, but the net effect
is to reduce further the inequality of income distribution.

Table 9.5 shows the effects of each stage of the compilation on all
households, taken together, in 1974. Because more tax than expenditure is allocated to households, the overall average household is
shown as paying £271 more in taxes than it receives in benefits.

If the overall process of redistribution between income groups is
clear from Table 9.5, other aspects of redistribution are concealed,
for example, differences between the working population and the
retired, and between those with large families and those without.
Some indication of these aspects of redistribution can be derived
from Table 9.6. Two final points of definition should be noted: all
persons over 16 count as adults (even though they may be at school
and receiving education benefits); and retired households are defined
as those in which the combined incomes of members who are over
60 and describe themselves as retired or unoccupied is equal to at
least half the total gross income of the household.

Distribution of Investment Income

The fourth Report of the Royal Commission on the Distribution of
Income and Wealth[1] includes data not hitherto published which
shows the distribution of investment income amongst persons.
Investment income, on the definition used, does not include imputed
income to owner-occupied houses. As can be seen from Table 9.7 the
distribution of investment income is particularly unequal. Less than
one quarter of the 'income units' had any investment income in
1973–74, but 86 per cent of the top 1 per cent of income receivers
had investment income. Over 30 per cent of investment income was
received by the top 1 per cent and over 60 per cent by the top
10 per cent.

[1] *Second Report on the Standing Reference*, Cmnd. 6626, October 1976.

Table 9.6 Estimates of Redistribution by Taxes and Benefits, United Kingdom, 1974: Average Net Total Benefits (+) or Net Total Taxes (−) for Typical Households.

Range of original income (£ per year)	Under 381	381−461	−557	−674	−816	−987	−1194	−1446	−1749	−2116	−2561	−3099	−3750	−4537	−5490+		Average overall
All households in the sample	+877	+785	+694	+607	+605	+547	+392	+361	+65	−87	−235	−379	−609	−844	−1204	−2012	−271
Retired households																	
One adult	+656	+467	+425	+440	+276	+198	+43	+166									+555
Two adults	+1016	+924	+775	+650	+566	+521	+473	+260	+65	−202							+750
Non-retired households																	
One adult	+814	+339	+222	+273	+125	−37	−207	−387	−625	−795	−900	−1215	−1519	−1852	−3020		−365
Two adults	+795	+883	+692	+660	+588	+372	+169	−213	−336	−549	−727	−1047	−1321	−1601	−2592		−837
Retired and non-retired households																	
Two adults, one child							+628	+4	+97	−254	−373	−551	−856	−1074	−1361	−3007	−642
Two adults, two children								+776	+185	−27	−172	−343	−511	−741	−980	−1756	−436
Two adults, three children									+453	+466	+89	+32	−148	−229	−763	−1646	−89
Two adults, four children										+838	+758	+512	+238	+4	−206	−1240	+425

Source: as Table 9.5.

Table 9.7   Distribution of Investment Income, United Kingdom, 1973–74.

Percentile group	Investment income in group as per cent of total investment income	Numbers in group Thousands	Numbers with investment income in each income group	
			Thousands	Per cent
Top 1 per cent	34.4	281	244	86.8
2–5 ,, ,,	21.0	1125	716	63.6
6–10 ,, ,,	7.5	1406	606	43.1
Top 10 per cent	62.9	2812	1566	55.7
11–20 ,, ,,	8.4	2812	960	34.1
21–30 ,, ,,	5.5	2812	782	27.8
31–40 ,, ,,	4.6	2812	703	25.0
41–50 ,, ,,	4.8	2812	693	24.6
51–60 ,, ,,	5.2	2812	738	26.2
61–70 ,, ,,	3.9	2812	635	22.6
71–80 ,, ,,	2.4	2812	451	16.0
81–90 ,, ,,	1.5	2812	301	10.7
91–100 ,, ,,	0.8	2812	116	4.1
Total	100.0	28,123	6945	24.7

Source: Royal Commission on the Distribution of Income and Wealth, *Report No. 4*, Cmnd. 6626, Tables 43 and 44.

This inequality in the distribution of investment income clearly reflects inequality in the distribution of wealth—the subject of Chapter 11.

Government Policy and the Distribution of Income

In looking at the post-tax and benefit distribution of income in the United Kingdom, and even to some extent in examining the pre-tax distribution, we have already been examining the consequences of government action, whether intentional or unintentional, on income distribution. Our main concern in this section is to look at the ways in which governments can change the distribution of income in a mixed economy, and in particular to examine the constraints on a government in so doing.

Almost any government policy will have some effect, however indirect or unintentional, on the distribution of incomes, but some policies are much more direct than others in their distributional effects. Policy, or lack of it, to maintain employment or combat inflation may exert a very powerful influence on income distribution. An incomes policy, which may be part of counter-inflation policy, is one such measure, and price and rent controls also imply restrictions on certain kinds of income. Monetary policy, apart from its indirect effects, acts directly on rates of interest and thus the income of the rentier. Minimum wage legislation is expressly designed to change the distribution of income to the benefit of the low paid and 'equal pay' legislation seeks to raise the proportion of income going to women. Education policy may have important effects on the pre-tax distribution of income, wider educational opportunities being associated with lower earned income differentials. However, whilst we shall touch on some of these topics in later chapters, here we shall concentrate on the effects of taxation policy, especially income tax, and on some of the direct consequences of government expenditure.

The Limits of Income Tax: the Theory

Let us look first at taxation. Inequalities of income can be reduced by progressive taxation. A progressive tax is one such that the higher the income the larger the *proportion* of it which goes in tax (other circumstances, e.g. the number of dependents, remaining the same). But to tax income alters the price of factors of production, and factor prices have a vital role in securing economic efficiency by acting as incentives to effort and inducements to workers and entrepreneurs to move into those lines of production desired by the community. The crucial question is, therefore, 'how far can a government go in altering the distribution of real income by taxation without destroying the efficiency advantages of the price mechanism?' There is a conflict, or potential conflict, between efficiency and the objective of reducing inequality. Let us concentrate on one main aspect of this issue, the effect of progressive income taxation on the supply of labour, and start by examining the effect on work effort of imposing an income tax or increasing an existing income tax. In analysing the problem we can use some of the concepts introduced in Chapter 4— the income and substitution effects of a change in price on the demand for goods. We can look at the problem from the point of view of the demand for leisure. If time is thought of as being divided between paid work and leisure, then an increased demand for leisure constitutes a reduced willingness to engage in paid work and vice versa.

The imposition of an income tax alters the price of labour and has both an income and a substitution effect. The income effect is that the tax makes the worker worse off—he can afford less of most things, including leisure.[1] He will thus tend to have less leisure, i.e. to engage in *more* paid work. Putting the point in another way, faced by a cut in income he will try to protect his living standard by doing more paid work. The income effect is thus not a disincentive but an incentive effect. The substitution effect is that the tax lowers the 'price' or the opportunity cost of leisure. If, before the tax, the worker received £1 for an extra hour of work, but after receives only 60p (£1 minus tax at 40 per cent) then if he takes that hour as leisure he sacrifices less other things after the tax than before. On this count he will tend to have *more* leisure, i.e. do less work. In other words he will substitute leisure time for work time and income. The substitution effect is thus a disincentive effect.

The observant student will have noted an important difference from the analysis in Chapter 4. When the price of a good changed, the income and substitution effects normally worked in the same

[1] Strictly speaking we cannot be sure that the taxpayer is worse off until we know how he has gained (if at all) from the way the government has used the tax revenue. But unless he has received cash benefits, or his normal purchases were subsidized, to an extent equivalent to his tax payments, he is at least worse off in terms of the goods and services which enter into his personal consumption. Moreover, because of the separation between cost and benefit which characterizes government expenditure, he will almost certainly *feel* worse off—and it is what he feels which affects his behaviour.

direction and, even if they did not, the substitution effect normally dwarfed the income effect which was negligible for small price changes of individual goods. We could thus say with confidence that a fall in the price of a good increased, and a rise in price reduced, demand.

With the change in the price of a factor of production, however, the income and substitution effects work in opposite directions. Moreover the income effect of even a small percentage change in price is not negligible. When the price of labour (and therefore of leisure) changes as a result of a tax we cannot say, on first principles, whether more or less work effort (or leisure) will result.

Even this negative conclusion is important, for it is often assumed that an income tax *must* have a disincentive effect—and this is plainly wrong. But our theory can take us further than this. The income effect works through the change in aggregate income as a result of the tax. The substitution effect is concerned with the terms on which income can be acquired at the margin—what I lose (or gain) by an extra hour more (or less) of leisure. Thus the more the aggregate effect relative to the marginal effect, the more the incentive (or the less the disincentive) effect. We can illustrate the difference by reference to the extremes. Suppose that everyone with an income was required to pay a lump sum in tax irrespective of the size of that income (in effect a kind of poll tax). Such a tax would have an income effect but no substitution effect since it would not alter the terms on which income could be acquired at the margin: if I worked an extra hour I would get just as much pay for that hour after the tax as before. A tax of this kind would have an incentive effect on all those who continued to earn. (If it was only paid by those with an income, it might discourage some people, e.g. married women, from entering the labour market at all). At the other extreme, let us imagine a tax with rates rising gradually with income to a maximum of 100 per cent. Anyone at the top rate would know only a disincentive effect. The substitution effect would be overwhelming since an hour of extra leisure would now cost nothing. The tax would clearly reduce income, but there would be no possibility of offsetting the income effect by working more, so that such a tax rate must be a disincentive.

Save in these extreme cases, theory cannot tell us for certain whether a particular income tax will have an incentive or disincentive effect, though we can say that, for the same revenue to the Exchequer, a proportional or regressive income tax will have more incentive (or less disincentive) effect that a progressive income tax: for a progressive income tax implies a rising marginal rate of tax. It is useful here to distinguish clearly between the marginal and the average rates of tax. The marginal rate is that paid on the last pound received (or, alternatively, what would be paid on an additional pound of income). It specifies the tax terms on which income can be acquired at the margin. The average rate of income tax is total tax paid expressed as a proportion of income. With a progressive tax the marginal rate is necessarily above the average rate.

Apart from the two extremes, to discover whether any particular tax acts as an incentive or disincentive we need to look at the real world and observe how people behave: in other words we must resort to empirical analysis. Let us start by describing the United Kingdom income tax.

The Limits of Income Tax: the Practice

There are three features of United Kingdom taxation of earned income that we need to appreciate. First, every 'tax unit' enjoys some tax-free income, the amount depending on the circumstances. There are tax allowances for a married couple, for single persons, for children and for a variety of other circumstances, e.g. owner-occupiers paying interest on house mortages. Once the allowances have been 'used up', tax is then paid over a wide band of income at 'basic rate'. Thereafter 'higher-rate' tax applies at rising rates. Also a surcharge is levied on investment income over a certain minimum. The situation, at 1976–77 tax rates, is set out in Figure 9.2. In that year the basic rate was 35 per cent; the maximum marginal rate of tax on earned income was 83 per cent and on investment income 98 per cent.

The vast bulk of taxpayers in the United Kingdom have incomes which place them in the basic rate band. Whilst the United Kingdom average rates of income tax are comparable with those in many other countries, the top marginal rates are exceptionally high by international standards. These features of the United Kingdom income tax should be borne in mind in considering the empirical investigations on the incentive/disincentive effects of income tax.

The first issue to emerge when we move from theory to the real world is that some people may not be in a position to adjust the amount of work they do in response to changes in income tax, at

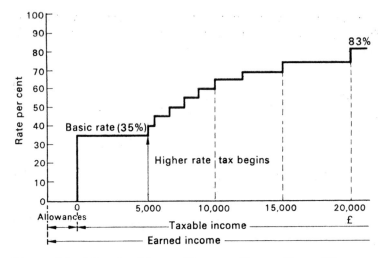

Figure 9.2   Marginal Rate of Income Tax on Earned Income, UK, 1976–77.

least in the short run, because their job is strictly confined to fixed hours. However, many people can change the amount of work which they do in one or more of the following ways: by taking more or less voluntary overtime; by more or less absenteeism; by accepting or refusing part-time work; by varying work effort within working hours (for those on piece rates or bonus rates); by advancing or retarding the date of retirement; if they are self-employed, by seeking or not seeking new business; by choosing to work or not (especially important for married women). Finally, in the long run, many people can adjust the time they work by influencing trade union policy about the relative importance of reducing hours of work amongst the union's negotiating objectives.

A number of empirical studies have been undertaken in this country and abroad, mainly in the form of surveys by interview or mailed questionnaire.[1] Each has limitations, e.g. it may have been confined to a particular income range or a small occupational group, so that firm generalized conclusions cannot easily be drawn. Nonetheless, taken as a whole the studies show a surprisingly

[1] Some of the best empirical studies on British data have been G. F. Break, 'Effects of taxation on incentives', *British Tax Review*, June 1957; D. B. Fields and W. T. Stanbury, 'Incentives, disincentives and the income tax, further empirical evidence', *Public Finance*, No. 3, 1970; C. V. Brown and E. Levin, 'The effects of income tax on overtime: the results of a national survey', *Economic Journal*, December 1974.

consistent pattern. The main conclusions may be summarized as follows:

1. For the large majority of the people surveyed, tax considerations were not a significant determinant of work effort.
2. Amongst those whose work effort was influenced, for some income tax acted as a disincentive, for others an incentive.
3. Little evidence emerges of any significant *net* effects, either incentive or disincentive, at basic income tax levels.
4. There is some evidence to suggest a net disincentive effect on those paying the top marginal rates of tax.[1]

Its effect on work effort is not the only way income tax may be detrimental to efficiency. It may discourage enterprise or retard investment by discouraging savings, especially for risk capital. But in each case the outcome is uncertain, for income and substitution effects will work in opposite directions: thus a heavy marginal rate of income tax encourages the substitution of consumption for saving; but, if I am saving for a future net income of a particular level, I need to save *more* as a result of the tax. Again, heavy income taxation may discourage mobility of labour both geographical and occupational—a person may be less willing to move to a new area for a job, or incur the costs of training for another better-paid occupation, because tax reduces the net benefit of the moves. On the other hand, if he seeks a certain net income, he may be prepared to move more often in order to attain it.

High income taxation encourages evasion (illegal tax dodging) and avoidance (arranging one's affairs within the law so as to minimize tax liabilities). It may generate inflationary pressures. Also, high income taxation may stimulate 'do-it-yourself' activities, for £1 saved is worth £2 earned at a marginal rate of income tax of 50 per cent. Such activities tend to break up the advantages to be derived from division of labour—that people do best those things in which they are trained and experienced.

We cannot pursue, at depth, these various issues, although we shall have more to say on inflation in Chapter 15. But, on the one important issue we have explored most fully, the effect of income tax on the supply of labour, it is clear that there is considerable scope for using income tax to reduce inequalities in the distribution of

[1] The surveys of accountants and solicitors by Break, *ibid.*, and by Fields and Stanbury, *ibid.*

income without running into serious economic disadvantages. It seems likely that the same conclusion would hold for the other possible detriments, where, as with work effort, there are often opposing tendencies. That is not to say, however, that economic disadvantages may not arise from the top marginal rates of income tax in the United Kingdom, which currently closely approach 100 per cent and are abnormally high by international standards. At such rates there may well be a significant loss in efficiency for a small gain in reducing inequality. More research needs to be done before we can be sure just what is the trade-off between the two; once that is known, it becomes a matter of personal value judgment how much loss of efficiency one would wish to sacrifice for how much gain in equality.

Disincentive Effects of Government Expenditure

It is also possible that government expenditure may generate disincentive effects. Thus, if unemployment pay or supplementary benefits for a man with a large family are nearly as much as the wage he can earn, he may be discouraged from seeking work. Means-tested benefits may particularly create disincentives. If earning more means the loss of benefits, or past saving reduces eligibility for benefits, then a disincentive to effort and to thrift may result. In the next chapter we shall examine such a situation in detail—the so-called 'poverty-trap'.

How Much Can the Rich Be Soaked?

We have already indicated one limit to a policy of 'soaking the rich' —whilst there is considerable scope for changing the distribution of income by taxation, there are practical limits imposed by efficiency considerations. There is some point, which may be very close to a marginal rate of 100 per cent, beyond which higher income tax rates will simply result in less output and income,[1] and at income tax rates near to that point, it is a matter of judgment whether the trade-off in efficiency is worth the gain in reduced inequality. But, even if this particular constraint did not exist, it can be shown that

---

[1] It should be noted that an extreme egalitarian might actually prefer a smaller national income more evenly distributed to a larger national income less evenly distributed *even if the poor had less income in the first situation than in the second.* The poorer society, in such a view, might be happier because it generated less feelings of injustice or envy even though the material standards of the poor were lower.

the scope for further reducing inequality of income in the United Kingdom by income taxation is very limited.

Let us refer again to the figures in Table 9.3. Suppose we decreed that no one should be allowed a post-tax income in excess of £6000 p.a. If we conveniently ignore the fact that to enforce the decree would reduce the amount of income forthcoming, how much income would be available for redistribution? The table shows us that, after present tax rates, 187,000 'tax units' had incomes over £6000, amounting in all to £1482 million. Allowing these 187,000 to retain £6000 each would account for £1122 million, leaving £360 million to redistribute. This is equivalent to £7 per year per person if equally spread over all men, women and children in the country. £360 million is just over half a per cent of total incomes in 1973–74 and less than 0.7 per cent of incomes which can be classified in ranges. The sum of £360 million, contrasts with £854 million from duties on alcoholic drinks in 1973–74 and £1030 million in tobacco tax; or £524 million, the cost of the mortgage interest concession to owner-occupiers in that year.

If we took £5000 instead of £6000 as the maximum permissible post-tax income, the numbers of those above the permitted income level would rise to 320,000 and the amount of income they possessed in excess of £5000 per unit would be £608 million. In fact, as we have already pointed out, the total available for redistribution would be less than £608 million if the attempt was made to enforce the maximum income provision.

The general validity of this conclusion is born out by evidence given to the Select Committee on a Wealth Tax by the Inland Revenue,[1] which demonstrates in a somewhat different way the relatively small amount of revenue derived from the top rates of income tax, essentially because the number of high income receivers is a very small proportion of the total. The memorandum states that 'The full year cost, at 1974–75 income levels, of abolishing the 83 per cent rate of income tax so that the top rate was 73 per cent would be £24 million; the cost of abolishing the 73 per cent rate, so that the top rate was 68 per cent would (including the previous figure) be £42 millions.'[2] In 1974–75 over £10,000 million of revenue was

---

[1] 'The Interaction between Wealth Tax and Income Tax', Memorandum submitted by the Board of Inland Revenue, *The Select Committee on a Wealth Tax*, vol. II, *Minutes of Evidence*, November 1975, p. 57.

[2] The rate structure of income tax in 1974–75 was somewhat different to that of 1976–77, set out in Figure 9.1.

derived from income tax; thus only 0.4 per cent came from the rates in excess of 68 per cent. In fact it is quite possible that the revenue cost of abolishing the top rates, as described, would have been substantially less than the Inland Revenue estimate, as their calculation assumes that the amount of taxable income is irrespective of the rates of tax; and it is not unlikely that a reduction in top rates might have had incentive effects which would have generated more taxable income.

This conclusion about the scope for reducing inequality of incomes by income taxation should not wholly be a surprise in view of the data we have examined on income distribution. Post-tax differentials in earnings between occupations are not large, at any rate amongst employees. High pre-tax earnings characterize only a very small proportion of the population and are heavily cut by taxation. Investment income *is* very unequally divided, but it represents only 5–6 per cent of total personal income when imputed rent is excluded.

If, like the author, you take the view that the present top marginal rates of income tax are too high (at 83 per cent and 98 per cent for earned and investment income respectively) and that, though the evidence is not conclusive, they probably have significant detrimental economic effects, does this mean that there is *no* scope for further reduction in inequality of incomes through taxation and, indeed, that the taxation on high income receivers should be reduced?

In reply to this question three comments may be made. First, even if we reduced top income tax rates, changes in the structure of the income tax could make it a better instrument for reducing inequality. Over the income ranges applicable to most of the population, income tax is not very progressive because of its high starting point and the wide band of income subject to the same (basic) rate of tax. A tax scale which started with lower rates and rose more evenly before the income at which higher rate now commences is more likely to serve the cause of distributive justice. The United Kingdom is possibly unique amongst advanced mixed economies in having such a high starting rate to its income tax and such a wide constant rate band.

Secondly, there is scope for modifying the tax base in ways which would reduce inequalities of income without increasing top marginal rates of tax. When allowances are given through the tax system, unless some special exception is made, the amount of benefit depends on the marginal rate of tax. Thus, suppose the child tax allowance is increased by £100; then every tax payer has an additional £100 of tax free income for each child. For the person paying basic rate, the benefit is £35. For the person whose income is below the tax threshold the benefit is nil. For the person paying at the top rate of income tax of 98 per cent the benefit is £98.[1] If a tax credit or cash grant were substituted for an income tax allowance the benefit could be the same for all.[2] To give another example, if the tax base was widened to include the imputed rent of owner-occupied houses this would tend to increase the proportion of tax paid by those with the highest incomes and the most expensive houses. A somewhat similar effect would result from ceasing to allow the mortgage interest on owner-occupied houses as a tax allowance. We shall have more to say on this topic in Chapter 14 on housing.

Finally, we pointed out earlier in the chapter that the main reason for differences in investment income was differences in the ownership of wealth. Policy to reduce inequality in the distribution of wealth, therefore, reacts on the distribution of income and specifically on that form of income which is most unequally distributed. Moreover, wealth, irrespective of the income which it yields and even if it yields none, gives its possessor advantages such as security, the opportunity of advantageous purchase, the chance to go on a spending spree, and additional independence. These advantages increase the owner's taxable capacity.

The scope for reducing inequalities in the distribution of wealth we shall examine in Chapter 11. Before that, however, we need to look at the problem of poverty, which is related to, but by no means identical with, the degree of inequality in income distribution.

SUMMARY AND CONCLUSIONS

Differences in earned income can best be explained by differences in 'productive capacity', differences in investment income by differences in the amount of wealth owned. There are conceptual problems in measuring the distribution of income, e.g. the choice of income unit and the 'life cycle' problem. There are statistical

[1] The benefits are calculated on the basis of the 1976–77 income tax rates.
[2] Both the Conservative tax-credit scheme and the Labour child benefit scheme involve the replacement of the child tax allowance by a cash payment (see Chapter 10).

difficulties in the United Kingdom stemming from the data available —mainly derived from income tax returns and the Family Expenditure Surveys. The after-tax range of earned incomes in the United Kingdom is among the narrowest in the world and the inequality is still farther reduced when allowance is made for allocable benefits and subsidies. Investment income is very unevenly distributed but it constitutes a very small proportion of total income. Whilst it seems likely that an income tax offers considerable scope for reducing income inequalities without serious economic effects, the present top marginal rates of income tax in the United Kingdom, abnormally high by international standards, may generate such adverse effects for little or no gain in tax revenue. Further reduction in inequality of income by taxation should be sought by widening the income tax base, introducing a more smoothly progressive rate structure into the income tax and possibly by an appropriate policy on the distribution of wealth, which would change the distribution of investment income.

10 The Poverty Problem

The Meaning of Poverty

The way in which income and wealth are divided up is clearly linked to the problem of poverty, but how closely partly depends on our definition of poverty and more than one definition is possible. In particular we need to distinguish between absolute and relative poverty.

Absolute Poverty

An absolute measure of poverty is an attempt to determine the minimum subsistence level: an assessment of the amount of income required to purchase what are regarded as the absolute essentials of life, a specified amount of food, clothing, shelter, and so on. In his classic investigations on the poverty in York in 1899, Seebohm Rowntree used such an absolute measure and distinguished between primary and secondary poverty. Primary poverty existed where income fell below what was required to purchase the absolute essentials in his minimum subsistence level.[1] Secondary poverty existed where, although income was sufficient, there was failure to acquire the essentials through an inappropriate or inefficient use of income, for example, as a result of gambling or drinking by the husband or ignorant housekeeping by the wife. To cover this possibility he added an additional income margin to his definition of primary poverty.

The Rowntree enquiry of 1899 was repeated in 1936 and again in 1950. The percentages in poverty in York fell from 28 in 1899, to 2 in 1950, reflecting economic progress and the welfare state provisions; and this substantial reduction occurred despite some

---

[1] Strictly speaking, Rowntree defined a family as living in primary poverty if its 'total earnings were insufficient to obtain the minimum necessaries for the maintenance of merely physical efficiency'. B. S. Rowntree, *Poverty—A Study of Town Life*, Macmillan, 1901.

relaxation in the later years of the original austere standard used by Rowntree to measure absolute poverty.[1]

Relative Poverty

There are a number of difficulties about trying to get an absolute measure of poverty and it is significant that even the Rowntree investigators could not resist the temptation to move from their original standard. The problems about an absolute measure are twofold. First, even an absolute measure is by no means clear-cut. An economist once calculated the number of soya beans that would be required to keep a person alive if they stayed in bed all day. But clearly we mean something better than this by minimum subsistence. More seriously, a particular diet may be sufficient to keep people alive and physically fit for the time being but improvements in diet might reduce their liability to disease and thus increase their expectation of life. Which measure should be taken as the minimum standard and just where do you draw the line with an absolute standard? Secondly, a minimum standard simply is not satisfactory. Poverty, as we generally think of it, always has an element of the relative about it. We can only define it in relation to the living standards of a particular society at a particular date. A poor Englishman would be regarded as one of the better-off persons if he lived in present-day India for example. Adam Smith, the father of political economy, recognized the relativity of poverty when he wrote in his *Wealth of Nations*, 'By necessities I understand not only the commodities which are indispensably necessary for the support of life, but whatever the custom of the country renders it indecent for creditable people, even of the lowest order, to be without.'[2] Once we move into this kind of definition, however, there can be in the nature of things no scientific objective answers. For example, is a man poor in present-day Britain if he cannot afford a radio, or a black-and-white television, or a car, or a colour television? The answer might be given differently by different persons according to their individual value judgments.

Nor do these distinctions end the complications about what constitutes poverty. Thus, for example, a neighbourhood may be

---

[1] D. Jackson estimates the value of Rowntree's poverty line as 36 per cent higher in 1950 than in 1899, see D. Jackson, *Poverty*, Macmillan, 1972, p. 25.

[2] *The Wealth of Nations*, Book 5, Chapter 2, Part II.

poor because its schools and hospitals are below standard or because it is heavily polluted, and so on.

There is also a depressing dynamic about poverty, often referred to as the cycle of poverty or the cycle of deprivation. As Dudley Jackson writes: 'A man with little education is likely to have only an unskilled job and a low income. Thus he may be able to afford only a slum dwelling in which living conditions may be so bad that his health and capacity to work suffer, and this may reduce his already low income. Eventually he may become unemployed and thus may lose his home, and this in turn may lead to a break-up of the family.'[1] The children of such a family are already part-way round the poverty cycle; moreover, without special action, the neighbourhood communal facilities, e.g. schools and hospitals, for such a family are likely to be inferior.

Whilst it is not possible to offer any fundamental and wholly satisfactory definition of poverty, the practical definition usually taken in this country is the supplementary benefit (formerly national assistance) level. This consists of a basic scale of money payments plus a variable allowance for rent and provision for payment for special expenses such as extra heating, special diet or essential domestic help. When the national assistance scale was introduced in 1948 it was set at a level roughly equivalent in terms of purchasing power with the poverty line used by Rowntree in his 1936 survey of York. Over the period since then the scale has risen in real terms more or less in line with average earnings, though somewhat erratically. The use of this measure is not taken to imply any judgment about its adequacy, but two implications of using it are significant. Firstly, as we have seen, the definition is a relative one. Secondly, defining poverty by reference to it has the paradoxical consequence that any attempt by the government to help low income families by raising the supplementary benefit scale increases the number defined as living in poverty.

Poverty in the United Kingdom

In Chapter 5, when we described the introduction of the wide-ranging national insurance provisions stemming from the report of Sir William Beveridge, we noted that Sir William envisaged a much reduced and diminishing role for national assistance/supplementary benefits, which were intended to act as a safety net. Yet, according

[1] D. Jackson, *Poverty*, Macmillan, 1972, p. 65.

to the Report of the Supplementary Benefits Commission,[1] supplementary benefit was being paid to some two and three-quarter million claimants on 3 December 1975, compared with just over a million in 1948; and this two and three-quarter million with their dependents numbered about four and a half million or 8 per cent of the total population of Great Britain. Why has this happened? Worse still, poverty is still widespread, affecting perhaps 3 per cent of the population. If our definition of poverty means those with incomes below the supplementary benefit level, and supplementary benefit is intended as a general safety net, how has this come about?

The explanation of the large and growing numbers of supplementary benefit claimants is very largely that the benefits under the national insurance scheme were never set at the levels that Sir William had envisaged. This was particularly true of retirement pensions; sixty per cent of the supplementary benefit claimants in December 1975 were pensioners, nearly all of whom received retirement pensions under the national insurance scheme, but needed supplementary pensions. The changing age-distribution of the population (described in Chapter 7) has swelled their numbers since 1948. A further important reason has been that the family allowances, which Beveridge saw as part of the overall welfare provision, were never set or maintained at an adequate level to eliminate poverty resulting from child rearing.

The answer to the second question—why is poverty still widespread—is related to that of the first. There is one category of persons not entitled to supplementary benefit and other categories who are entitled but who have not invariably taken up that entitlement. We can distinguish three main groups of persons whose income may be below the supplementary benefit level. Firstly, a number of people in full-time work with low wages, who are not eligible for supplementary benefit because they are working. Especially where there are large families, such persons may fall below the poverty line. This situation has arisen partly because of inadequate family allowances, which have been well below the supplementary benefit rates for children. The family income supplement, introduced in the early 1970s, was introduced to try to deal with poverty from this cause. FIS is available to those in full-time work, with at least one child, whose income falls below a prescribed level; the payment under FIS

[1] This and subsequent references to the Report of the Supplementary Benefits Commission refer to *Supplementary Benefits Commission Annual Report 1975*, Cmnd. 6615, 1976.

is half the difference between actual pay and the prescribed level, subject to a maximum. Its success has been limited by low take-up, which the Report of the Supplementary Benefits Commission suggests has now risen from around 50 per cent of those eligible in 1972 to about 66 per cent in 1975. A second group of persons are those not covered by national insurance who are eligible for supplementary benefit but have not always taken it up. These include one-parent families other than widows, and unemployed people who have exhausted their national insurance entitlement to unemployment pay. The take-up by such people appears to be about 70 per cent. Finally, there is a large group of retired persons in receipt of state retirement pension but whose income is below supplementary benefit levels and who, in about 25 per cent of cases, have not taken up their entitlement to supplementary benefit. In some instances the short-fall between their income and the supplementary level may be very small.

The recognition that there are many people at or near the poverty level has led over the past decade or so to the introduction of a large number of means-tested schemes designed to benefit the poorest households, or at least to shelter them from some new charge or the increase of an existing charge. Such benefits have been introduced by different government departments and by local authorities. At the same time the lack of coordination between the social security provisions and the tax system, by which the income tax threshold has not kept above the supplementary benefit level and has been falling as a proportion of the average real wage, has created the situation which has become known as the 'poverty trap'.

The Poverty Trap

To quote David Piachaud,

> There are literally dozens of means-tested benefits and it has been estimated that over 1,500 different methods of means-testing are used by different local authorities and central government departments. Most of these only come into operation when there is a special need, such as for a home help, or a school uniform allowance, but many households, particularly those with children, may in normal circumstances be eligible for four or five means-tested benefits.[1]

[1] David Piachaud, 'Poverty and taxation' in B. Crick and W. A. Robson (eds.), *Taxation Policy*, Penguin Books, 1973.

It is in the nature of a means-tested benefit that if income rises entitlement to benefit may be reduced or cease. At the same time a deduction will be made from the increase in income for national insurance contributions and possibly for income tax. The net result may be that a wage earner who receives a pay rise may be left little better off or even can actually finish up worse off.

Let us illustrate by reference to tax and benefit rates applicable in mid-1975 and taking account of family income supplement, rent and rate rebates, school meals and milk.[1] A man with a wife and three children might have had a weekly income of £30 and be paying £6 in rent and £2 in rates. If his weekly earnings rose by £5 he would then have paid an additional £1.75 in income tax and 27p in national insurance contributions. At the same time he would have been liable to lose benefits as follows: FIS £1.80, rent rebate 67p, rate rebate 22p, school meals 75p, and free milk 42p—a combined loss of benefit of £3.86, total deductions amounting to £5.88. Such a person could thus have finished up 88p worse off as a result of a £5 per week increase in earnings.

Professor A. R. Prest has referred to the loss of benefits consequent upon the receipt of an extra £1 of income as an 'implicit' marginal tax rate.[2] In this case the combined implicit and explicit tax rates (including national insurance contributions) amounted to 118 per cent.

Such a situation means that poverty is not being adequately relieved. It becomes almost impossible for the poor to drag themselves out of poverty by their own efforts, thus accentuating the poverty cycle. In addition there is a strong disincentive to work effort. The substitution and income effects in this situation work in the same direction. The tax rates encourage a worker to substitute leisure for extra work and he is actually better off if he does so.

In practice the situation is mitigated by time lags and lack of comprehension. Income tax and national insurance contributions will become payable immediately a tax payer receives a pay rise, but there will be a time lag (of up to twelve months) before he has to re-apply for a particular benefit and by then it is possible the benefit scales may have risen. Nonetheless, the situation is completely unsatisfactory. It illustrates a characteristic of complex government to which we have already referred—lack of coordination.

[1] The data for this example is drawn from a letter to *The Times* in August 1975, from Mr Ralph Howell, M.P.

[2] A. R. Prest, *Social Benefits and Tax Rates*, Institute of Economic Affairs, 1970.

Needs and Possibilities

Requirements of a Satisfactory System

A satisfactory system must be capable of relieving poverty. It must do so in a way compatible with the dignity of the recipient of benefits, both the total cost and the administrative cost must be as low as possible, the system must be as free as possible from abuse, and it must not exercise pronounced disincentive effects. The present system has singularly failed to meet these criteria. The poverty of many has not been relieved. The low take-up of some benefits suggests that some people see a stigma attaching to supplementary benefits. The total cost is high and there are particularly high administrative costs in operating means-tested benefits. Recent examples suggest that the system is not free from abuse. The poverty trap provides a strong disincentive to work effort, whilst a means-test on accumulated saving as a condition of receiving supplementary benefit may discourage thrift. What can be done to improve the system?

Possibilities and Problems

There have been no lack of suggestions for reform, varying from major reconstruction of the whole national insurance and income tax systems to piecemeal reform. We shall look at three approaches. First the most grandiose, the social dividend scheme; then negative income tax and tax credit ideas; finally the piecemeal approach, based mainly on a return to Beveridge principles.

1. *Social Dividend Schemes*

The idea of amalgamating the income tax and national insurance systems in a social dividend scheme was originally advocated by Lady Rhys Williams in 1942, and since then others have offered variants of the scheme. The principle is that all families, irrespective of means, would receive weekly sums related to family size and other appropriate characteristics, for example, a payment for disablement or for adult dependents. In the purest form of the scheme, these payments would replace all national insurance and supplementary benefits and all tax allowances. Income tax would then be levied on all income (excluding the dividend) at a flat proportional rate, possibly with a surtax on higher incomes. Such a system aims at securing redistribution from the expenditure rather than the income side. Its workings are illustrated in Table 10.1.

Table 10.1   Example of the Operation of the Social Dividend Scheme for a Married Couple with Two Children.

Annual income (£)	Social dividend (£)	Tax (at 50 per cent)	Net income (£)	Effective tax rate (%)
500	400	250	650	−30
1000	400	500	900	+10
2000	400	1000	1400	+30

Social dividend: married couple, £200; each child, £100.

The attractions of the scheme are that payments would be uniform without means-testing; there would be a high take-up and no stigma; and there would be no implicit marginal tax rates, for no one would lose benefits as their earnings grew. The disadvantages are that it would require a complete reform of the income tax system, and all those with incomes would need to file a tax return because an essential element of the scheme is that all should be taxed; secondly very large gross flows of revenue would take place through the Exchequer; but most important and significant, the proportional tax rate would need to be very high on all income, possibly of the order of 50–60 per cent, if benefits were to be adequate. The combination of the income effect of the dividend received, with the substitution effect of a relatively high marginal rate of tax, might result in a significant disincentive especially for lower income groups. In practice too, it is most unlikely that all the complex benefits designed to meet individual circumstances could be incorporated in such a scheme.

2. *Negative Income Tax and Tax Credit Schemes*

There is more than one variant possible within this umbrella heading. Let us briefly look at a scheme for tax-free graduated benefits and then examine in more detail the proposal for tax credits put forward by the Conservative Government in the early 1970s which would have become law by 1977 had the Conservatives won the 1974 election.

The first negative income tax scheme would involve that benefits to households with low incomes would be made through the income tax machinery, the amount of benefit being directly related to the income assessed for income tax purposes. If the income of a person fell short of the tax allowances due to him then a proportion of the difference would be paid out through the income tax machinery. If on the other hand his income exceeded tax allowances, then he would receive no dividend but would pay income tax. An example of the operation of this scheme is set out in Table 10.2.

Table 10.2   Example of the Operation of a Negative Income Tax Scheme for Tax-Free Graduated Benefits for a Married Couple with Two Children.

Annual income (£)	Tax allowances (£)	Tax (50 per cent negative/ 30 per cent positive)	Net income (£)
500	1000	−250	750
1000	1000	nil	1000
2000	1000	300	1700

Tax allowances: married couple, £700; child, £150.

The result of this system is that benefits are not uniform but vary inversely with income. The scheme has advantages similar to those of the social dividend scheme: there is no take-up problem, everyone would file a return and all would receive the same treatment whether paying tax or receiving supplement. It would resolve the problem of overlap between the national insurance system and income tax. But, as with the social dividend scheme, there would be administrative problems in requiring everyone to file a tax return. Most important of all there would be a conflict between the requirements for relieving poverty and for economic efficiency. The higher the level of negative income tax, the greater the benefit to the poor but the bigger the disincentive effect. If the tax allowances were set at the poverty (supplementary benefit) level, the negative income tax would need to be at a rate of 100 per cent to relieve poverty adequately; but a rate of 100 per cent would be a massive disincentive to all those around or below the poverty line. As the income tax exemption levels for many households are currently below supplementary benefit level, even with a negative tax rate of 100 per cent, it would not be possible to raise these families above a poverty level without a major upward shift in exemption levels and a radical change in the income tax schedule.

An alternative scheme, worked out in sufficient detail to ensure that it was practicable even if initially limited in extent, is the Green Paper Proposals for a Tax-Credit Scheme published by the Conservative Government in October 1972,[1] as modified in the light of the recommendations of a House of Commons Select Committee.[2]

The Conservative Tax-Credit scheme involved the partial replacement of tax allowances and social security benefits by tax credits, administered through the income tax system, except for child credits, which, following the recommendation of the Select Committee, were to be paid to the mother through the Post Office. The proposed new credits were to replace personal tax allowances, family allowances and FIS, but not national insurance benefits nor, at any rate initially, other means-tested benefits. The credits were to be uniform and non-taxable, but national insurance benefits not at present taxed for administrative reasons, e.g. unemployment and sick pay, would be taxable. Credits would be paid to employees through their employer; to occupational pensioners through their employer and to people drawing national insurance benefits through the Department of Health and Social Security or the Department of Employment. The employer (or other paying agency) would deduct tax at basic rate from the wage (or other income) add the tax credit and then pay over the net sum which might be more or less than the wage. Table 10.3 gives examples of how the scheme would work with a basic rate of income tax of 30 per cent (the rate at the time the scheme was proposed), and the illustrative rates of tax-credit contained in the Green Paper.

Various other proposals made possible the elimination of most of the remaining tax allowances, the few outstanding having to be reclaimed at the end of the year. The administration of the income tax was simplified by providing that all deductions of tax by employers and other paying agencies should be at 30 per cent from all income, higher-rate tax being paid in arrears at the end of the tax year.

At inception the scheme was to cover all employed persons earning (in 1972) above £8 per week, all main national insurance beneficiaries and most occupational pensioners. It excluded the self-employed, for administrative reasons, and those with under £8 per

[1] *Proposals for a Tax-Credit System*, Cmnd. 5116, October 1972.
[2] *Select Committee on Tax-Credit*, HC 341-I, 1973.

Table 10.3   Examples of the Operation of the Tax-Credit Proposal.

	Weekly pay (£)	Less tax (at 30 per cent) (£)	Plus credit (£)	Pay after tax and credit (£)
Single person	10	3	4	11
	25	7.50	4	21.50
	50	15	4	39
Married without children	10	3	6	13
	25	7.50	6	23.50
	50	15	6	41
Married with two children	10	3	10	17
	25	7.50	10	27.50
	50	15	10	45

Credits: single person £4; married couple £6; child £2. A single-parent family was to receive the married couples' allowance as well as child allowances.

week, because it would have been too costly to have raised benefits sufficiently high to have taken them off supplementary benefit. The Green Paper expressed the hope that means might be found to enable them to be incorporated in the scheme at a later date.

The Conservative government did not claim that the tax-credit system offered a complete solution to the problems of poverty. But for those within the scheme it was claimed that if offered a simple, readily comprehensible, system of family support; that it was largely automatic and therefore offered a high take-up with no suggestion of stigma; that it gave benefit to those with incomes too low to gain from the existing tax allowances; that, as a result of its introduction, hundreds of thousands of pensioners would be relieved of the necessity to claim supplementary benefits and millions of pensioners, just above that margin, would receive significant increases in income, and that it would help many families of working age, especially those with children. Although some means-testing would remain, its role in the social services would be reduced. The greater coordination of tax and social security provisions and the abolition of FIS would at least have eased the poverty trap for many currently caught in it.

On the negative side the scheme did not cater for substantial sections of the population and many means-tested benefits remained. Perhaps more crucially, there was no satisfactory explanation in the Green Paper of where the net cost of the scheme (£1300 million on the basis of the illustrative figures) was to be found—yet this was vital to its effect on poverty and the distribution of income. Further, on the basis of the illustrative figures, much of the benefit went to those not in poverty. Many critics considered the scheme insufficiently flexible to make it possible to direct help to those most in need, whilst others feared that it would tie the income tax irretrievably to a rate structure lacking in progression over most of its range, with all income taxed at a flat rate save for the few per cent of incomes in the higher rate band.

By a majority the Select Committee gave its blessing to the tax-credit scheme, but when the Labour Party won the 1974 election the scheme was shelved, if not abandoned. It would undoubtedly have been a big improvement on the present (1976) situation, though whether it is the best practicable solution to the poverty problem in the United Kingdom is much more debatable.

3. *Piecemeal Reform*

The piecemeal approach considers the particular ways in which poverty arises and attempts to deal with them individually, thus gradually, but only gradually, ridding the system of its present deplorable features. It is largely based on a return to the principles of Beveridge.

1. The major group of recipients of supplementary benefits are pensioners. Beveridge had considered that state retirement pensions should be set at a level at which no state retirement pensioners should need to resort to supplementary benefits. Raising the level of retirement pensions to supplementary benefit levels would thus move off supplementary benefit many now on it and also move out of poverty pensioners eligible for supplementary benefit who do not claim it. But it would mean paying higher pensions to *all* retirement pensioners and this would be very expensive. As a result of increased occupational pensions and the graduated pension scheme the Supplementary Benefit Commission's Report does indicate some decline in the proportion of pensioners requiring supplementary pensions.

2. Another cause of poverty is large families. Family allowances,

which Beveridge always envisaged as an adjunct to national insurance benefits, have risen only fitfully since their introduction in the 1940s; and the poorest do not benefit, or at least obtain full benefit, from child tax allowances. The Labour Government in 1976 committed itself to introducing a child benefit scheme which would replace both child tax allowances and family allowances and be paid through the Post Office to the mother. This scheme, in effect, takes over one component of the Conservative tax-credit proposals. The child benefit scheme was shelved because of the possible effect on the 1976 pay policy, for switching to child credits would have reduced the 'take-home' pay of fathers. At the time of writing a compromise appears to have been reached by which child credits will be phased in gradually. Eliminating 'child poverty' will help those in work on low pay and provide the possibility of eliminating FIS.

3. Another proposal to help those on low pay in work is legislation for a national minimum wage, advocated by many leading trade unionists. The purpose is to set a floor to wages above the level which would be brought about by the forces of supply and demand. A national minimum wage raises three kinds of problems. Firstly, conceptual and administrative: are we talking of a weekly wage or rate per hour? This is obviously important where different working weeks apply. Is it to be a common minimum for men, women and young persons? If so, women and young persons stand to benefit most. Further, how should one deal with regional differences? The same wage is worth more in Cornwall than in Bristol and more in Bristol than in London.

Secondly, there is the possibility of adverse employment effects on the low paid, especially on women. Employers, seeking to maximize profits (which may mean avoid losses) will seek to substitute other factors for unskilled labour if it rises in price, or they may even contract their operations. Economically rational employers will take on workers up to the point at which the additional receipts from selling the products of the last worker employed are equal to the addition to the wage bill—in economists' language, the value of the marginal product equals the marginal cost of labour. It follows that unless employers can increase the value of the marginal product— either by increased labour productivity[1] or *by selling as much as before at a higher price*—they will employ less labour. The possibility of unemployment amongst the low paid is increased because many of

[1] This might conceivably happen because the higher pay improved labour fitness (unlikely in a developed country) or labour morale.

them employed in manufacturing appear to be in contracting industries or industries expanding less rapidly than the average.[1]

The third problem is the possible effect on wage costs in general. Obviously wage costs in industries employing the low paid would rise, but the vital question is how far this would react on other wage costs: would there be a chain reaction in an attempt to restore differentials? Such an attempt is most likely from workers with wages just a little above the minimum and in industries where the low paid work alongside better paid workers. Because many of the low paid in British industry are to be found in relatively small proportions in the labour force of large industries, relatively widespread repercussions on wage costs are more likely. Experience of national minimum wage legislation in other countries such as the USA and France is not encouraging; it suggests an initial narrowing of differentials but their general restoration over a period of four or five years.

There must be serious doubt whether a national minimum wage would result in any long-term benefit for the lower paid, and it would be bound to raise the general price level to some extent. But the outcome depends very much on the level and nature of the minimum adopted.

We have largely had to omit from this brief general review some special groups in poverty, for example, the disabled, single-parent families and deserted wives whose maintenance payments are not kept up. Also we have said nothing about piecemeal reform in the shape of administrative changes such as the standardization of means-tested benefits amongst local authorities or the conversion of all means-tests to a post-income-tax basis. One other very relevant issue is housing. Many of the means-tested benefits—rate rebates and rent rebates and allowances—relate to housing, and because of the variation in housing costs and the difficulty of obtaining certain kinds of housing provision, the standardization of rent allowances as a component of supplementary benefits is impracticable. The resolution of the present chaos of housing policy would make a major contribution to the solution of problems of poverty. We shall say more about housing in Chapter 14.

Will the Poor Always Be with Us?

The answer to this question in part depends on how poverty is

[1] J. Marquand, 'Which are the lower paid workers?', *British Journal of Industrial Relations*, November 1967.

defined. If we use an absolute standard, similar to that of Rowntree in 1899, and if we are talking only of primary and not secondary poverty, then we could say that poverty has already been virtually eliminated in Britain.

On the other hand, whatever poverty level we set, unless all our lives are rigidly controlled, there will always be some secondary poverty: some people will always dissipate their income.

Between these extremes lie the practical issues of ensuring that all have an income above a poverty line determined on relative criteria. If we take the supplementary benefit level as such a level, provisions to ensure that no one is in poverty very largely exist, but in a form unacceptable to some and with other consequences—the poverty trap—which are deplorable. Solving these problems is likely to require both administrative skills and additional public expenditure. Changes in related policies, especially in housing, could help both by easing the practical administrative problems and by transferring benefits from the less to the more needy.

A relative poverty level is necessarily a subjective standard. If we set the level at a high proportion of average wages, as our analysis of income distribution in Chapter 9 showed, poverty can only be eliminated by a redistribution of income at the expense of those who are only moderately well off. As Professor Robert Pinker has written, 'In the past, the pattern of social justice was a product of the tyranny of rich minorities over a mass of poor people. In the future the persistence of injustice in our kind of society is more likely to arise from the indifference of a relatively prosperous majority to the welfare needs of a minority of poor people.'[1]

SUMMARY AND CONCLUSIONS

We need to distinguish absolute and relative, primary and secondary poverty. Poverty, defined by the supplementary benefit level, continues to exist on an appreciable scale in Britain mainly because national insurance benefits, especially retirement pensions, are below supplementary benefit levels and not all eligible persons claim; also because those in work are not eligible for supplementary benefit and child allowances have been inadequate. Although it was only intended as a safety net, a total of claimants currently approach-

[1] Robert Pinker, 'Social policy and social justice', *The Journal of Social Policy*, No. 1, Vol. III, January 1974, pp. 1–19.

ing 3 million receive supplementary benefit. Attempts to ease the lot of the poorest by a variety of means-tested benefits, together with falling tax thresholds and rising tax rates, have created a 'poverty trap'. Suggested solutions include social dividend schemes, negative income tax and tax-credit proposals (notably those of the Conservative Government of 1972), and a gradual piecemeal approach incorporating higher retirement pensions and child benefits. The value of a national minimum wage is dubious. There is no good reason why the poor should always be with us.

11 Inequality in the Distribution of Wealth

Causes of Differences in Wealth Distribution

We can distinguish four main ways in which wealth is acquired which are to some extent interrelated: saving, enterprise (combined with saving), good luck, and inheritance.

Saving. We know from national income statistics that normally about 8 per cent of total income after tax is saved. Besides saving in the form of government securities or shares in firms, millions of people save by means of life insurance, through pension funds and by purchasing a house.

Enterprise. A man may start a business and build it up and because he is producing a product which people want at that time, has anticipated a need or has commercialized an innovation. The business may grow rapidly. Its growth will be assisted by his saving in the form of ploughed-back profits, but the rise in the value of the business will be more than the savings he has put into it. In other words, he is likely to obtain a substantial capital gain on the business assets.

Good luck. Acquisition of wealth by good luck may take a number of forms, such as winning the football pools, coming up on 'Ernie', or obtaining capital gains on stocks and quoted shares or increases in land value as a result of community developments.

Inheritance. There is substantial empirical evidence to suggest that this is the most important cause of inequality in the distribution of wealth. Following a line of research pioneered by Josiah Wedgwood[1] in the 1920s, Professor Colin Harbury[2] has examined the relationship between the size of estates left by rich men with the estates left by

---

[1] Josiah Wedgwood, *The Economics of Inheritance*, Penguin, 1937, Chapter 9.

[2] C. D. Harbury, 'Inheritance and the distribution of personal wealth in Britain', *Economic Journal*, December 1962; C. D. Harbury and P. C. McMahon, 'Inheritance and the characteristics of top wealth leavers in Britain', *Economic Journal*, September 1973; C. D. Harbury and D. M. Hitchens, 'The Inheritances of top wealth leavers', *Economic Journal*, June 1976.

their fathers. He looked at the years 1956–57, 1965 and 1973. In the first two periods he found that more than two-thirds of the sons with estates over £100,000 had fathers who had left estates of over £25,000 (measured in terms of the prices of the year in which their sons died) There were no significant differences between the proportions of sons having rich fathers in these two periods and these proportions were very much the same as Wedgwood had found in the 1920s Professor Harbury's latest findings (relating to 1973) suggest that there has been a statistically significant decline (of over 10 per cent) in the proportions of top wealth leavers who were preceded by fathers who died rich. Even so, the main conclusion remains, that one is more likely to die rich if one had a moderately rich father

Measurement of Inequality in the Distribution of Wealth

As with income, so in looking at the distribution of wealth we run into conceptual problems and statistical difficulties.

Conceptual Problems

The conceptual problems closely parallel those we met in looking at the distribution of income.

What is wealth? In the introduction to this section we provisionally defined wealth as a stock of goods and (from the point of view of the individual) financial assets of various kinds. But there is scope for different interpretations of precisely what should be included and the definition we take makes an enormous difference to the picture of the distribution of wealth in a society.

How should we treat wealth which is held in trust for particular individuals? More particularly, to whom should we attribute the wealth held in discretionary trusts, where the beneficiaries may be one of a large class of persons and it is the trustees who determine which of these shall receive the income and the capital from the trust? In practice our treatment is very much conditioned by the statistics available, but there is no entirely clear-cut solution even if we had full statistical information.

A second problem is that of human capital. We shall see, when we come to Chapter 12, that education can be regarded as an investment in human capital, with the same sort of income benefits that might be obtained from an investment in machinery. Should we therefore, count the present value of future earning power as wealth to the individual? There is a strong theoretical case for this treatment, but in practice it would be very difficult to do.

A third and more practical issue is the treatment of pension rights. Much saving takes the form of contributions to pension funds where the individual does not have control of a stock of goods or financial assets but has the guarantee of an income in retirement. Indeed, such a guarantee may be provided for some people, for example civil servants, who are not themselves required to contribute to it, but who nevertheless need to save less because of this guaranteed retirement income. Such pension rights are very much on a par with the saving undertaken by those with no occupational pension rights, who take out insurance policies or buy shares to provide an income for their retirement. Again, if we regard the right to an occupational pension as wealth, should we not treat rights to state retirement pensions in the same way?

What unit of wealth-holding? What is the most appropriate unit to use in analysing wealth-holding? Is it the individual? If so it would seem sensible to take not the whole population but adults, for we would not expect children to have much wealth. But what age is most suitable for measuring adulthood in this context? Should it be 18 or 21 or 25? There is no clear-cut answer and the statistics of wealth distribution will vary according to the definition taken. But it might be better to take a family unit rather than the individual in looking at the distribution of wealth. A family might be expected to benefit as a whole from the wealth possessed by the head of it. Moreover, it is increasingly common for a husband and wife to hold what is often their main form of wealth, their house, jointly. But again if we take the family unit, where should we draw the line? Should it be only members of a family living in one residence together? There is evidence of past avoidance of death duty by gifts made to younger members of a family who may not be resident with their parents but whose acquisition of their parents' wealth might make it more sensible to treat the whole as one unit. In practice the figures available relate to individuals, but this may not necessarily be the most significant unit.

The snapshot problem: variations in life-time wealth. The only figures of the distribution of wealth which we have are in the form of a snapshot for a particular year. At that point of time many people will be shown to possess little wealth who, twenty years later, might be large wealth-holders. Quite apart from the possibilities of acquiring wealth by inheritance or luck there is a life-cycle of saving; people save during their working lives and might be expected to reach a peak of wealth at retirement, thereafter gradually drawing down their wealth. Some part of the inequality in the distribution of wealth at a point of time simply reflects the differences of wealth associated with differences of age.[1]

Measuring inequality. We can use the same method of percentile analysis as with income, with precisely the same problem of deciding which is the more unequal distribution when Lorenz curves cross.

Statistical Inadequacies

We meet the familiar problem that the statistics on the distribution of wealth are collected as a by-product of administration and are not designed for the purposes of the social scientist. Our main source is data collected by the Inland Revenue in the course of administering estate duty (in the past) and capital transfer tax (currently). Estimates of the distribution of wealth are made on the assumption that the sample of estates assessed to death duty in any one year is typical, for each age and sex group, of estates held by the living. The method is to take the figure of estates of each age and sex group which are collected for death duty purposes in the particular year, and then to multiply each by the reciprocal of the mortality rate for that age-sex group. Suppose, for example, that in the year in question ten estates in the range £100,000–£200,000 totalling £1,600,000, owned by women aged 75–76, became liable to death duty. If the mortality rates for that year for women of that age were 100 per 1000 (one in ten), then it is assumed that in that year there were 100 (10 × 10) estates in the population as a whole amongst women aged 75–76 of a size 100,000–200,000 and that these estates together totalled £16 million (£1,600,000 × 10). Such calculations for each age-sex group can then be totalled for each property range.

There are three main groups of deficiencies in the method

---

[1] A recent article, 'The distribution of wealth and the relevance of age', by J. A Astin in *Statistical News*, No. 28, February 1975, suggests that the life-cycle theory only goes a small way to explaining the existence of inequalities in wealth distribution in present day Britain. For the year 1972 he found that average wealth increased slightly from age 25 to age 64 (but only from £3,800 to £4,300) and decreased slightly in the age group 65–74 (to £4,100). He then found that it increased in the next two age categories to reach a peak at 85 and over of £5,300. He suggested that possibly this increase in wealth in the very old reflected their acquisition of inheritances at a time when death duties were low compared with present levels.

adopted: omissions, errors derived from the grossing-up process, and valuation problems. In addition there are particular problems in making comparisons over time.

The omissions are particularly serious. The evidence collected covers rather less than half of total deaths in any year. It excludes deaths where transfer of property can take place at death without a grant of representation being required. This occurs where the property left is small in amount or where there are joint owners of property such as houses. Secondly, assets held in the form of trusts are either not covered or only incompletely covered in the statistics. Further, pictures and other items benefiting from death duty relief on items of national, artistic, historic or scientific interest, only come into the reckoning if they are ultimately sold.

Secondly, the grossing-up process itself creates errors. There are likely to be sampling errors especially amongst the very large estates because the total number of such estates becoming liable for death duty in any one year is very small and random fluctuations may have a considerable effect. In particular, large estates held by those dying young may be unrepresentative of their age and sex group (for which the mortality rates are low and therefore the reciprocals, used as multipliers, are high). As Professor Atkinson has vividly put it: 'A wealthy young man crashing his sports car could add 1000 to the estimate of the total number of people with wealth over £200,000'. Another problem is that the use of different mortality rates affects the result, but mortality rates vary between occupations. The Inland Revenue has adopted a compromise between the general mortality rates and the lowest occupational rates, but clearly the appropriate rates are a matter of judgment.

The third category of deficiency is in valuation. For example, the value of life insurance policies taken at death (when they mature) is very much higher than such policies possess in the hands of the living. As life insurance is a very widely used form of saving amongst the less well-off, this valuation issue may bias the figures in the direction of understating the degree of inequality. On the other hand, the value of household durables is likely to be undervalued for estate duty purposes and probably houses as well. As these figures are a larger proportion of small estates than of large, this creates a bias towards overstating inequality, a bias accentuated because officials will be less keen to check that such items are valued accurately for the smaller estates, which contribute little or nothing to revenue, as compared with the larger.

Comparisons over time are affected by changes in death duty legislation; by the fact that the geographic coverage of the Inland Revenue statistics was limited to England and Wales until 1938, when figures for Scotland were compiled, and is still restricted to Great Britain as figures have not yet been published for Northern Ireland; and by the different bases on which earlier researchers made their calculations before official figures were produced by the Inland Revenue.

In the light of these deficiencies it may be asked, are the figures meaningful? Whilst comparison of the various estimates spanning the century as a whole must be treated with extreme caution, many of the other major deficiencies can be largely made good; for example, estimates can be made of 'missing wealth' based on national balance sheet data (the statement of the various forms of asset for Great Britain as a whole, derived from the original sources) and allocated to the various property ranges. The most recent and thorough study of the 'estate duty method' of arriving at the distribution of wealth, after tests of the sensitivity of the results to varying assumptions relating to the main areas of difficulty, confirms the substantial validity of the Inland Revenue figures for the shares of the top wealth groups.[1]

Distribution of Wealth in Great Britain

Let us start with some absolute numbers before moving on to percentile analysis. The form of the Inland Revenue figures on wealth-holding does not enable us to give the number of millionaires in Britain, but we can say that in 1974 there were 26,000 individuals with wealth of £200,000 or more and 91,000 with wealth of £100,000 or more. Now let us turn to percentages.

The data in Table 11.1 is derived from the Fourth Report of the Royal Commission on the Distribution of Income and Wealth.[2] It shows the distribution of personal wealth in 1974 on various assumptions. Column 1 simply uses the unadjusted figures derived from the Inland Revenue. Column 2 attempts to adjust both for the wealth of those with little or no wealth who were excluded from the figures and also attempts to take into account wealth held in settlements and trusts. In column 3, an allowance is made for occupational pension rights, whilst column 4 also makes an allowance

---

[1] A. B. Atkinson and A. J. Harrison, *The Distribution of Personal Wealth in Britain*, Cambridge University Press, 1977.

[2] Cmnd. 6626, October 1976.

for state pension rights. The figures show, for example, that excluding pension rights and allowing for adjusted wealth holdings, the top 1 per cent of adults owned 25 per cent of the wealth, the top 5 per cent about 47 per cent of the wealth. At the other end, the bottom 80 per cent owned 22 per cent of the wealth. The picture changes markedly if one includes pension rights: if both occupational and state pension rights are included the share of the top 1 per cent falls to 14 per cent of the wealth, while the share of the bottom 80 per cent more than doubles, rising to 45 per cent. It should be stressed, however, that the bases for calculating the value of accrued pension rights and attributing it to income ranges is necessarily somewhat arbitrary.

Table 11.1   Concentration of Individual Wealth, Great Britain, 1974.

Percentage shares of estimated personal wealth of total population of Great Britain aged 18 and over

	(1) *Assuming persons not covered by Inland Revenue figures have no wealth* %	(2) *With adjusted wealth holdings* %	(3) *Including occupational pension rights* %	(4) *Including state pension rights* %
Top 1%	25.3	25.0	20.2	13.8
Top 5%	49.9	47.4	42.0	30.0
Top 10%	66.0	61.5	56.0	41.1
Top 20%	85.5	78.1	73.6	54.8
Bottom 80%	14.5	21.9	26.4	45.2

Source: Royal Commission on the Distribution of Income and Wealth, *Report No. 4*, Cmnd. 6626, Tables 23, 35, 37 and 39.

Table 11.2, derived from the same source, shows trends in the distribution of wealth since 1960. These suggest a substantial decline in the amount of wealth held by the top 1 per cent of the population, but a much smaller decline held by that of the top 10 per cent and very little decline in the amount held by the top 20 per cent. Earlier studies, though not directly comparable, make it clear that these same trends have been at work throughout the century.

Table 11.2   Trends in the Distribution of Individual Wealth in Great Britain since 1960.

	1960 %	1965 %	1970 %	1971 %	1972 %	1973 %	1974 %
Top 1%	38.2	33.0	29.0	27.6	29.9	27.6	25.3
Top 5%	64.3	58.5	56.3	52.1	56.3	51.3	49.9
Top 10%	76.7	73.3	70.1	67.4	71.9	67.2	66.0
Top 20%	89.8	88.8	89.0	85.7	89.2	86.4	85.5
Bottom 80%	10.2	11.2	11.0	14.3	10.8	13.6	14.5

Source: Royal Commission, *Report No. 1*, Cmnd. 6171, Table 45; *Report No. 4*, Cmnd. 6626, Table 29. The figures are based on Inland Revenue data and assume that people not covered by the Inland Revenue data have no wealth.

The decline in the proportion of wealth of the very wealthy seems mainly to have been to the benefit of the moderately wealthy, rather than the least wealthy.

Reasons for the Reduction in Inequality in Wealth Holdings

We can suggest a number of reasons for this decline in inequality, although it is difficult to determine their relative importance. Firstly, there has been a growth in affluence amongst the population as a whole, particularly associated with the rise in savings by means of insurance and also with the growth in home ownership. The Royal Commission estimated that domestic property now represents over 40 per cent of total personal wealth and just over half of all householders are house owners. Secondly, we should expect that high death duties have played a part in reducing inequality though (as we shall discuss below) the loopholes in the former estate duty meant that it was a less effective instrument for reducing inequality than might have been expected.

Other factors have also been at work. In Chapter 7 we pointed to the increasing longevity of women as compared with men, and one reason for the reduction in inequality may well have been the inheritance by women of part of their husband's estates. A more even division of property within marriages would likewise have reduced inequality measured in terms of individual wealth holdings.

A further potent influence has been changes in relative prices, partly accentuated by the effects of inflation which have tended to raise some prices more than others; in particular, in the mid-1970s, the rise in house prices and land prices and the relative fall in the value of stocks and shares has brought about a redistribution of wealth which has favoured the owner-occupier of houses and the owner-occupier in agriculture (who, during the century, has come to own about half the total of agricultural land). Fluctuations in asset prices may be a particular cause of fluctuations in the distribution of wealth from year to year and the figures of a single year therefore need to be interpreted with caution. For example, the exceptional fall in stock market prices in 1974 explains most of the decline in wealth holding of the top 1 per cent in that year, ownership of personally-held securities being heavily concentrated amongst top wealth holders.

One crucial factor to assessing the significance of the changes in the distribution of wealth is how far they result from a transfer from the wealthy to their children in order to avoid estate duty. Such transfers would not represent a redistribution of wealth in any very fundamental sense. There is evidence of considerable gifts *inter vivos* which would have avoided estate duty completely or in part, but their total must be a matter of conjecture.[1]

Government Policy and the Distribution of Wealth

A number of government policies, intentionally or unintentionally, affect the distribution of wealth, for example encouragement of owner-occupation in housing and in agriculture, and the success (or failure) of policy to check inflation. In this chapter we shall concentrate on the direct effects of taxation. The main taxes bearing on the distribution of wealth are wealth transfer taxes, annual wealth taxes and capital gains tax.

Wealth Transfer Taxes

Wealth transfer taxes are paid when wealth changes hands by gift between the living or at death. There are two basic and different forms of death duty with each of which a gift tax may be associated: estate duty and inheritance tax.

An *estate duty* is levied on the total amount of property a person leaves at death, irrespective of how it is divided up amongst heirs. Britain had an estate duty as its main (and for much of the time its

---

[1] See, for example, E. G. Horsman, 'The avoidance of Estate Duty by gifts *inter vivos*', *Economic Journal*, September 1975.

sole) death duty, from 1894 to 1974. Over this period it became a heavy and progressive tax and at the time of its abolition the maximum marginal rate was 75 per cent on an estate of £500,000. As a method of reducing inequality in the distribution of wealth the estate duty had certain defects: (1) it was never very successfully applied to trusts, especially to discretionary trusts; and (2) it could be avoided wholly or in part, especially by the use of gifts, gifts between the living not being taxed unless they took place within seven years before the death of the donor, in which case the value of the gift was added to the estate when death duty was levied. Besides these defects many of its critics would maintain that it was 'the wrong way round', that an inheritance tax form of death duty would have been more appropriate.

An *inheritance tax* is levied on the legacies received by the beneficiaries irrespective of the total estate from which they come. It would seem fairer to tax in relation to benefits received. Moreover an equivalent inheritance tax might be expected to be more effective in reducing inequalities in the distribution of wealth than an estate duty in two ways. Firstly, it is large receipts, not large estates as such, which perpetuate inequality; hence an inheritance tax strikes at the heart of the matter. Secondly, an inheritance tax provides an incentive to people to distribute their property more widely at death, because if the property is widely distributed in small parcels amongst a large number of people, less duty is paid than if it is left in a concentrated parcel to one or a small number of people. An inheritance tax has the incidental advantage too, that because tax is related to the recipient, it becomes easy to take account of particular circumstances of the beneficiary, such as his relationship to the deceased, or the fact that he may be a minor or disabled child inheriting from a deceased parent, and grant a special exemption or rate.

In 1974 the Labour Government replaced estate duty by a *capital transfer tax*. Based on the estate duty principle, the capital transfer tax incorporated a tax on gifts, and provided for cumulation, so that the rate paid by the donor on any gift and on the estate left at death, was determined by reference to the total amount given, up to and including the gift in question or, finally, the estate. Cumulation meant that the tax could not be avoided by a series of small gifts (apart from those permitted by the annual exemption). Capital transfer tax also dealt more effectively with trusts. As a means of reducing inequality, capital transfer tax was thus an improvement on estate duty. However, many reformers would have preferred an *accessions tax*, the correspondingly sophisticated form of an inheritance tax, incorporating gifts and cumulating in such a way that the rate of tax paid by the recepient of any gift or legacy is determined by the total received in legacies and gifts. An accessions tax would have hit hardest the big receipts by gift and inheritance and encouraged people to give or leave their wealth to those who had received little by way of previous gifts or legacies.

Annual Wealth Tax

An annual wealth tax is a tax levied regularly on the total stock of personal assets less liabilities. In 1976 Britain does not have an annual wealth tax, but the Labour Government is committed to introduce one. A wealth tax might be a light tax, proportional or mildly progressive, as in many continental countries, which would replace the investment income surcharge. Alternatively it could be a much heavier tax, intended to reduce inequalities in the distribution of wealth, imposed as such a level that the wealthy could not meet the combined weight of income tax and wealth tax from income. Then each year would see a decline in the wealth of the wealthy as they had to dispose of assets to meet the tax.

Capital Gains Tax

A capital gains tax is more accurately thought of as a tax on a particular kind of income than as a tax on wealth. It is levied on the appreciation in the value of assets, tax being charged when assets are realized on the difference between the acquisition and the realization value. Thus, if I bought some shares in 1970 for £5000 and sold them in 1974 for £8000 I would pay capital gains tax on the appreciation in value, i.e. £3000. In 1976–77 the United Kingdom rate of capital gains tax was at 30 per cent with a somewhat lower rate for those with modest incomes. A capital gains tax is a useful adjunct to a tax policy designed to reduce inequality of wealth, but wealth and wealth transfer taxes are far more significant, and it is on those we shall mainly concentrate.

Which tax or taxes a government should employ to reduce inequality of wealth should rest very much on the philosophy about wealth which it holds, administrative practicality and likely economic effects.

What Philosophy of Wealth?

An annual wealth tax is a suitable medium to reduce inequality of wealth if there is no desire to take account of the source of the wealth. On the other hand a more discriminating policy may be intended. Wealth acquired by saving and enterprise may be considered acceptable and indeed desirable, whereas wealth acquired by inheritance and by good luck may be considered appropriate for heavy taxation. Then the relevant taxes are death duties (supported by gift taxes to prevent avoidance) to strike at inheritances and capital gains taxes (perhaps extended to include large gambling winnings) to strike at wealth acquired by good luck. Another attitude might be that inequalities of wealth are acceptable as long as they do not lead to inequalities of consumption. For example, there may be no objection to a farmer owning a farm worth £250,000 (even if he acquired the farm by inheritance and its value has risen largely by capital appreciation unconnected with his own efforts) if he works hard and lives frugally as many such farmers do. But the conspicuous consumption of the West End playboy, who might have less wealth than the farmer, might be condemned. To match that approach a very progressive expenditure tax might be the most suitable—not a tax on particular commodities, but a tax levied on the individual, like income tax, having as its base income minus saving plus spending from wealth.

Another consideration is the kind of society which is sought. A heavy annual wealth tax and a capital transfer tax reduce inequality almost solely by transferring assets from the rich to the state. Inequality is reduced because concentration ratios are less (e.g. the top 1 per cent of wealth holders now own a smaller proportion of total wealth) but there has been no 'redistribution'—this wealth has not been added to the wealth of the least wealthy members of society.[1] There is a difference with an accessions tax. Whilst it

---

[1] Because these taxes will be largely paid by a disposal of assets, they will not reduce private claims on the national output, so that the government cannot use the tax yield as ordinary revenue but as an addition to its capital account, reducing the borrowing requirement. Saving on ordinary revenue is the (net of tax) interest on what would otherwise have had to be borrowed. Even if all the benefit from the revenue saving could be concentrated on the poor in the form of tax reductions or increased public spending, the effect on their holdings of wealth would be minute. For example, if debt interest was 10 per cent and income tax on debt interest averaged 50 per cent, for every £100 million raised annually in wealth or capital transfer tax, £5 million would be available to increase the incomes of the poor. If they saved 10 per cent of this increased

partly operates by the transfer of assets from the private to the public sector, it also reduces inequality by offering a positive incentive for the wealthy to spread their wealth within the private sector.

Thus if a government wishes to see an increasing public sector, then an annual wealth tax and a capital transfer tax are the appropriate taxes; but if a wider diffusion of personal wealth is sought within the private sector, an accessions tax is more appropriate. It is also clear that any major policy to redistribute wealth requires an emphasis not just on taxation, but on ways of building up the wealth of those with little or none. Governments hitherto have been singularly ineffective in devising such methods. Encouragement of home ownership through the tax system has worked to some extent in this way, but, as we shall see in Chapter 14, it suffers from defects: it is discriminatory, helping only those who wish to hold their wealth in one particular form, and it fails to help the very poorest who are unlikely to be able to buy houses.

Administrative Practicality

All wealth taxes, whether imposed on transfers, or on wealth stock, or on capital gains, raise administrative difficulties, especially in the valuation of assets such as personal chattels, private companies and land. Because of these difficulties capital gains taxes are levied when gains are realized (e.g. when the asset is sold, giving rise to a valuation) instead of annually as the gains accrue (which would require an annual valuation).

In three respects the valuation problem is more severe for an annual wealth tax than a wealth transfer tax. Firstly, with a transfer tax only a small proportion of total personal wealth becomes liable to tax in any one year, much less than with an annual wealth tax with a comparable threshold. Secondly, when transfers take place at death, an inventory and sometimes a valuation of property is required to carry out the will of the deceased or implement the law of intestacy, so in contrast to an annual wealth tax, listing and valuing the property is required irrespective of taxation purposes. Thirdly, there is a particular difficulty with an annual wealth tax which does not occur with a transfer tax: the treatment of pension

---

income, the annual increase in their wealth would be £0.5 million. The wealth of the rich would have fallen by £100 million for a £500,000 increase in that of the poor.

rights. The issue can be presented most vividly by contrasting a self-employed businessman with a senior civil servant. The businessman may have made no specific pension provision during his working life but have reinvested all available funds relying on selling the business on retirement; he is liable to wealth tax on all his business assets during his working life and on the assets he acquires to provide himself with an income in retirement. If the value of pension rights are excluded from the wealth tax base, then the civil servant is clearly very favourably treated by comparison. He has a guaranteed non-contributory inflation-proof pension, does not have to accumulate savings (which would have been taxable to wealth tax) during his working life to provide for retirement, nor does his retirement income come from a capital sum which attracts wealth tax. On the other hand pension rights are not normally realizable either during working life or in retirement nor, unlike the businessman's assets, can they be freely given or bequeathed. Moreover it would seem hard if a man had been required to pay wealth tax on pension rights but died before reaching retirement. If, which is probably right in principle, it is decided to include pension rights in the tax base, valuing them fairly raises possibly insuperable problems.

Economic Effects

No advanced mixed economy imposes such a heavy annual wealth tax that it is impossible for the wealthy to pay income tax and wealth tax together without disposing of assets. It seems reasonably certain that, whilst such a tax would reduce inequality in the distribution of wealth, it would also have seriously harmful economic consequences.

First, it would damage incentives to enterprise and saving. With a wealth tax of this kind net saving by the wealthy would be impossible; the only gain to the rich man from reducing consumption would be a slower rate of decline of his stock of wealth. In these circumstances consumption spending by the rich might be stimulated, for, in economists' language, the opportunity cost of consuming wealth would be very small.

Secondly, a heavy wealth tax would threaten the growing points of new enterprise—businesses which are owned by one or a small number of persons whose wealth consists predominantly of business assets. Establishing a business would be more difficult because wealth tax would have to be paid on the value of machinery and plant even before the business had become profitable. If an established business ran into a loss-making situation, the continued payment of wealth tax would increase its current difficulties. Further, a heavy wealth tax would make it very difficult, if not impossible, for the owners to build up a promising business by ploughing back profits.

Thirdly, agriculture would be particularly hard hit because of the high proportion of farms in individual ownership. At best a heavy wealth tax would bring down land prices, creating difficult transitional problems especially for owner-occupiers who had bought on mortgage at higher price levels. At worst investment in agriculture might be impaired and farms fragmented as parcels of land were sold to raise funds to meet the tax.

Fourthly, a wealth tax of this level, out of line with taxation elsewhere in the western world, could hardly fail to stimulate tax avoidance, including the emigration of the rich with their wealth.

In short, a heavy wealth tax, which had to be paid by a disposal of assets, could undermine private enterprise and upset the balance of the mixed economy.

Are the same consequences likely to follow from wealth transfer taxes? Firstly, consider the incentive to save. People save for many reasons and only if the motive is to bequeath will a wealth transfer tax influence saving. Such a motive will be particularly important for the aged wealthy, but it is not certain that a heavy death duty must *reduce* the incentive to save. Once again we meet income and substitution effects working in opposite directions. On the one hand high marginal rates of death duty make saving for heirs less worthwhile, and on this score the property owner may be inclined to substitute consumption for saving. On the other hand, if people wish to pass to heirs a capital sum sufficient to provide a particular level of income, then a high death duty makes it necessary to save more, not less. Two other factors differentiate a transfer tax, which only has to be paid at death, from a heavy annual wealth tax. First older people, who are those most affected by death duty considerations, are also those most likely to find departures from previous modes of living unwelcome. A consumption spree is therefore less likely. Further, the very uncertainty of death defies a rational calculus of action and the sanguine view which people often take of their life expectation may dissuade them from engaging in close planning in relation to their own demise.

Secondly, the effect on the growing points of enterprise. Unlike an annual wealth tax there is nothing about a death duty which hampers new enterprise or prevents the growth of a business in the hands of its creator. Handing it on to a second generation is more difficult, however. We do not know how far the founders of businesses are impelled by the dynastic motive; some research evidence suggests that this motive has been overstated.[1] Moreover, there is nothing in the process of inheritance which guarantees that the son of the founder of a business is necessarily the best person to carry it on. If it has to be sold on the death of the founder, it might end up in more, not less, efficient hands than if it went to his heir. If there is a competent successor to a flourishing business it also seems likely that the private capital market can ensure that the business survives and remains under his management.

The case of farms is not dissimilar, save that the forms of ownership which make it easier for a unit to remain intact in the management of a successor have not developed to the same extent, though there are signs that they may.[2]

Finally, whilst some people do emigrate to avoid death duties, it runs counter to the characteristics of the old and is much less likely to be serious than with a heavy annual wealth tax.

In short, there is a crucial difference in economic effects between a heavy annual wealth tax and a heavy transfer tax. The latter does not impinge on saving, enterprise and business behaviour in the way that an annual wealth tax necessarily does.

Let us take this line of argument somewhat further in the next section by posing the question of the compatability of a heavy transfer tax with a large private sector in a mixed economy.

Is a Heavy Inheritance Tax Compatible with Private Enterprise?

We suggested earlier that the most suitable form of transfer tax for reducing inequality in a mixed economy was an accessions tax, so let us take that as our form of wealth transfer tax.

Whilst we must register some small reservations because of ignorance about the importance of the desire to bequeath, especially amongst the creators of businesses, there are at least three general reasons why a heavy accessions tax is compatible with the continu-

---

[1] Jonathan Boswell, *The Rise and Decline of Small Firms*, Allen and Unwin, 1972, especially Chapter 5.

[2] For example, the kind of proposal made by the Agricultural Mortgage Corporation for 'co-ownership'—the purchase from an owner occupier of an undivided share (10–49 per cent) in his farm which would then be leased back to him.

ance of a large and flourishing private enterprise sector in a mixed economy.

First, inheritance is not integral to the private enterprise ethic. Such an ethic, as inferred from our description of the market mechanism in Chapter 4, is that economic rewards should be directly related to contribution to output, the value of that contribution being determined by members of the community acting through free markets. Whilst some rights of inheritance may be necessary as an incentive to the property accumulator, the receipt of large inheritances and gifts, against which no contributions to output can be set, can be regarded as inimical to the basic rationale of a free enterprise economy.

Secondly, the development of the stock exchange and of specialist facilities within the capital market have reduced the economic disadvantages of death duties. The development of public joint stock companies with readily marketable shares has made the diffusion of the ownership of a business after its owner's death far less open to economic objection. The most rapidly expanding firms can expect to 'go public' in the lifetime of their founder. Where private firms affected by death duties are too small to go public, specialist credit facilities, developed within the private capital market,[1] have much reduced the chance that an efficient business with good prospects and good management succession will be seriously impeded by death duties. If agriculture is not yet as well served by the capital market, there are signs of developments to meet the need.

Thirdly, an accessions tax form of transfer tax, by encouraging the wider dispersion of private wealth in smaller units, may give more people the means of starting their own businesses.

SUMMARY AND CONCLUSIONS

Wealth is derived from saving, enterprise, good luck and inheritance. Inheritance is almost certainly the most important cause of inequality in the distribution of wealth. There are a number of conceptual problems in measuring such inequality and a number of deficiencies in our statistics, both of which leave scope for dispute about the extent of inequality. If a government wished to reduce inequality in the distribution of wealth it could do so by wealth transfer taxes

---

[1] In the United Kingdom, most notably the formation of EDITH (Estate Duties Investment Trust) now incorporated in Finance for Industry.

and/or an annual wealth tax. The choice of tax should be related to the philosophy on the distribution of wealth and the kind of society which is desired. For those who wish to preserve a large private enterprise sector in the mixed economy an accessions tax has much to commend it. It strikes directly at the perpetuation of inequality through inheritance (and related gifts) and unlike other forms of wealth tax it encourages a wider diffusion of wealth within the private sector; it also has less detrimental economic effects than a heavy annual wealth tax.

Part IV

ECONOMIC ASPECTS OF SOCIAL SERVICES

Introduction to Part IV

In this part of the book we examine some of the economic aspects of some of the social services—education, health and housing. The subject matter of these three chapters has much in common as does the treatment, though there are also significant differences. We begin each chapter by examining the growth of public expenditure on those services in the United Kingdom expressed as a percentage of GNP to give us a perspective. In each case we say something about the policies underlying the expenditure changes—though we shall use a broad brush as it is not our purpose to consider the details of policy.

Each of these services or goods comes into what we described in Chapter 5 as the quasi-public/quasi-private category: goods with externality effects, which could be provided publicly, privately, or both, and where decisions about public or private provision are much affected by non-economic criteria. We spend some time in analysing the economic characteristics of these goods, which have an important bearing on policy.

In the United Kingdom each of these goods or services is provided partly through the public sector, very largely for education and health and significantly for housing. In addition there is some government expenditure and major tax concessions for housing provided in the private sector, and some very limited government financial assistance for privately-provided education. Thus the main decisions on how many resources to allocate to education and health care, and how to use them within those services, are made through the political system, whilst the political machinery also plays a dominating role in the control and direction of the resources applied to housing.

When allocation decisions are taken out of the market, as we pointed out in Chapter 5, there ceases to be any direct relationship between cost and benefit. Although public opinion, expressed through the media and the ballot box, has some influence, public opinion is necessarily amorphous, general, and imprecise save for organized pressure groups with an axe to grind. Actual decisions on how much to spend on what are made by ministers and officials. Because there are no clear-cut criteria, the danger is that these decisions are largely the outcome of political bargaining and personal whim and that they do not represent an economic use of resources in any or all of the following senses: they do not accurately reflect the community's wishes about which services should have priority; nor about what weight should be given to the different programmes within a service; nor secure that a specified programme objective is being achieved with the least expenditure of scarce resources. To illustrate the problem: in 1956 public expenditure on education and the NHS was almost identical; since then education expenditure has risen at almost twice the rate of expenditure on health services despite the growing proportion of old people in the community. Can anyone say with conviction that this is an accurate reflection of the community's priorities and needs? Or again, currently expenditure on higher education is being cut back in real terms whilst nursery education continues to expand despite the falling birth rate. Is this a result of anything more than political whim? Or again, are all the relevant costs considered in a decision to replace county out-patient clinics by expanding city centre clinics?

It follows that techniques or approaches which could increase the economic rationality of decision-making are of vital importance. It is for this reason that we look at output budgeting as it might be applied to education and some examples of cost-benefit analysis in health care. We shall also examine rate of return analysis in education, which could be used to define a *lower* limit for education expenditure and also to provide guide-lines as to the direction of expenditure.

Finally, in the light of our analysis we query how far present methods in these services are appropriate for the objectives, and, indeed, how far the objectives themselves need clarifying. Thus, would it be more appropriate to finance higher education by loans rather than grants? Why not use vouchers for education? Are there any clear objectives to current housing policy?

12 Education

Public Spending on Education

Education has been one of the big growth industries of the post-war period. The figures of money expenditure are not very meaningful because of the continuous rise in prices, estimated to have increased about three-fold over the two decades from 1956. But Table 12.1 indicates that expenditure on education had grown from 9 per cent in 1956 to over 13 per cent of combined central and local government spending by the 1970s. Still more significantly, the share of education in the national product more than doubled between 1956 and 1975.

**Table 12.1 Public Expenditure on Education,
United Kingdom, 1956–75.**

Education expenditure	1956	1961	1966	1971	1972	1973	1974	1975
At current prices (£m)	636	1012	1768	3023	3559	4083	4746	6840
As % of total public spending*	9.02	10.23	12.17	12.96	13.41	13.33	12.16	13.32
As % of GNP at factor cost	3.45	4.14	5.28	6.09	6.41	6.30	6.34	7.27

* Public spending is here measured as combined central and local government spending including expenditure on financial assets. (Measure 2 in Chapter 5, p. 61.)

Source: *National Income and Expenditure, 1967* and *National Income and Expenditure, 1965–75*, HMSO.

Why this enormous increase in education expenditure? To some extent it reflected demographic changes. In 1956 the peak age groups resulting from the 'post-war bulge' were in the junior schools and beginning to work through into the more expensive secondary education and would later move into still more expensive further and higher education. Another factor was 'the trend'—the growing proportion of the relevant age-groups which chose to stay on at school to 'A' level and sought higher education thereafter. Further, evidence from other countries suggests that education is income-elastic, that, whether education is provided in the public or the private sector, as a community becomes better off it wishes to spend an increasing proportion of income on education. But other influences were also at work. The 1960s saw economic growth elevated to a policy objective as never before, and education was encouraged as a means of promoting growth. Linked to this was the desire to keep up with the international Jones's in science and technology and a feature of education spending was expansion of the (very expensive) facilities for educating more scientists, technologists and technicians. Yet, when all these points are listed and weighed as well as they can be, there remains a residual question mark about why education expanded so much. The arguments for expenditure on the health services seem equally convincing, yet they expanded much less.

What seems clear is that the expansion is coming to an end. The Public Expenditure White Paper, *Public Expenditure to 1979–80*[1] proposed a big reduction in education estimates from 1977 as compared with previous plans and provided for a roughly constant level of expenditure to 1980 measured in real terms. Education expenditure as a percentage of GNP would therefore fall given any growth in GNP from 1976 to 1980. As the White Paper explained, 'The planned expenditure figures reflect not only the restraints necessary in view of the economic situation but also changes in the prospective demand for education at a number of levels compared with the projections of Cmnd. 5879.[2] Latest projected numbers of births show a further fall and somewhat lower growth rates are also expected, on the basis of observed trends, in the number of pupils remaining at school beyond the statutory school leaving age and in the demand for higher education.'[3] On the other hand some increased demand for non-advanced higher education was expected. Naturally, in view of the continuing birth rate fall, new building

---

[1] Cmnd. 6393, February 1976.

[2] *Public Expenditure to 1978–79*, January 1975 (the Public Expenditure White Paper of the previous year).

[3] *Public Expenditure to 1979–80*, Cmnd. 6393, February 1976.

took the biggest cut. After the 1976 Public Expenditure White Paper was written the economic situation deteriorated, the birth rate continued to fall and further economies were announced including further cuts in building programmes and the projected closure of more colleges of education.

Characteristics of Education

Externality Effects

One underlying reason for the state's interest in education is the existence of social benefits over and above private benefits from education expenditure. Such beneficial externality effects do not necessarily require the state to provide education. As we pointed out in Chapter 5, the state can promote education by regulation and finance instead of, or as well as, by provision, and indeed, the earliest state encouragement to education in the nineteenth century took the form of grants to voluntary bodies. But in the United Kingdom the state's hold on education has been tightening and the state is now a near monopolist in providing education services.

What are the social benefits of education over and above private benefits? There are a number of possible benefits, some intangible, some disputable and all defying quantification.

One of the most solidly-based is the benefits of higher productivity and hence of incomes which education brings over and above the benefit which a worker would derive from his own education. A minimum standard of literacy and numeracy in a society is necessary for the running of a complex advanced economy; people need to be able to make simple calculations, read advertisements about products and jobs, and follow simple written instructions. If such skills are widely diffused in a population each member gains from the education of the others because the higher levels of output and productivity benefit all, even the few who may not have acquired the skills of literacy and numeracy.

Connected with the output advantages of education, but going beyond them, is the benefit resulting from research—leading to new knowledge and understanding. This may be knowledge in the field of technology directly promoting innovation and productivity; knowledge in the social sciences, increasing our ability to control our environment so that we are able to reduce unemployment or curtail inflation more effectively; or advances in medicine some of which might have no effect on output but, for example, make life more tolerable for the chronically sick.

Benefits of a social character are also claimed for education. Thus it is maintained that a more educated population makes for more stable government and enables democracy to function more effectively. Much more disputable is the assertion that education reduces crime, a view which seems to be supported by very little evidence. Indeed, some statistics point in the opposite direction, though, as we trust the reader will need no reminding, a correlation does not prove a causal relationship. Thus, the age-group in its last compulsory year at school has shown the highest rate of juvenile crime in recent decades, whatever the school-leaving age has been; and university libraries are notorious for book thefts. With other alleged social advantages we move very much into the realm of value judgments. Thus education may, or may be used to, promote social cohesion or, indeed, to inculcate particular attitudes. Whether such matters are social benefits or social costs depends on judgments first about whether education systems should be used for such purposes, and if so, about the nature of the views propagated.

Private Benefits of Education

The private benefits of education are of several kinds, in line with three of the four kinds of goods we distinguished in Chapter 3. Firstly, there is a single-use consumption benefit—at least, those of us who are teachers like to think so—in other words, the person being taught enjoys the process. This is certainly true of some pupils and students, but not necessarily of all. Secondly, there is a durable-use consumption benefit. Education offers a continuing consumption benefit because the greater knowledge and understanding which education gives enables those who receive it to live richer lives: because they can read they can enjoy great literature; their education may help them to appreciate the visual arts or increase their delight from music; they gain a heightened awareness and appreciation of what is going on around them and are better equipped to take part in it. Thirdly, there is that aspect of education which corresponds to the durable-use-producers' good, which is generally termed the investment benefit of education expenditure (although the continuing consumption benefit could also be so regarded). Spending on education can be likened to spending on equipment. Buying new machines results in a flow of output and hence income throughout the working life of the machine. In the same way, spending on education, which can be termed 'investment in human capital', results in a flow of output and income to the educated over and above what they would have received had they not possessed the skills which education confers. This conception of education as investment in human capital can provide many helpful insights. Thus there is a parallel between a machine rendered obsolescent by a new invention and a worker whose skills are made redundant because of a change in technology. Again, it should be no surprise that doctors and dentists receive relatively high salaries; because their education is relatively lengthy, the costs of investment in it (including income forgone during training) are relatively high and the returns need to be correspondingly greater.

Rate of Return Analysis

This investment benefit of education expenditure lends itself to measurement; we can at least make an attempt to quantify and compare the costs of education and the investment benefits. In doing so we need to distinguish between the benefits and costs to the individual, the private rate of return to education, and benefits and costs to a society as a whole, the social rate of return.

The kind of question we are attempting to answer in private rate of return analysis is: 'What rate of return can a person expect to obtain from expenditure on additional education?' Just as a person may lend money to a firm (which uses it to buy new equipment) and receive interest on that money or a share in the profits, so, instead he could use it on education and expect to obtain a return in higher net earnings as a result.

We know that there are many factors, not excluding luck, which influence personal earnings, so the appropriate procedure is to take an average as a guide to what the individual might expect. The private costs of education are not too difficult to determine. Let us illustrate by taking higher education in the form of a first degree course. Then the private costs of education are monetary expenditure on books, stationery and the like, fees if any, and the earnings foregone during the three years of university study, minus government grants or scholarships. (For some forms of education, notably qualifications gained by evening study, there will also be a cost in terms of leisure foregone, and leisure is difficult to value, partly because there is likely to be some element of consumption benefit from using leisure in this way and partly because of a general difficulty of knowing what value to put on non-work time.)

On the benefit side what we are seeking to measure is the extra life-time earnings which result from a first degree. Ideally, we should like to be able to compare the life-time earnings of two 'matched samples' of the population alike in all respects, such as intelligence and family background, save that one group has read for a first degree and the other has not. In practice our nearest approximation is to base our comparison on the earnings in different age cohorts of the population. Thus we can look at the earnings differences of those aged 20–21, 21–22, 22–23 and so on throughout the working age groups, comparing those who took the highest secondary school qualification, 'A' level, but went no further with their formal education, with those who went beyond 'A' level to take a three year full-time course for a university degree. We must then 'adjust' for that part of the difference in earnings at each age group which results from factors other than education; we are then left with the education differential. When measuring the private rate of return we have to calculate this education differential net of income tax.

The next step is to compare in a meaningful way the costs which are wholly or mainly incurred during the first three years post 'A' level, with the net of tax earnings resulting from the extra education, which will be spread over a lifetime (and may well influence income in retirement through pension schemes). To compare like with like we must put both costs and benefits on to the same time basis; we must make allowance for the fact that, apart from any question of inflation, £100 in the future is worth less than £100 now; if I have £100 now I can lend it out at interest and, for example, with interest at 10 per cent compound, my £100 will become £110 next year and £121 the year after. The method adopted is to calculate the present value of both costs and benefits by 'discounting' them, which is precisely the same process as compound interest in reverse. Thus, if the rate of discount is 10 per cent, the value of £121 in two years time is £100 now.

In fact we can adopt either of two procedures. To see if the expenditure on higher education was a good investment we could discount private costs and benefits by the market rate of interest and then see if the sum of the present value of the benefits was greater than the costs. Alternatively, we could adopt a slightly more complicated procedure, but one which gives the answer in a more convenient form and discount the net returns less costs each year by such a rate of discount as would make the present value of the returns less cost equal to zero. That rate of discount is then the private rate of return on higher education—the rate of return over and above costs—and it is in a form (e.g. 12 per cent) in which it can be compared with the return to be expected from alternative forms of investment.

There are certain obvious snags in this procedure. First, what we have calculated is the average rate of return on past education expenditure, whilst what we wanted was the marginal rate of return on current or future education expenditure. If the past is a good guide to the future in this respect and the marginal return is much the same as the average then this does not matter. Historical indications are that, in the past there has been little difference between the average and marginal rates of return to education and that the rate of return has remained at a fairly consistent level over time (at any rate in the USA, where most of the calculations have been made). But there is no certainty that this will remain so for the future.

Secondly, the adjustment to separate out the educational component of the earnings differential is difficult. Calculations of the rate of return to education in the United Kingdom have tended to rely on American studies for various scatters of ability and class origins which suggest that about 40 per cent of the earnings differences result from other factors and 60 per cent from education.

Another important omission is differences in non-monetary advantages in the occupations of graduates and non-graduates. We should expect graduates on average to enjoy net advantages—longer holidays, perhaps certain 'perks' and certainly more interesting jobs —than non-graduates; but these benefits are not taken into account in rate of return analysis. The private rate of return calculations thus almost certainly understate the private investment advantage of education.

Calculations of the social rate of return follow similar lines to that of the private rate of return but differ somewhat in the costs and benefits included, because we are looking at the costs and benefits to society, including the individual. On the costs side, as well as private expenditures we must count state expenditures. Thus we need to include maintenance grants and scholarships paid by the state to the individual and the cost of the education itself less the student's contribution (if any). In the United Kingdom the fees for higher education represent only a small proportion of the cost; the rest is paid to the universities by the Government through the University Grants Commission or to the Polytechnics, etc. by the Department of Education and Science. On the benefit side we take the earning differential gross, and not net of tax, as the community benefits from government expenditure of the tax revenue. Thereafter we discount to get the rate of return in exactly the same way as before. Ideally in measuring the social rate of return we should take into account the beneficial externality effects we discussed earlier in this chapter. In practice the difficulty of measuring them precludes us from so doing.

Rate of Return Calculations for Great Britain

Most of the calculations of rates of return to education have been made in the USA. Britain has lacked data on earnings and education at different age groups. However, some studies have been made on British data. Mr D. Henderson-Stewart on 1963 data made a provisional estimate of the private rate of return on the three years to complete secondary education, which came out at about 13 per cent, and on three years of higher education, at about 14 per cent.[1] These yields represented about 50 per cent more than could be earned by investing in debentures (loans to industry carrying a fixed rate of interest) or in ordinary shares. Since then better data has become available from the 1966 (10 per cent) Sample Census on Population, which included a question on education qualifications, and a follow-up sub-sample postal enquiry on earnings in 1968. Social rates of return have been calculated from this data for a number of educational qualifications over the preceding educational stage.[2] The social rate of return for a first degree for a man came out at 12.5 per cent, for a woman 6.9 per cent (lower mainly because of part-time working and lower participation in the labour market). The Higher National Certificate (HNC), a qualification gained from part-time study, had the strikingly high social rate of return of over 20 per cent, mainly because of the small expenditure costs and earnings foregone, whilst at the other extreme the social rates of return for higher degrees were remarkably low at 2.8 per cent for a master's degree and 2.7 per cent for a doctorate. No private rates of return were calculated in this study. Both these series of estimates

---

[1] Contained in an Appendix to 'The rate of return on investment in education in Great Britain', by M. Blaug, *The Manchester School*, September 1965.

[2] V. Morris and A. Ziderman, 'The economic return on investment in higher education in England and Wales', *Economic Trends*, May 1971.

used the coefficient derived from the American studies to adjust earnings differentials for factors other than education.

It should be stressed that no great precision can be attached to the particular figures but they can be taken as broad indications of the investment return to education.

Policy Implications

Could we use such calculations, perhaps refined, as policy tools to aid decision-making?

There are two main policy implications. First, social rates of return to education can be regarded as setting a *minimum* to spending on particular sectors or kinds of education. If the social rate of return is above the return which can be expected from investment elsewhere, then there is a strong case for further investment in education. However, if the rate of return is less than can be obtained from alternative investments, it does not follow that expenditure on the relevant education sector should be cut back, because the social rate of return takes account neither of the externality benefits nor of the consumption benefits of education. Because these cannot be measured they should not be treated as unimportant. Thus, it might be argued that post-graduate education, although it has a low social rate of return calculated by the methods we have indicated, is that aspect of education most likely to generate the externality benefits in the future of the kind associated with increased knowledge from research.

The second policy implication relates to the private rate of return. A high private rate of return means that the extra life-time earnings resulting from education are high in relation to the costs of incurring that education. One reason for high private rates of return to higher education to first degree level in Great Britain is that much of the cost is met not by the individual receiving the education but by the state, i.e. the general body of taxpayers. The beneficiaries of higher education are amongst the top 10 per cent or so of the population in terms of their intellectual endowment and, even without education, would earn life-time incomes well above average. Heavy state expenditure on this select élite enables them to earn still more. Indeed, it could be argued that the state is accentuating inequalities in earnings by its heavy education spending on a relatively small proportion of the relevant age-groups. Further, it should be remembered that the rate of return calculations take no account of consumption benefits (single-use and durable-use) which the educated enjoy. Thus the question is raised in an acute form: should not the beneficiaries of higher education pay more of the cost themselves? The most realistic way to bring this about would be to finance a proportion of education expenditure by loans repayable on fairly generous terms. This, indeed, is what happens in a number of countries other than the United Kingdom.

Output Budgeting in Education

There are many aspects of the economics of education. We could examine schools, colleges and universities adopting the same kind of approach that we outlined in Chapter 1 when considering the economics of a church, analysing efficiency in the use of labour or of plant. Again we could look at the location of educational institutions or, in principle, at optimal methods of teaching. Or we could examine some case studies in cost-benefit analysis in education of the kind we shall be considering in the next chapter on health services. Instead we are going to analyse output budgeting or planning, programming budgeting (PPB) as it might be applied to education. Our main reason for choosing this aspect of the economics of education is twofold. Firstly, it links with the crucial issue of effective decision-making in the public sector where the criteria for determining the amount and direction of expenditures are not clear-cut; output budgeting is intended to provide a broad framework for more effective decision-making over a whole policy area. Secondly, it is convenient to choose education because of a feasibility study undertaken for the Department of Education and Science in Britain.[1] In what follows we naturally draw heavily on that study.

Traditional budgets set down spending or proposed spending on materials of various kinds, on staff of different categories and skills and on buildings of various types. The essence of output budgeting is to relate inputs or costs to defined objectives. A number of stages are involved. The total budget for an activity such as education has to be broken down into a series of sub-budgets, programmes, sub-programmes and detailed elements (of which there may be many hundreds) so that the decision-maker can make detailed and mean-ingful decisions at the margin. The objective of each of the components must be specified and the costs of achieving each objective must be identified and measured. Further, a full output budgeting

---

[1] *Output Budgeting for the Department of Education and Science*, Education Planning Paper No. 1, 1970, HMSO. Referred to hereafter in the text as the feasibility study.

system requires continual studies to assess the validity of the objectives, to test their achievement, and to present alternative ways of attaining the specified objectives.

These points can be clarified by reference to how output budgeting might work in education. The feasibility study divided the total education budget into three sub-budgets: (A) Education—concerned with acquiring knowledge and skills; (B) Research—concerned with new knowledge and understanding; (C) Cultural—concerned with the enrichment of leisure. Each of these was then further divided into programmes. If we take (A) Education, there was a programme for each educational stage: A1, Nursery education; A2, Education during the compulsory school ages and so on to A6, Higher education to first degree level and A7, Postgraduate education. It should be noted that the presentation is related to the objective (e.g. a first degree) rather than to the institution (e.g. university or polytechnic). Within each of these major programmes expenditure was set out in various elements, covering the costs of catering: (a) for present numbers at existing cost levels; (b) for increase in numbers in the relevant age groups; (c) for population shift; (d) for forecast changes in participation rates; and (e) for changing standards in provision. Thus the programme elements would contain the estimated costs (current and capital) of improving pupil/teacher ratios in primary schools by a specified amount in a specified year; or making the same improvement in Educational Priority Areas (EPAs) only; of improving staff-student ratios in all subjects in universities by a specified percentage point; or doing the same thing only in certain subject areas, and so on.

The purpose is to present ministers and officials with the costs of achieving alternative objectives so that, if more money could be found for education, they could make realistic choices about how to spend it—if a cut-back was necessary, they could decide on rational grounds which policy objectives to sacrifice or postpone, rather than adopting crude percentage cuts across the board.

At the same time the objectives would continually be under scrutiny; methods would be studied to define and test them more effectively (perhaps, for example, the use of rates of return analysis); and studies would take place of alternative ways, with different cost structures, of achieving a particular objective (e.g. fewer teachers and more teaching machines in teaching children to read).

There are difficulties about any output budgeting system. There are particular difficulties as applied to education; and there are still more difficulties as applied to education in the United Kingdom. We can do no more than illustrate each of these facets. First, most output budgeting systems face problems of joint costs—that a particular form of expenditure contributes to more than one objective. Consider, for example, the broad division in the feasibility study between the objectives of Education (A) and Research (B). A university teacher is expected to contribute to both objectives and university teachers' salaries must therefore be divided between them. But on what basis? The most obvious answer is a salary division proportional to a time division and university teachers could be (and in fact have been) asked to specify what proportion of their time is teaching-related and what proportion research-related. But this is almost impossible to answer: teaching and research go hand in hand; time spent on reading feeds into both. At best any division must be somewhat arbitrary.

Secondly, a particular problem in education is that of defining the objective or the output in meaningful and measurable terms. In some sectors of education there may be examinations, the results of which might be taken as a tolerable measure. In other sectors, like primary school, a series of tests of the three Rs and of other subjects could be used as a help to defining and measuring objectives. There are dangers in gearing an education system too closely to performance in examinations or tests, yet there are also dangers in not having clearly defined or measurable objectives. Currently we often use as a proxy for improvements in quantity of output an input measure such as pupil/teacher ratios, so that a decline in pupil/teacher ratios is taken as the equivalent of an improvement in output; yet little or no studies have been made to try to assess what difference is made by a small change in these ratios and what are the critical levels. Elsewhere in the economic system it is a general economic objective to obtain the same output with less workers, i.e. to increase labour productivity.

Finally, there is the particular problem of applying output budgeting in Britain where the DES and its Scottish and Northern Ireland equivalents are planning, guiding and monitoring agencies rather than agencies of detailed control. Britain has a small private sector of education subject to broad regulation by the state, local authorities have considerable areas of discretion, as have universities, and to a lesser extent schools. It is clearly much more difficult to apply a satisfactory budgeting system for the DES than in some other departments of government. It is no accident that the one ministry in the United Kingdom with a full output budgeting system is Defence, which is unaffected by problems of diffused and devolved responsibilities.

It was not within the terms of reference of the authors of the feasibility study to recommend whether an output budgeting system should be adopted in the DES. As a framework for rational choice it is attractive. Yet it is perhaps more difficult to apply a full output budgeting system in education than in any other area of central government responsibility and whether a full system could be implemented which would be sufficiently accurate and useful to justify the costs of setting it up must be doubtful. There is, however, no doubt of the value of some of its components. One can move in the direction of output budgeting without going all the way; and there may well be scope for effective and economical systems of output budgeting at the level of the local authority, or of educational units such as universities.

Why Not Vouchers for Education?

A very different approach towards responsible decision-making about the amount and direction of expenditure on education is offered by the scheme for education vouchers. This approach would put more of the decision-making on the individual—parent or student—and tilt the balance of the state's contribution more towards finance and less towards provision.

The general idea is that at, say, the secondary stage of education there should be a voucher system by which the parents of a child in the relevant age groups would receive each year an education voucher. A voucher is a coupon of a particular money value encashable only against a particular good or service (thus a health voucher scheme has been proposed which could be used to buy medical insurance, and some American states have used food vouchers as part of their anti-poverty programmes). The value of the education voucher would be set at that level at which it would purchase an education at the current average cost of providing it in state schools. The voucher could then be used to buy education in state schools or in private schools which met specified standards, being supplemented by those parents who wished to spend rather more than the basic minimum on their children's education. The choice of school would rest with the parent. It would be expected that the scheme would bring many new private schools into existence.

The voucher scheme is attractive to those who are concerned with the growing size and power of the state and the dangers of state monopoly of education, dangers to democratic freedoms, to efficiency, to diversity and to standards. It is a way of giving more say to parents in the education of their children and providing an incentive to maintaining and improving standards: parents can vote with their feet and poor schools are likely to lose children. It is argued that it is also a way of bringing more resources into education. Despite the huge increase in expenditure on education over the past few decades, there is some evidence to suggest that expenditure might have been even greater had it been possible for parents to supplement the state's contribution to education expenditure. Currently parents either have to send their children to state schools or pay the whole economic cost of sending a child to private school; there are many parents who cannot afford the latter who would nonetheless be happy to make some contribution.[1] It would end the situation, seen by many as absurd, that Parents' Associations at state schools can buy unlimited frills for the education of their children but are debarred from improving what are seen as essentials, for example, an extra teacher to reduce class sizes.

Arguments against education vouchers fall into two categories, the practical and the ideological.

There are those, attracted by the scheme and its objectives, who fear it is administratively costly and impracticable. Distributing vouchers and collecting them in again would put up administrative costs. There would be a cost to the state of providing vouchers for children at present at private schools. There are problems in parental freedom of choice which might swamp popular schools with applicants whilst the unpopular were left empty. Expanding the popular by new building, or even mobile class rooms, would put up costs, and the very process of expansion might change the character of the school. Over-provision to allow for choice could prove wasteful. Whether these difficulties are overstated is a practical matter which could be determined by a feasibility experiment. Such experiments are taking place in the USA, notably at Alum Rock in California; in Britain, Kent County Council is undertaking a study of the possibilities in its area.

The more fundamental objections come from those who consider a voucher scheme in education undesirable. They argue that buying

[1] Surveys conducted by the Institute of Economic Affairs in 1963, 1965 and 1970 bear this out.

education is buying privilege. Their objective is state education for all as a common badge of citizenship. They believe that the poorest and those with uncaring parents would suffer from the voucher system because state schools offering the basic cost provision would deteriorate once the more caring, energetic and enterprising parents had sent their children elsewhere. Thus the opponents of the voucher system consider that it would lead to a deterioration of the education of the poorest and accentuate class divisions in society.

The advocates of the voucher scheme claim that these objections are misguided. That, if it is desired to raise the general standard of education and give particular benefit to the poor, vouchers could count as part of taxable income. The poor households with incomes below the income tax threshold would thus gain most and a surplus of revenue would be available for raising standards in state schools in general or for pumping into the Educationally Deprived Areas. They also hold that it is misconceived to believe that class divisions would be accentuated. On the contrary, they claim, it is the present structure which accentuates such divisions where there is no inter-mediate position between the (necessarily) high-priced private school and the 'free' state school; the voucher system would make for gradations rather than marked divisions. They point to survey evidence which suggests that many 'working class' parents would like to supplement spending on their children's education if this was an option open to them; and they marvel at an attitude which would allow people to spend without limit on drinking, smoking and gambling but prevent any private spending on education.

This is very much the realm of value judgments. Whilst some issues may be resolved by experiment, the extreme individualists and collectivists are unlikely to be brought to a common mind by reference to fact, or by any arguments about the economics of education.

SUMMARY AND CONCLUSIONS

Public expenditure on education in Britain, measured as a per-centage of GNP, has more than doubled over the past twenty years. That expansion is now abruptly ending. Education expenditure generates beneficial externality effects, though some benefits claimed are highly disputable. Education offers both short-term (single-use) and long-term (durable-use) private consumption benefits and private investment benefits. The investment benefits of education expenditure can be calculated by means of rate of return analysis; but, at best, rates of return calculations can only offer orders of magnitude. The social rate of return for a particular sector of education can be a guide to *minimum* expenditure on education, and private rate of return calculations raise questions about the appropriate ways to finance education. Output budgeting offers an attractive framework for rational decision-making in public policy areas but it is doubtful if a full system could usefully be attempted in education. A voucher scheme for education may or may not be practicable; attitudes to such a scheme depend very much on personal value judgments.

13 Health Services

Public Spending in Health Services

Public spending on the National Health Service, as a percentage of GNP, grew some 62½ per cent during the two decades from 1956, the rate of growth accelerating somewhat in the latter part of the period. Thus the growth was substantial but much less than that of education expenditure over the same period. The figures in Table 13.1, of course, take no account of private expenditure on health which has grown quite rapidly over the period mainly in the form of insurance, through non-profit-making bodies such as BUPA, for consultancy services and hospital treatment.

Of the total of public spending on the NHS, less than 5 per cent is financed from charges on prescriptions, dental treatment and spectacles; the remainder is financed by the Exchequer from the proceeds of taxation including national insurance contributions which contain a health component.

**Table 13.1   Public Expenditure on the NHS,
United Kingdom, 1956–75.**

Expenditure on NHS	1956	1961	1966	1971	1972	1973	1974	1975
At current prices (£m)	633	930	1401	2289	2642	2984	3903	5260
As % of total public spending*	8.98	9.41	9.46	9.82	9.96	9.74	9.98	10.24
As % of GNP at factor cost	3.44	3.81	4.18	4.62	4.76	4.60	5.21	5.59

* Public spending is here measured as combined central and local government spending including expenditure on financial assets. (Measure 2 in Chapter 5, p. 61.)

Source: *National Income and Expenditure, 1967* and *National Income and Expenditure, 1965-75,* HMSO.

Much of the growth in NHS expenditure can be accounted for by the needs of the steadily growing proportion of old people in the population during the period. Evidence from other countries supports the view that, like education, health is an income-elastic service—that as national income rises, so a community wishes to spend a growing proportion of it on health care. In fact international comparisons suggest that Britain is well down the league table of advanced countries in the proportion of GNP spent on health care.[1] This does not necessarily mean that Britain devotes a lower proportion of real resources to the health service; it could be that health services are relatively dearer compared with other goods and services in these other countries (e.g. that doctors and consultants are, relatively to other occupations, more highly paid abroad than in Britain). Casual evidence suggests that this is part of the explanation, but it would be very surprising if it explained the whole difference.

In view of the differing significance of demographic changes for the two services, public expenditure on the NHS has not been subject to the same cutback as education expenditure. The Public Expenditure White Paper of February 1976,[2] whilst providing for some reduction in the estimates contained in the previous White Paper, especially on capital account, envisages a continued rise in expenditure in real terms on the NHS sufficient to maintain standards for the increasing number of old people and to permit the continued spread of new methods of treatment.

Characteristics of Health Services

Externality Effects

As with education, so with health, we can identify beneficial externality effects from health expenditure—social benefits over and above private benefits. But with health we can distinguish more sharply than with education the kinds of expenditure which do and those which do not give rise to externality benefits. The clearest externality effects arise from the treatment of contagious and infectious diseases, the kind of disease with which public health programmes have been concerned—plague, typhus, smallpox,

---

[1] *International Health Expenditure II*, Information Sheet No. 22 of the Office of Health Economics, May 1973.

[2] *Public Expenditure to 1979–80*, Cmnd. 6393.

diphtheria and the like. Many of these have now been stamped out in Britain, but there remain some—influenza, V.D. and the common cold, for example. Successful treatment of one person for such endemic and epidemic diseases reduces the risk to the rest of the community and thus confers a social benefit over and above the private. Expenditure on medical research also can clearly bring widely-diffused social benefits.

On the other hand many health expenditures bring purely private benefit. Treatment for broken limbs, operations to remove diseased kidneys or swollen appendixes, manipulations to replace a slipped disc or treatment for arthritis, these and many more bring benefit of a purely personal kind.

Private Benefits of Health Expenditure

As with education, private benefits from health expenditure are of both the consumption and investment kind. Although, unlike education, undergoing health treatment is not something usually enjoyed, at least there is a short term consumption benefit in the sense of a 'utility' or satisfaction from the easement of pain or discomfort. A consumption benefit (comparable to a durable-use consumption good) is gained from successful treatment of illness which leaves the patient able to enjoy life thereafter.

There is also a private investment benefit from health expenditure, but, as with the consumption benefit, of a rather negative kind. For someone who starts out healthy, health care does not provide any differential increase in earnings, but may restrict the loss of earnings which illness could bring.

Rate of Return Analysis

There are no precise parallels in health spending to the rate of return analysis of the investment benefit on earnings and output which has been applied to the various stages of education, but a number of attempts outside the United Kingdom have been made to calculate the cost and benefits of particular health programmes, taking into account effects on output. American cost-benefit studies have examined mental illness, peptic ulcer, alcoholism, polio, tuberculosis, cancer and syphilis on those lines.[1]

[1] See for details on these and comparable studies an admirable article by Jennifer A. Roberts, 'Economic evaluation of health care: a survey', *British Journal of Preventive Social Medicine*, 1974, 28, pp. 210–16.

In Britain, there have been no comparable studies of particular health programmes. Broad attempts have been made to justify expenditure on health in general on grounds of its benefits to production, and we shall return to this point in the final section of this chapter. Historically, arguments in general terms have also been presented to justify particular public health programmes on broad cost-benefit grounds; thus, in the seventeenth century Sir William Petty was advocating public expenditure to reduce the ravages of the plague as money well spent in relation to the return it would yield; and Edwin Chadwick, the great apostle of sanitation, used similar arguments in the nineteenth century. But the more scientific cost-benefit studies in the United Kingdom have been concerned with smaller, though important, issues—various ways in which resources within the health service can be used more efficiently. To these we now turn.

Cost-Benefit Studies in Health Care

Cost-Benefit Analyses in General

The measurement of the rate of return to education, which we described in the previous chapter, was a particular kind of limited cost-benefit analysis in which benefits occurred solely in the form of additional earnings. A full cost-benefit study seeks, in principle, to take account of all costs and benefits. An industrialist deciding whether to introduce a new product or buy a new machine will weigh up the costs against the benefits in the form of the extra revenue he expects to get from the sale of the product. Cost-benefit analysis differs from this in two main ways: it seeks to take account of externality effects by including items which enter into social but not into private costs and benefits. Secondly, the method is applied in situations where the product is not sold so that there is no market price to reflect the value put on the product by the purchaser.

Cost-benefit analysis has established itself most firmly in transport studies. The M1, the Victoria Line and the site of a third London airport are the best-known studies, but there have been many other less publicized cost-benefit analyses on roads and bridges and in connection with possible rail closures. Undoubtedly such studies can assist decision-making in public investment in transport; but even in transport considerable difficulties have arisen, all of which recur, sometimes in accentuated form, in attempts to apply cost-benefit analysis to other aspects of public expenditure. It is worth, therefore, examining the methods and limitations of the technique in relation to an area of application where it has proved its value, before turning to the more recent applications in health care.

There are three stages in a cost-benefit analysis: (1) the listing of the costs and benefits to be taken into account; (2) their evaluation, in money terms if possible, so that there is a common measuring rod; and (3) their conversion, if necessary, into a form which compares like with like and facilitates decision-making. At each stage difficulties may arise.

Ideally all costs and all benefits should be taken into account, but in practice this is impossible, and the investigator determines what to include partly on the basis of his own judgment about what is important, partly on the basis of the data available. Thus, for example, the M1 study, whilst it took into account the effect of the motorway on the traffic of other roads, did not consider the effect on rail traffic. Inevitably in a cost-benefit analysis there is an element of subjectivity and arbitrariness about which costs and which benefits are considered.

At the second stage a number of difficulties arise. One of the benefits of road investment is a reduction in accidents and the saving of human lives; but how does one value a human life? To some, the very idea of putting a monetary value on life is repugnant; but it sometimes has to be done by a judge awarding accident damages. Furthermore, people such as divers and steeplejacks do implicitly put a value on their lives in so far as they accept increased risks in return for higher monetary and other rewards. One way of putting a value on life, recognized as imperfect but currently used by the Ministry of Transport in traffic studies, is to calculate the present value of the expected future earnings of the deceased. The same kind of problem arises with someone maimed but not killed. Another difficulty is the value to be placed on time. Working time saved by transport improvements can reasonably be valued at the appropriate wage-rate, but leisure time has no such clear-cut value. Most people would argue that it has a positive value but less than the wage-rate; but precisely what value is ascribed to it may be crucial. In the Victoria Line study a large part of the benefit consisted of the saving of leisure time and the value given to that time determined whether the Victoria Line should or should not be regarded as an economic proposition. A further difficulty is the valuation of intangibles: we may be able to put an acceptable figure on loss of earnings from death or handicap caused by accidents, but we cannot hope to do anything more than list the fact of personal grief and sorrow they cause. A slightly less difficult intangible is the value of amenity considerations—affected by pollution of various kinds, eyesores, noise or air pollution. Such amenity considerations were the vital issues in the study of alternative sites for a third London airport.

Finally, at the third stage, the main problem is that some costs and benefits extend well into the future: a bridge, for example, will require maintenance throughout its life but, if maintained, will provide benefits over a very long period. Usually an arbitrary cut-off point in the future has to be taken; then the benefit and costs to that date are reduced to present values by the kind of discounting methods used in rate of return analysis.

Finally, there is the overall consideration that acquiring the necessary information and undertaking the study is not itself costless; in some cases the costs of undertaking a sufficiently accurate cost-benefit analysis to be decisive will be too large for the exercise to be worthwhile.

In considering cost-benefit analysis in health care, we shall start by looking at the range of applications, indicate how the same kind of problems arise as in transport studies and finally proceed to examine two case studies which demonstrate both the success and the limitations of cost-benefit analysis in health services.

Range of Applications in Health Care

Jennifer A. Roberts in her survey of applications of cost-benefit analysis to the alternative use of resources in health care[1] distinguished three categories: alternative types of care, alternative places of care, and alternative times of care. The distinctions are not absolute—for example, alternative types of care necessitate alternative places of care—but they provide a convenient expository framework.

Studies of alternative types of care include American analyses of the alternative ways of caring for the mentally ill by institutional treatment or by new intensive therapies; a study of the alternatives of renal dialysis and renal transplantation for kidney failure; and a recent British study of alternative ways of treating varicose veins, which we examine as one of our case studies.

Cost-benefit analyses of alternative places of care include work

[1] *Ibid.*

on the evaluation of home and hospital care; the costs of different regimes for maternity care; the costs of caring for elderly persons with various degrees of disability, either in their own homes with supplementary services or in residential accommodation; the efficiency of different sizes of residential homes;[1] and the relative costs and benefits of small outpatient country clinics as compared with large urban clinics.

With alternative times of care we are in the realm of preventive medicine including both primary prevention concerned—as with vaccination programmes—to prevent or lower the risk, and secondary prevention where the object is early detection and treatment and where predominantly we are concerned with evaluation of screening procedures, such as mass radiography. A recent British example of secondary prevention is a study on screening to prevent the birth of infants with Down's syndrome (mongolism).[2] Our second case study, on birth control, could be thought of as coming into the primary prevention category.

From the studies briefly reviewed it is clear that all the problems of the transport studies emerge. To give some examples. In deciding what costs and benefits to include it is rarely possible to take account of benefits to medical technology which may result from one form of treatment rather than another. The value of life may figure crucially in choice between alternative methods of treatment if each is associated with somewhat different chances of mortality. The value of leisure time is important in many of the studies, for example the time taken to travel to clinics; and, in comparisons between domiciliary and institutional costs, the valuation of the time of 'voluntary' nursing is important. Intangibles are many: the different degrees of pain, discomfort, convenience or anxiety to the patient from different forms or places of treatment; the possible dehumanizing effects of large institutions which may be economical to run. Studies concerned with treatment at different times raise acutely the need to discount future costs and benefits to present

[1] Both the comparison of domiciliary and residential care and the economics of different sizes of residential institutions are considered in a recent British study, R. Wager, *Care of the Elderly*, Institute of Municipal Treasurers and Accountants, 1972.

[2] Spencer Hagard and Felicity A. Carter, 'Preventing the birth of infants with Down's syndrome: a cost-benefit analysis', *British Medical Journal*, 27 March 1976; see also N. Glass, 'Economic aspects of the prevention of Down's syndrome (mongolism)', from N. T. J. Bailey and M. Thompson (eds.), *Systems Aspects of Health Planning*, North Holland Publishing Company, 1975.

values. Another problem, which arises more in health than in transport studies, is an accurate assessment of costs: health studies are generally based on the costs of a particular hospital, clinic or institution; but that may or may not be efficient. Valid comparisons between alternative methods or places of treatment require that each should be as efficient as possible for that kind of place or method. Finally, more than in transport studies, cost-benefit studies in health care raise ethical considerations, e.g. applying the conclusions from the study on Down's syndrome would require a programme of voluntary abortion.

At best cost-benefit studies in health care can lead to clear-cut conclusions of considerable help to policy-makers; at worst they can seriously mislead if their limitations are not understood and they are not carefully presented and interpreted. The two case studies which follow show in more detail the methods of the cost-benefit analyst. The first is relatively straightforward; the benefit from one method of treatment rather than another is clear-cut. The second shows the application of the technique in a more dubious way in a more doubtful area.

The Alternative Treatment of Varicose Veins[1]

The study compares the costs and benefits of alternative treatments of varicose veins by (1) surgery requiring a stay in hospital and (2) injection-compression sclerotherapy, requiring out-patient attendances.

In the experiment some 200 patients were divided randomly into two approximately equal groups similar in all relevant respects, e.g. height, weight, age and sex, save that of the treatment given. As, on the basis of a three-year follow-up, there was no significant difference in the results of the two methods of treatment, the comparison resolved itself into one of costs.

For neither form of treatment was it considered possible to estimate the capital costs, though it was clear that the capital costs of the facilities utilized for in-patient surgical treatment would have been higher than for the out-patient injection-compression treatment. The cost comparison therefore took account of (1) the running costs of the alternative forms of treatment and (2) the time

[1] D. Piachaud and J. M. Weddell, 'The economics of treating varicose veins', *International Journal of Epidemiology*, 3, 1, 1972

costs to the patient. The comparative running costs of the methods are set out in Table 13.2:

The average stay of a varicose veins patient in hospital was 3.7 days. The average number of clinic attendances per patient for the injection-compression treatment was 7.3.

Table 13.2 Average Cost per Patient of Alternative Treatments for Varicose Veins, 1967–68.

Injection-compression		Surgical	
	£		£
Medical staff	2.88	Medical staff	2.02
Nursing staff	1.12	Nursing staff	2.02
Secretarial staff and			
medical records	1.04	Medical records	2.76
Cost of rooms	0.03	Operating theatre	13.71
Materials for treatment	4.70	Pathology	1.19
		X-rays	5.80
		Drugs and pharmacy	0.26
		Dressings	1.08
		'Shared' costs*	15.38
Total	£9.77	*Total*	£44.22

* Covers domestic staff, catering, heat and light, maintenance, etc.

The mean number of days taken off work at the time of treatment and for convalescence was 6.4 for those treated by injection-compression and 31.3 for those treated surgically. The corresponding average losses in earnings for those in full-time employment was £29 and £118. No attempt was made to calculate in money terms the value of the time lost for those not in full-time employment but it was calculated that, allowing two hours for travelling time, the injection-compression treatment took a maximum of 30 hours of patient's time compared with 100 hours taken up in surgery.

It was further calculated that if the surgery had been conducted in a cottage hospital instead of a large general hospital, whilst the in-patient costs would have been lower, they would still have substantially exceeded the costs of the out-patient injection-compression treatment.

The study concludes: 'It is clear that injection-compression treatment involves substantially lower costs to the community than surgical treatment.' A comment in the *British Medical Journal* whilst pointing out that there would still be special cases where surgical treatment was advisable, recorded that 'Since the 1966 figures for bed-occupancy by patients undergoing treatment for varicose veins was 32.6 beds occupied daily per million of population in the UK, and since this exceeded the provision needed for treatment of appendicitis, the scope for economy is substantial.'[1]

Costs and Benefits of Family Planning[2]

The author of this study, W. A. Laing, approaches his subject from the point of view of investment by local authorities in family planning services. He argues that if family planning services are not readily available, not only is there likely to be much human suffering, but also very substantial expenditure by public authorities. The essence of the argument is that 'unwanted' children make demands on the health and welfare services over and above those made by the average child. He claims that research suggests that a large percentage of later children in families of four or more are unwanted, and the same is true of illegitimate children. He then points to evidence that these children will generate very significantly greater demands than average in four sectors of the health and welfare services: (1) supplementary benefits, (2) child care

Table 13.3   Costs of Preventing Unwanted Children Compared with Benefits.

	Costs per unwanted child prevented per year (1971–72 figures)	Benefits per unwanted child prevented in 1971–72*	Benefit/cost ratio
	£	£	
Illegitimate child	34	4346	128:1
4th child	34	675	20:1
5th child	34	755	22:1

* i.e. the expected cost of excess usage of health and welfare resources by the unwanted child. Sums saved in future years are discounted back to 1971–72 present value.

[1] 'Economics of varicose veins', *British Medical Journal*, 16 June 1973.
[2] W. A. Laing, *The Costs and Benefits of Family Planning*, P.E.P., 1972.

services, (3) sickness benefits and (4) temporary accommodation for the homeless. Table 13.3 reproduces his summary findings.

The author concludes,

> It is quite clear from this table that the benefit of family planning to public funds alone is very high indeed, without taking into consideration the social and personal benefits to the individuals and families themselves. Although the figures in themselves can only be estimates, they reflect certain hard facts: that about one-half of unmarried women with children depend on supplementary benefits; and that the child from a home which has never been complete or which has been broken by divorce, separation or death can be expected to use nine times as much in child care resources as the average child.

Within the confines he has prescribed for himself Mr Laing's figures rest on some heroic assumptions. Should one really treat fourth and fifth children as 'unwanted'? Surely many children, perhaps unwanted on arrival, will become wanted when they make their own place in the family. Mr Laing never satisfactorily explains why he has assumed that the child goes on making 'excess' demands on the health and child care services for some eighteen years of dependency, even though for most of that time it will have ceased to be a fourth or fifth child because its elder brothers and sisters will have moved into adulthood. Does the high supplementary benefit expenditure on fourth and fifth children reflect anything other than poor family allowances and the need for more child support in our social security system for wanted and unwanted children? Having assumed a rise of (for example) 13 per cent per annum in current terms in supplementary benefit provision in the future, is it reasonable to take a rate of discount of only 8 per cent to get present values? And what of the costs of preventing the unwanted child? The figure of £34 is based on a £4.85 charge made by the Family Planning Association for one year's non-domiciliary service including medical examination, advice and the supply of contraceptive substances and appliances; this figure is then multiplied by seven on the assumption that the effect of the service is to prevent one birth in seven years—so the cost of preventing an unwanted birth in one particular year is seven times the annual cost. Not only is the assumption, resting on tenuous evidence, very arbitrary but we are never told how the sum of £4.85 is derived. Is it the economic cost of the service or is it a subsidized figure—subsidized by donations to the FPA and by voluntary labour, which nonetheless has a positive opportunity cost?

Even more serious objections can be made to the narrowness of the framework which Mr Laing has chosen for himself. On at least two quite different grounds it can be argued that this is a cost-benefit study of Hamlet without the Prince of Denmark. A full cost-benefit study would have faced up to issues which Mr Laing largely ignores.

On Mr Laing's figures it is the illegitimate child whose excess demands on the health and welfare services are most heavy—six times those of other unwanted children. Now it can be hypothesized and is certainly believed by some persons that the growth of FPA services and Brook Advisory Clinics, *in so far as they are directed towards the unmarried* as they must be if they are to achieve the prevention of illegitimate children, have helped to create illegitimacy, since they have contributed to a loosening of sexual morality in the community with their implied assumption of the acceptability, even normality, of sexual relationships outside marriage. This hypothesis is certainly compatible with the statistical evidence. Whilst the activity of the FPA and the Brook Clinics has grown and been directed increasingly towards the unmarried over the years, so the illegitimacy rate has grown too from 5 per cent of all live births in 1951 to 6 per cent in 1961, to 8 per cent in 1971 and (provisionally) to 9 per cent in 1974.[1] Abortions have also increased, totalling nearly 120,000 in 1973, well over half of which occurred to the unmarried.[2] If, indeed, the activities of the FPA have contributed to the social climate of opinion from which the illegitimate births and the abortions have sprung, then all Mr Laing's arguments can be turned on their head!

Another comprehensible approach in this delicate area would be to say, 'A plague on all your figures'. On personal welfare grounds, unwanted children should be prevented if this can be done by encouraging contraception; the dubious calculations of economic benefit are a misleading irrelevance. Indeed, it can be pointed out that if the items Mr Laing takes into account are the only, or even the most important, then, on parallel arguments, there is an overwhelming cost-benefit case for exterminating all retired persons! The benefit/cost ratio would be very high. Euthanasia would cost little

[1] *Social Trends*, No. 6, 1975, Table 1.7.
[2] *Ibid.*, Table 1.10.

and these people make heavy above-average demands on the health and welfare services not to mention their claims on pensions and supplementary benefits.

Mr Laing has written a controversial pamphlet and the reader must judge for himself whether, within its own terms of reference, it is a help or a hindrance to public policy-making.

Health Producing and Wealth Producing?

In a famous dictum, the Guillebaud Committee[1] described NHS expenditure as 'Wealth-producing as well as health-producing'. The Committee was using 'wealth' in its loose rather than its more specific economic sense; 'income'-producing would have described more accurately what they had in mind, but 'income' would have destroyed the assonance and hence the impact of their phrase! The point at issue, however, is how far does health expenditure generate income? How important is the investment benefit of health expenditure as compared with the consumption benefit?

We can distinguish three ways in which health expenditure might be income-generating: by increasing the rate of economic growth; by reducing hours of work lost through sickness; and by increasing the fitness of workers whilst at work.

Despite the doubts cast upon the medical evidence,[2] it is fairly clear that, to some extent in the eighteenth century and throughout the nineteenth century, expenditure on health reduced mortality rates and this in turn promoted economic growth; reductions in mortality, especially the big reductions in infant mortality, swelled the size of the working population. Today the position is very different. In Chapter 7 we saw how the expectation of life had risen, for example, from 40 in 1851 to 69 in 1971 for males at birth. In the latter year 19 per cent of the population of Great Britain was over 60 compared with around 7 per cent during the nineteenth century. The change was summed up by the Royal Commission on Population in 1949: 'Most of the wastage of human life has now been cut out. Only among the old could further reduction in mortality have really considerable effects on numbers.' Because of past success in reducing death rates there is now a large and growing proportion of the elderly in the population who make increasing demands on the health and welfare services. In the absence of an increase in

[1] *Report of the Committee of Enquiry into the Cost of the National Health Service* (under the Chairmanship of Mr C. W. Guillebaud), 1956, Cmnd. 9663.

[2] See Chapter 7, p. 94.

retirement ages none of the benefit of additional expenditure on the old can be regarded as income-creating.

There are no reliable figures of hours of work lost through sickness, but in 1971 it was estimated that there were some 300 million days of certified absences from work of those entitled to claim national insurance benefits.[1] Whilst this figure appears to offer some scope for increasing the effective labour force by health expenditure, in fact the trend has tended to be upwards despite increased NHS expenditure. It is doubtful if much can be gained from this source.

As to the third aspect, whilst there may be many workers in the Third World whose productivity is seriously reduced by debilitating disease, it is very doubtful if much increase in productivity can be gained by health expenditures which, in some sense, increase the fitness of the British worker.

In British society a century ago and in other societies today, it may well be true that health expenditure is 'wealth-producing', but in British society today health expenditure is predominantly consumption expenditure, mostly for the benefit of the elderly. This does not mean that we should not expand health spending; nor does it mean that there may not be some particular health programme which could find its justification wholly or partly in terms of investment benefit. It does mean that the case for any general expansion of health care must rest on other grounds than its effect on future income.

SUMMARY AND CONCLUSIONS

Public expenditure on the NHS as a proportion of GNP grew by over 60 per cent in the twenty years from 1956, and growth in real terms is likely to continue for demographic reasons. Some health expenditures, notably those on infectious and contagious diseases, have beneficial externality effects; other forms of health spending yield only private benefits. Such benefits may be consumption or investment or both, but, taken as a whole, additional spending on the NHS is likely to yield predominantly consumption benefits; the investment potential of health spending in the United Kingdom is largely exhausted. Cost-benefit studies in Britain have been applied

[1] 'Sickness Absence', *Information Sheet No. 26*, April 1975, Office of Health Economics.

to alternative forms, places and times of health care. Such studies raise the same kind of problems as in transport, often in a more acute form and sometimes with the added complication of moral judgments; their value to the policy-maker varies widely.

14 Housing

Complexity and Confusion

No aspect of social policy is more complex or confusing than housing policy. The complexity springs partly from the wide ramifications of housing. Housing is an 'essential' on which most households spend a substantial proportion of their income. It is quantitatively the most important form of personal investment and a very important national investment. Housing is inter-related with monetary policy because of the sensitivity of housing costs to changes in interest rates. Housing policy is confusing because of the variety of housing tenures and the legal complexities of tenants' and landlords' rights. New housing raises issues of planning controls, development gains and the taxation of such gains, and community ownership of land. There are complexities associated with housing standards which raise questions about time preference, e.g. should standards be lowered to meet immediate needs more quickly at the cost of heavier future expenditure on up-grading? Not least confusing is the variety of the financial support for housing.

Another feature of housing which complicates policy-making is the part which non-economic factors play in conditioning the attitudes of citizens and politicians. Housing seems to arouse irrational emotions. It is only a slight exaggeration to say that some people see the private landlord as a greedy anachronism whose interests can be disregarded; that others regard living in a municipal housing estate as a form of serfdom; and that many see virtues in home ownership of a metaphysical kind. Such attitudes do not beget clear thinking or rational policy.

Finally one cannot study the present housing situation without knowing something about housing history. Whilst this is true of all the subjects of social policy, it is perhaps particularly true of housing because of the longevity of the product—a house. Housing has been much affected by population growth and movement and the deprivations and devastations of wars. Moreoever, policies have varied over the years and have sometimes even been reversed by successive governments. Whilst most government measures have been well-intentioned, changes in housing policy have sometimes been prompted by sheer expediency and far too often dominated by short-term considerations.

In one chapter we cannot hope to thread our way through the whole of this jungle. We must be selective. We shall attempt, first, to indicate the extent and range of government support for housing, direct and indirect; then analyse the economic characteristics of housing and proceed to relate them to the 'mainstream' of housing policy, indicating the main consequences of that policy; in so doing we shall incorporate the minimum of historical background necessary for understanding and, even at the risk of over-simplification, concentrate on economic principles rather than on legislative details, for the principles will remain valid when the legislation has changed. By this means we would hope to raise some of the crucial questions which must be answered if a more rational housing policy is to prevail in the future. We shall have to ignore, wholly or partly, a number of important aspects of housing policy: standards, planning controls, ownership of development land and new forms of ownership or co-ownership such as housing associations.

Public 'Subsidies' for Housing

We were able to present fairly comprehensive figures of the support from public funds for education and health services and the proportion of GNP devoted to these services. We can provide no such comprehensive figures for housing. There are, of course, a number of statistics of housing expenditure of various kinds, including figures of public investment in housing and public sector loans for house purchases, but the available figures do not tell us anything like all we want to know. We should like to know the annual cost of housing policies to the public sector ignoring self-financing expenditure. For example, if a local authority borrows money to build council houses which it lets at an economic rent[1] we would not wish to include that as a cost to the public sector, for government would simply be acting as an agent in a self-financing enterprise; but if a lower rent was charged, the difference being made good from public funds, we would wish to know the annual cost of this subsidy. Moreover,

[1] We can define an economic rent as a rent sufficiently high to enable the interest and the capital of the loan to be repaid over the life of the house, and to meet maintenance and management costs.

besides explicit subsidies, we want to know the costs of implicit subsidies in the form of revenue foregone in tax concessions, or in other ways, as a result of housing policies. It is convenient to distinguish three categories of 'subsidy' in this wider sense: (1) explicit subsidies for council houses and other purposes; (2) tax concessions to the owner-occupier; (3) a group of more complex revenue losses resulting from housing policy.

The official figures of housing subsidies, by central and local authority, which constitute a continuous series in the National Income and Expenditure Blue Books, amounted to £1051 million in 1975, representing 1.12 per cent of GNP. In 1956 the figure had been 0.57, and it did not rise much above that level until 1974 when it jumped to 0.99 per cent from 0.60 per cent the previous year. This big rise was primarily a product of the Labour Government's rent freeze, for which it had to compensate local authorities. The Public Expenditure White Paper of February 1976[1] provides further details of explicit government subsidies to housing. In the year 1975–76, measured in 1975 price levels, subsidies for local authority housing were expected to be £1329 million. The 'option mortgage scheme' by which the government subsidizes the interest paid on mortgages by owner-occupiers who do not claim the income tax concession was estimated to cost £99 million. Grants to housing associations were set at £120 million. Improvement grants, to modernize old housing, were estimated at £86 million for private sector housing and £389 million for local authorities. Thus the explicit subsidies to housing, largely but not wholly for council housing, were expected to amount to over £2000 million in 1975–76.

We can identify three tax concessions to an owner-occupier. Firstly, since 1963, the practice has ceased of imputing an income to his house, equivalent to a rent; secondly, although interest payments on private loans are not generally allowed against income tax, he has been allowed to deduct from taxable income the interest payments on his mortgage; thirdly, the owner-occupier has been exempt from capital gains tax on the sale (or gift) of his house, provided that it was his principal private residence. We shall examine the nature of these concessions more fully in the final section of this chapter; here we are primarily concerned with the value in terms of revenue forgone. We can only make very rough estimates. On the basis of the figures of imputed income in the national income and output estimates, and assuming all such income paid tax at basic rate, the

[1] *Public Expenditure to 1979–80*, February 1976, Cmnd. 6393.

revenue forgone could be around £1000 million in 1975—and if anything these imputed rental figures based on rateable values are likely to err on the underside. On the value of the mortgage interest concession we can be more definite; official figures (given in answer to parliamentary questions) were £700 million in 1974–75 and £865 million in 1975–76. Finally, with the capital gains tax, a figure of around £1500 million might be a reasonable 'guestimate' for 1975–76.[1] Apart from the speculative nature of two of the estimates, a further caveat about these figures should be entered. It is invalid to add them together to get a total value of the tax concessions to owner-occupiers for two reasons. Firstly, if an imputed rent were attributed to owner-occupied property, as we shall see later in the chapter, there would be a good case for continuing the mortgage interest concession. Secondly, if an imputed rent had been charged to income tax or the mortgage interest concession had not existed or been withdrawn, the rise in house prices would have been less and hence the loss of revenue from capital gains tax would have been less.

Finally, there is the third group of more complex losses to the public revenue arising from housing policy. The most important of these is the loss of tax income from private landlords. As we shall see, the rental income received by private landlords of unfurnished property is less than they would receive in the absence of government controls on rents. Whilst most of the loss is incurred by the landlords themselves, part is incurred by the government which loses the income tax revenue which would have been paid on the higher income.[2] In two other ways, also, there may be small elements of subsidy for housing. Building societies pay to the Revenue authorities a composite sum in lieu of income tax on behalf of their depositors, which is at a somewhat preferential rate; in effect, this helps to keep down the rate of interest to borrowers and thus is a further subsidy, if a very small one, to owner-occupiers buying through building societies. A further possible element of subsidy may enter into the charges which borrowers from local authorities pay for home loans. It is simply not possible to put realistic figures on these items.

As to the immediate future, although it is intended that there shall

[1] Assuming all the increase in the value of owner-occupied houses in that period had been liable to tax at half the basic rate of income tax (the lowest rate of tax chargeable on capital gains).

[2] Since the introduction of rent allowances (see below) there is a partial offset in that, without this implicit subsidization of private tenants by means of rent control, the cost of rent-allowances to public funds would have been higher.

be some decline in the next few years in the proportion of the rent of council tenants met from subsidy, the White Paper on Public Expenditure envisages some expansion in explicit subsidies in real terms. With high interest rates and rising owner-occupancy, 'expenditure' on tax concessions is also likely to rise, being only partly offset by a diminished loss of revenue from further decline in the private rented sector.

It is not possible to give an accurate figure for the total subsidization of housing, in the widest sense. But we are talking about the same order of magnitude as expenditure on the NHS, probably upwards of £5000 million in 1975 prices. To set against this, we must record that some £1300 million was raised in local rates on domestic property in 1974–75 and some £1800 million was expected in 1975–76.

Characteristics of Housing

Externalities

As with education and health, so it is argued that expenditure on housing generates social benefits over and above private benefits. The main kinds of benefit alleged are negative, arising from the removal of bad housing, with beneficial externality effects on public health and on crime, especially juvenile delinquency. The argument is not wholly convincing. It is difficult to separate out the effects of poverty from the effects of housing. In so far as the argument is valid it would seem to constitute a case for, say, state subsidization of slum clearance programmes rather than more general support for housing throughout the community. But even here we must be careful. Crime has been at least as prevalent in some new housing estates as in the slums they replaced; and often the environmental influences on juvenile delinquency are subtle, relating more to the nature of the new buildings and the communal provisions than to the amount of expenditure on them.

There are also external benefits of a more positive kind. Expenditure by an individual householder to improve his property helps to raise the quality of the whole neighbourhood and the value of *all* the houses in it. Some would also hold that there is a widespread, if vaguely formulated, view that everyone ought to have a minimum housing provision; and if such provision is ensured to all, there is an externality consumption benefit—we all feel better as a result.

Others would disagree and maintain instead that this external consumption benefit properly related to a minimum *income* provision which provided the opportunity for all households to enjoy certain minimum standards not only of housing but of food, clothing, warmth etc; and that to single out housing confuses rather than clarifies the issue.

The Nature of the Product

Housing has a number of important characteristics which need to be borne in mind in reviewing and formulating housing policy. Like food and clothing some sort of shelter is an essential of life, moreover one on which most families spend a significant proportion of their income. Consequently, in terms of demand analysis, a change in the annual costs of housing may have a significant income effect as well as a substitution effect. A poor tenant could suffer a severe cut in living standards as a result of a 20 per cent rise in rents. A potential house purchaser might have to abandon or postpone his objective and move to inferior rented accommodation as a result of a per cent rise in building society interest rates. The annual costs of housing are particularly sensitive to changes in interest rates, though their effect on rent-controlled private accommodation or subsidized council houses is likely to be cushioned.

Another obvious, but very important characteristic of a house[1] is that it lasts a very long time. The existing stock of houses is therefore very large in relation to the annual supply of new houses. Currently the total stock of dwellings of all kinds in the United Kingdom is just over 20 million; the number of new dwellings per annum has averaged under 300,000 in recent years, less than 1.5 per cent of the stock; allowing for slum clearance and other losses the net gain in housing stock has been between 200,000 and 250,000 per annum during the past five years. It is clear that even a big increase in supply in any one year, say 50,000 houses, would have a very small effect on the total stock, only 0.25 per cent. Such an increase would be very considerable because houses take quite a long time to build, especially if we include in the construction time the acquisition of the land and construction of the amenities, like roads and drainage, required on most developments. As a result of these characteristics housing is said by the economist to be in very inelastic supply— in the short run almost completely inelastic and considerably

[1] The term 'house' will be used as a convenient shorthand to include 'flat'.

inelastic even over a long period. A rise in price will therefore not call forth much increase in housing supply. Consequently, the price of houses and house-room in a free market, is much affected by changes in demand. If demand increases price will rise considerably; if demand were to undergo a continued fall, house prices could drop very substantially.

The volatility of house prices in response to changes in demand links with two other features of the market for house purchase. A house is the most important type of durable-use consumers' good. With the possible exception of the value of pension rights it is the most important form of personal wealth. The value of a house is normally a multiple of, at the least, twice the annual income of its occupier. Few people who contemplate buying a house can do so without borrowing much or most of the purchase price. It follows that the ease with which funds are available for house purchase influences the demand for housing which in turn affects the price significantly. If building society funds dry up then house prices will falter or fall; if funds are plentiful, house prices may boom.

Because a house has a degree of permanence and the land on which, and within which, it stands has even more permanence, it is the kind of asset people turn to for security in times of high inflation. If paper assets lose their value, at the end of the inflation the bricks, the mortar and the land will still be there. In inflationary times there is thus a tendency for house prices to rise more rapidly than prices in general.

Finally, a house is characterized by immobility. Most forms of house cannot readily be transported from one place to another. Taken in conjunction with the long life and inelastic supply it means that housing prices may differ very much from one part of the country to another. In the absence of mobility of houses differences in house prices vary between localities with changes in the mobility of people. If travelling becomes cheaper, quicker and easier, people can more readily travel longer distances to work and the differences in house prices between localities are reduced; if the converse happens to personal travel, the differences are increased.

Whilst all that we have said is true and very important, there are ways in which the supply of housing can respond to variations in price: the total stock of buildings may be more or less fixed but the utilization can vary. For example if house prices and rents rise, a family living in a large house might decide it would be worthwhile converting part of their house into a flat and selling or letting it

Conversely, if housing is cheap they might prefer to retain the extra room for themselves; and with cheap housing some families will more readily go in for second houses in the country or at the seaside. Moreover the 'housing market' is not monolithic, but really consists of a number of overlapping markets. Because of the immobility of housing there are regional markets. There are also markets for different sizes of houses: to take an extreme example, the man with a large family has housing needs very different from those of the retired married couple or spinster. In particular, because of the way housing policy has developed in this country we need to think in terms of three sectors corresponding to different tenure systems: the owner-occupied sector in which houses are bought and sold; the council house sector of tenanted accommodation; and the private rented sector which in turn divides into the furnished and the unfurnished.

Housing Policy and its Consequences

The background to a consideration of housing policy in the United Kingdom is what has happened to the relative sizes of these sectors. Table 14.1 summarizes the information. In 1914 the total stock of dwellings for Great Britain was estimated at 8.5 million; at the end of 1974 the estimate for the United Kingdom was just over 20 million dwellings.

This fundamental change which has taken place in the balance of tenures has been largely the outcome, part intentional part un-

Figure 14.1 Stock of Dwellings by Tenure (per cent).

	Owner-occupied	Rented from private owners*	Rented from local authorities**
1914 (GB)	10	90	negligible
1950 (UK) (end)	29	53	18
1974 (UK) (end)	52	17	3J

* Includes 'other tenures', e.g. occupied by virtue of employment; rented from housing associations.
** Includes new town corporations.
Sources: M. E. H. Smith, *A Guide to Housing*, Housing Centre Trust, 1971; *Social Trends*, No. 6, 1975, C.S.O., HMSO, 1976.

intentional, of the policies of successive governments. For most of the period there has been a sufficient degree of common ground between the parties for it to be possible to identify the main strands of policy whichever of the two major parties has been in power. But there are differences in emphasis: the Conservatives are particularly tender to the owner-occupier and have more sympathy for the private landlord than Labour, which is especially favourable to council tenants. Recent years have possibly shown more divergence between the parties than formerly. At the time of writing the government is awaiting the report of a Committee set up to review housing finance.

Features of Housing Policy

The main elements of current housing policy, as they have developed over the years, can be listed as follows:

1. *Subsidization of council housing*. From the end of the 1914–18 War the building of council houses (permissible from 1851) has been encouraged by a wide range of subsidy schemes, some relating to special needs such as rural housing or slum clearance, and others of a more general nature. As well as Exchequer subsidies, local authorities have been able to subsidize council housing from the rates. Until the Housing Finance Act of 1972, local authorities were left free to use the subsidies as they thought fit; rents differed for similar houses as between councils not only because the average level of rent was higher in one locality than another, but because of different ways in which the subsidies were applied. Before that Act, 90 per cent of the subsidies was used to reduce the general level of rents regardless of the needs of tenants and only 10 per cent was used to grant rebates to poor tenants. The Act provided for the introduction of rent rebates (see below) and also sought to remove the discretion from local authorities on rent policies and gradually move all rents to the 'fair rent' level which applied to private tenants. But the latter provisions were repealed by the incoming Labour administration in 1974. Both the Conservatives (in 1973) and Labour (in 1974) froze council rents as part of counter-inflation policies, thus increasing the element of subsidy. The Public Expenditure White Paper records that in 1976–77 'The percentage of costs borne by rents, after rebates, will stay at about 43 per cent. Thereafter it is assumed

that the percentage will rise so as to exceed 50 per cent by the end of the period,'[1] i.e. by 1980.

2. *Tax concessions to owner-occupiers.* For part of the inter-war period grants were available for small houses built by private enterprise, many of which were purchased by owner-occupiers. The big boom in private housebuilding in the later 1930s, however, owed nothing to direct subsidy but resulted from low building costs and low interest rates. Subsequently, benefits to owner-occupiers have mainly taken the form of tax concessions, though owner-occupation was also encouraged by a provision in a 1959 housing act by which the government lent money to approved building societies which advanced additional funds for the purchase of older, cheaper houses.

The tax concessions to owner-occupiers have gradually built up over the years. From the earliest days of the income tax until 1963, tax was charged on the annual value of houses whether they were let or owner-occupied. The annual value was fixed at intervals and was supposed to reflect the rent at which the house could have been let, with a deduction allowed for repairs. In practice the valuations lagged well behind an economic rent and hence an element of subsidy crept in. In 1963, partly because of the complications of the procedures for claiming repairs and maintenance which generated inequities and partly to encourage home ownership, the charge on owner-occupiers was abolished by Conservative Chancellor Mr Selwyn Lloyd.

The next concession to owner-occupiers came with the capital gains tax introduced by Labour Chancellor, Mr James Callaghan, in 1965; a taxpayer's principal private residence was exempted from the charge.

In 1974, when Labour Chancellor Mr Denis Healey introduced the provision that interest paid on private (as distinct from business) loans should not qualify for relief from income tax, loans to acquire or improve a principal place of residence were specifically excluded; they continued to rank for tax relief.

Meanwhile, to provide a benefit to home-buyers whose income was too low to enable them to get the full benefit from the income tax relief at standard or basic rate, an 'option mortgage scheme' was introduced (from 1968) by which they could choose a lower rate of interest, as an alternative to the tax concession, with the government making up the difference to the building societies.

One small move to curb the benefits to owner-occupiers has been

[1] *Public Expenditure to 1979–80*, Cmnd. 6393, February 1976, p. 68.

made by the Chancellor, Mr Denis Healey. The deductibility of interest payments for new mortgages for owner-occupiers has, since 1974, been limited to the principal (or only) private residence and to an amount of £25,000.

It is not possible to say, in the same precise way as with subsidies to council houses, the extent to which owner-occupation has been subsidized but it is very considerable. The basic rate taxpayer in 1976–77 has 35 per cent of his interest charge met in effect by the state and the higher rate taxpayer anything up to 98 per cent. Not only does the benefit to the individual rise as his personal rate of tax rises, but the benefit to all owner occupiers rises if income tax rates go up or if interest rates rise. The assistance is thus, to some extent, in the form of an open cheque by the government.

One other aspect of home-ownership has tended to be a matter of party dispute—the sale of council houses to their occupants. Whilst Conservatives have favoured such sales Labour has been much less sympathetic and some Labour councils positively hostile.

3. *Rent controls and tenant rights.* Whilst the cost of housing has been kept down for council house tenants by direct subsidization and for owner-occupiers largely by tax reliefs, it has been held down for private tenants by rent controls. First introduced during the First World War to try to hold the cost of living and prevent a situation of shortage resulting in big rent increases, rent controls, though abolished on some properties between the wars, have remained ever since. Some attempt was made by the Conservative Government in 1957 to ease the controls and they were made less rigid by the Labour Government's Fair Rent Act of 1965. This Act provided that rent officers should arbitrate between landlord and tenant in unfurnished private rented accommodation; in the absence of agreement, a rent assessment committee would fix a 'fair rent'. A fair rent was never defined in the Act, except to say that it must have regard to all the relevant circumstances (e.g. the age and state of repair of the property) but *not* take account of any scarcity value. Once fixed the 'fair rent' is registered and cannot normally be altered for three years.

The rents payable to private landlords of unfurnished dwellings have remained below what they would be in the open market and below what would have been necessary to give a return comparable to alternative forms of investment.

Clearly, landlords of rent-controlled property have a strong incentive to try to switch their property to the uncontrolled or less controlled sectors, i.e. either to sell it or to let it furnished. To prevent their evicting tenants or harassing tenants so that they leave, the rent control legislation has been supported by measures to give tenants security of tenure in private unfurnished rented accommodation.

Furnished property has not been subject to rent control to the same extent as unfurnished. In 1946 it became possible for a tenant of furnished property to appeal to a rent tribunal, but the furnished tenant lacked the security of tenure of the unfurnished. In 1974, following a rent freeze which included furnished tenancies, furnished property was made subject to the 'fair rent' provisions applying to unfurnished, and the same security of tenure was granted to furnished tenants, but only where the landlord was not living on the premises.

4. *Improvement grants.* Since the Second World War and especially since 1959 when standard instead of just discretionary grants were introduced for supplying certain specified basic amenities, grants have been made for improvements and, later, for conversions, provided the property had a life of more than a specified period. The cost of this attempt to make better use of the existing housing stock, is met partly by the Central Exchequer and partly by the local authority.

5. *Rent rebates and rent allowances.* The 1972 Housing Finance Act had the merit that it sought, on a consistent basis, to relate assistance towards rent to the circumstances of the tenant instead of the class of property. Subsidies to council housing were to be directed into rent rebates by all local authorities and for the first time assistance was to be given to needy tenants in the private rented sector, called rent allowances, also administered by local authorities. This attempt to apply help where it was most needed had the disadvantages of means-tested schemes which we considered in Chapter 10: the take-up is less than 100 per cent and the scheme helped to create the poverty trap. In 1975–76 £134 million was paid out in rent rebates and £27 million in rent allowances.

Consequences of the Policies

On the credit side there can be little doubt that the large majority of the population is better housed than it would have been without these policies. In so far as there are beneficial externality effects from housing they should have been amply achieved. But this result had been attained at a very high cost in resources (which could have been devoted to other purposes such as a thorough-going policy to deal with poverty), with considerable distortions, wastes and inequities and without 'solving' the housing problem. The effects, indeed, are a classic example of what an economist, from his demand and supply analysis, would expect from such price distortions for a good with the characteristics of housing. We can group the outcome under several headings.

1. *Changes in the supply of house-room in the different sectors.* Whilst it was deliberate policy to increase the supply of council houses and, especially latterly, to encourage owner-occupation, which would have grown anyway with rising incomes and wealth, both changes were accelerated by the unintended effects of rent control on what was by far the biggest sector of the housing market in the 1940s. Because of the controls, private landlords of unfurnished dwellings were faced with rents which had often fallen very heavily in real terms whilst repair costs had soared and they inevitably took what opportunities they could to move into the unrestricted areas of the market. Mainly this meant selling, sometimes to sitting tenants at a reduced price, more often when the property became vacant because tenants left or died. The converse was that, there being no unfurnished rental accommodation available for other than sitting tenants, those seeking housing were forced to buy or go on the council waiting lists. Thus owner-occupation was stimulated, willy-nilly, and councils were encouraged to build more to try to accommodate those on their lists.

To a lesser extent when their unfurnished property became vacant landlords re-let on a furnished basis.

The security given to tenants also tended to dry up the supply of unfurnished accommodation. Those with a house which they did not wish currently to occupy (perhaps because accommodation went with their job) but which they would subsequently need, dared not let it unfurnished because of the difficulty of repossession.

2. *Deterioration in the housing stock.* Rent controls tended to affect the source of supply in another way, in extreme cases to reduce it but more generally to lower its quality. Rent control left the landlord with little real income and no incentive to maintain and improve the property. Hence ensued a deterioration in the quality of the housing stock in the private rented sector. The subsequent scheme for improvement grants was a direct outcome of this result; without rent control, or if the levels of rent had been set more realistically,

much government expenditure on improvement grants would have been unnecessary.

3. *Reduced mobility of labour.* The mobility of labour of those in the unfurnished rented accommodation sectors has been, and is, much reduced. Whether they live in accommodation supplied by private landlords or by councils they enjoy a substantial subsidy; but it is a subsidy dependent on staying where they are. Exceptionally they may be able to arrange an exchange with a tenant of another council; otherwise if they leave one council house they have no guarantee of being able to get another in another district, except perhaps after a long wait on the council lists. Similarly a tenant leaving unfurnished accommodation with a controlled rent is most unlikely to find similar accommodation elsewhere. Those buying houses are not so much affected because they can buy elsewhere. But even they find a move more difficult as there is little chance of taking unfurnished accommodation to tide them over until they have had the chance of a good look round for a house that suits them. Thus labour mobility is reduced. This reduces the efficiency of the economic system: there are less applicants for jobs and hence less chance of getting the best man for any particular vacancy; and there will tend to be a higher level of unemployment because the unemployed will be less willing to move house to get a job.

4. *Under-occupation.* A result of holding down the price of housing is that people buy more of it. If anyone is offered an unfurnished house to let larger than they want, they will not turn it down when the controlled rent brings it well within their pocket. Owner-occupiers too are encouraged, especially in times of inflation when bricks and mortar seem a good investment, to buy larger or more luxurious houses than they otherwise would or to extend those they have. Thus scarce building resources are used up without increasing the supply of housing for those who need it most. At the same time there is evidence of under-occupation or over-provision in other directions. People's housing needs change. When families have grown up and departed married couples no longer need such big houses. When the old people die for whom the spinster daughter has been caring, her housing needs are reduced. But the low price of housing and the difficulties of finding a suitable alternative encourage people to stay in houses which have grown too big for them.

The General Household Survey[1] contains evidence which strongly

[1] *The General Household Survey 1973*, HMSO, 1976, Table 2.12.

suggests under-occupation in Great Britain. Thus 45 per cent of all two-person households in the 16–59 age range live in houses with at least two bedrooms more than they would normally need for personal use; the same is true of 38 per cent of two-person households where at least one of the persons is over 60; and 34 per cent of individuals aged 60 or over living on their own are in houses with at least three bedrooms.

5. *Failure to meet housing needs.* For all the resources that have been poured into housing over the past thirty years, there remains evidence of unsatisfied demand and of housing needs not met; this can be seen in the long local authority waiting lists, homelessness, the key money paid for unfurnished accommodation in the private sector and squatting. The people who have fared least well under the system are often those with most need: the floating population which is never in a local area long enough to be able to take up a local authority house; the immigrant population. These have tended to be forced into often unsuitable furnished accommodation. For others, too, the policies have made life more, not less difficult. The young couple, if they want anything other than furnished accommodation, are almost bound to have to buy. Yet the extent of assistance given to owner-occupation in general acts to their disadvantage as first-time house buyers. Because of the inelasticity of the supply, whilst the stimulation of demand for houses to buy may have had some influence in increasing the total of the housing stock over a period, it has certainly forced up the price, thus making purchase more difficult for the first-time buyer.

6. *Haphazard distribution of income.* Many people might be prepared to overlook these defects in housing policy if the effect had been to distribute real income more equitably in the community. But the redistributive effects of housing policy have been haphazard and possibly, overall, regressive rather than progressive. We saw that in the council house sector the vast bulk of subsidy has been used to lower rents irrespective of income. In the private rented sector rent control has resulted in a transfer of real income from landlord to sitting tenant. Sometimes this will have been from the better-off to the less well-off but not invariably and not systematically.[1] Within the owner-occupied sector the effect has definitely favoured the

---

[1] In the 1950s the author knew well an old retired weaver, a single person who had put her lifetime savings into four cottages to provide a retirement income. She lived in one and let the others. The controlled rents did not cover the cost of repairs. Her tenants were workers receiving an average industrial wage.

better-off. If an imputed rent had been charged to income tax those with the highest incomes and the most expensive houses would have paid at the highest rate of tax. With the concession on mortgage interest, the basic rate taxpayer at 35 per cent pays £65 net of tax for every £100 interest charge; the taxpayer with over £20,000 of taxable income, including investment income, whose tax rate is 98 per cent, pays only £2 for every £100 of interest (though subject to the limits imposed in 1974). The biggest injustice is done to the household which gets no subsidy and lives in furnished accommodation. They lose compared with those in all the other housing sectors and they will often be amongst the least well-off.

No consistent policy on income distribution is possible by manipulating benefits as between persons in different classes of tenure. The General Household Survey gives the following mean weekly incomes for head of households in different tenure systems in 1973:

	£
Owner-occupied owned outright	28
Owner-occupied with mortgage	46
Rented from local authority	24
Rented privately unfurnished	22
Rented privately furnished	27
	—
Total of all in sample	31
	—

Within each tenure group incomes spanned the whole range from the lowest category in the survey, up to £7.50, to the highest, over £80.00. To illustrate the overlap: between 48 and 56 per cent of the owner-occupiers who were outright owners, and between 7 and 13 per cent of owner-occupiers with a mortgage had incomes less than the average income of local authority householders. Although the Survey is subject to the same kind of errors and limitations as the Family Expenditure Survey (see Chapter 9) the general accuracy of the picture is not in doubt.

The Direction of Reform

In seeking to find an improved basis for housing policy, the crucial decision is how far it is desired to support expenditure on housing as such (because it is thought to have beneficial externality effects or some special merit which makes it desirable that people should buy more housing than if left to themselves) and how much the sub-sidization of housing has been thought of as a way of improving the distribution of income. As we have seen, existing policy probably does nothing to reduce inequalities in the distribution of income and no policy based on support to different tenure systems could produce any consistent pattern of income redistribution. At the same time such policies have many undesirable effects.

If agreement could be reached on the support to be given for housing as such, the way would be open to move to that level of support. If, as one would believe, it was considerably less than the present level, the degree of subsidy in all sectors of the housing market could gradually be reduced thus releasing resources for other purposes. If some of the released resources were so channelled as to benefit those losing subsidies, especially the poorest, then the rate of change could be more rapid. But, as has been stressed, changes in the cost of housing have a considerable income effect and one must make haste slowly.

Besides the reduction of the explicit and implicit subsidies and the easing of rent controls, one suggested way in which new building might be most effective in generating additional housing would be by making small purpose-built dwellings available to the elderly. Not only would this be directing resources to one of the growing sectors of the population, but it would bring about the release of accommodation too big for their needs and which they under-occupy at present. Further, as Wager points out, 'The benefit to the community's housing problem arises irrespective of whether the accommodation released is local authority or privately owned; this suggests that the optimum use of the community's housing resources is not served by the practice . . . whereby some local authorities do not consider applications for accommodation by owner-occupiers'.[1]

Should Owner-Occupiers Have Tax Concessions?

Many of the arguments relevant to answer this question have already appeared in this chapter, but it is useful to pull them together and perhaps add some further clarification as well as some suggestions.

The general and interconnected arguments for subsidizing owner-occupiers are: (1) that home ownership is an inbuilt desire of most families which should be fostered; (2) it promotes a 'property owning democracy'; (3) it encourages a wider diffusion in

[1] R. Wager, *Care of the Elderly*, I.M.T.A., 1972, p. 59.

the ownership of wealth and with it a healthy independence; (4) it helps to ensure that the national stock of housing capital is well looked after because people take more care of property they own than property they rent.

On the other side, the tax concessions granted in the United Kingdom have had unfortunate consequences: (1) they have given most benefit to the well-off; (2) they have encouraged the demand for housing by the better-off, diverting building resources from the less well-off and driving up the prices of houses and land[1]—a result particularly, of the inelasticity of housing; (3) they have discouraged building for letting as distinct from building for sale; (4) they have narrowed the income tax base which means higher tax rates to raise a given revenue; (5) in conjunction with inflation (see Chapter 15) they have helped to bring huge capital gains to existing owner-occupiers with the danger of opening up a new division in the distribution of wealth, which splits the nation in two, between those who own their own houses and those who do not.

If home ownership is to be subsidized at all, the question is how much and by what method. Many people would be happy to see some concessions for home ownership but not as much as at present, and not such as particularly to benefit the high income receivers.

A reasonable compromise would be to bring back by stages the taxation of an imputed rent but, as in many continental countries, to let the value of the rent be a cautious one calculated simply and without the reductions for repairs which complicated the previous 'Schedule A' tax; such a rental might be, say, 2 or 3 per cent of the capital value of the house. If that happened it would be reasonable to allow interest mortgage payments to be deductible (up to but not beyond the imputed rental income) as a cost of acquiring the income, as with business interest.

The other concession to owner-occupiers, exemption from capital gains tax, has something to commend it in terms of its effect on labour mobility. If capital gains tax were charged on the sale of owner-occupied houses it would discourage people from moving. A

---

[1] It is often thought that high land prices cause high house prices. The reverse is true. When a developer is seeking to buy land for a housing development he considers first how many houses he can put on the plot and how much he can sell them for: he starts with the demand for the houses. He then calculates his building costs including a minimum profit and deducts this from what he expects to get for the houses. This then sets the maximum he is prepared to pay for the land. If demand for the houses rises, so does the price of the land.

compromise might be a 'carry forward' provision by which gains tax was not paid as long as the proceeds of the sale were used to purchase another house.

The partial removal of the tax reliefs to owner-occupiers could be eased by some general tax reductions made possible by the increased revenue—concessions which would benefit all taxpayers. Such action could be expected to check the rise in housing prices. For this reason, and because of the effects on the income of owner-occupiers, a very gradual approach is desirable.

SUMMARY AND CONCLUSIONS

Subsidization of housing at the expense of the public purse takes three main forms: (1) explicit subsidies, mainly to council house tenants; (2) tax concessions to owner-occupiers; and (3) more complex and hidden costs, most notably loss of revenue from the policy of controlling rents in the unfurnished private sector. The total cannot be assessed accurately, but it could easily equal the cost of the NHS. The extent of externality effect of housing is arguable. Housing has certain distinct characteristics which bear on policy, e.g. the annual cost is an important part of household budgets; it is very inelastic in supply. Rent restriction in the private unfurnished sector of the housing market has generated owner-occupation and council house building, which have also been greatly fostered by 'subsidization'. Some unhappy consequences of United Kingdom housing policy have been a deterioration of housing stock, reduced labour mobility, under-occupancy, a failure to meet some housing needs and a haphazard, probably regressive, effect on the distribution of income. Reform of housing policy must rest on a clarification of how far we want to support housing as such and how far we seek a more even distribution of incomes; housing policy is not a suitable medium for the latter objective.

Part V

STABILIZATION AND GROWTH

Introduction to Part V

In this part of the book we examine two vital aspects of the economy as a whole: stability and growth.

By stability we mean the avoidance of excessive fluctuations in output, prices and employment with their disruptive effects on the economy and on people's lives. It was argued (in Chapter 4) that a defect of the unregulated market economy was that it was subject to instability—cyclical fluctuations in output, employment and prices. For twenty-five years after the Second World War it appeared that 'demand management' by the state had, if not eliminated fluctuations, at least kept them very largely under control. The experience of the past decade has dispelled that belief. Fluctuations in employment and prices have become much more marked in recent years and, in particular, there is an overhanging threat of price increases at such a rate as to undermine both the economic and the political systems of the mixed economies of the Western world and of the United Kingdom in particular.

Economic growth—the increase in national product—has also been the subject of attack. In the early 1960s the desirability of economic growth was taken as axiomatic. The problem was how to maximize growth. Since then the 'doomsters' have raised doubts: to them the choice is not growth or grief, but growth and grief, not just for Britain but the world. Where does the truth lie and what action, if any, should be taken?

To these vital matters we address ourselves, with the proviso that we cannot in two chapters of an introductory text do more than scratch the surface of issues of formidable breadth and complexity, about which there is much controversy and disagreement.

15 Unemployment and Inflation

Evils of Unemployment and Inflation

Unemployment was the economic scourge of the inter-war years in Britain and in the other mixed economies. The inter-war figures are not precisely comparable with current employment statistics but the broad dimensions of the problem are not in doubt. For nearly all the inter-war years unemployment in the United Kingdom exceeded 10 per cent of the insured population and at its worst was more than 20 per cent; in the peak year of 1932 there was an estimated $3\frac{3}{4}$ million unemployed. In marked contrast, from early in the Second World War to the end of the 1960s the employment record was very good with unemployment rarely rising above 2 per cent of the insured population, or some half a million persons. However, at the end of the 1960s unemployment was rising. It topped a million in 1972, fell back in 1973 only to begin a further climb. At the time of writing—the end of 1976—the rise is still continuing and has brought unemployment to a new post-war peak at 5–6 per cent, or between $1\frac{1}{4}$ and $1\frac{1}{2}$ million persons, the exact figure depending on which categories are included.

Inflation can be defined as a sustained upward pressure on prices resulting in a general rise in the price level[1] and the rate of inflation can be measured as the percentage increase in the general price level per period of time, e.g. month or year. In the inter-war years after a post-war boom and slump ending in 1922 prices were fairly steady, fluctuating inversely with the level of unemployment. In the early years of the Second World War prices were about the same level as

[1] Inflation is often defined simply as a general price rise; but, strictly speaking, the price rise is the symptom. Prices could be held down by a comprehensive system of controls, but then inflation would show itself in the form of shortages, queues, black markets, a haphazard distribution of goods and services, and particularly large price increases in whatever products were not covered by price controls, e.g. second-hand goods. This situation is often termed suppressed or repressed inflation. Its unhappy consequences are no less than those of open inflation.

in 1922. From the end of the Second World War to the late 1960s the average annual rate of inflation was just under 4 per cent. Thereafter, as with unemployment, the position worsened. From mid-1970 to mid-1971 the general price level rose about 10 per cent. At the time of the General Election of February 1974 inflation was running at an annual rate of about 12 per cent, having fallen somewhat in between. From mid-1974 to mid-1975 prices in general rose over 25 per cent, to fall somewhat thereafter. In the autumn of 1976 the general price level was about 15 per cent higher than a year before. Thus in 1976 both unemployment and inflation were serious problems.

The relevance of unemployment to the subject matter of social economics hardly needs to be stressed; its evils are well understood. When people lose their jobs they and their families may be pushed down to the poverty line (or, conceivably, below it). A person becoming unemployed in Britain in 1976 moves from a wage or salary to unemployment pay and later, if the unemployment lasts so long that their entitlement to unemployment benefit expires, they become dependent on supplementary benefit. But it is not only the individual unemployed and their families who lose by their unemployment. The standard of living of the whole community is to some extent reduced. Unemployment means that labour resources are not being productively used. This loss to the community is reflected not only in the lower living standards of the unemployed, but in the contribution the rest of the community makes through public funds for their support and in the reduced tax contribution to public funds by the unemployed. Long-term unemployment has further consequences. The unemployed may feel a sense of failure and despair. They may feel that they are being stigmatized as layabouts. Long-term unemployment can sap morale and the will to work and undermine skills; and, perhaps especially amongst the younger, the enforced idleness may breed crime.

The evils of inflation are different—more insidious, less widely appreciated but not less serious than those of unemployment. Even a mild rate of inflation, like the 3 or 4 per cent annual average of the twenty-five years following the Second World War in Britain, if unanticipated, will bring about a redistribution of income and wealth which has no regard to social justice. A higher rate of inflation will accentuate these distributional consequences and disrupt economic life generating bankruptcies and unemployment. Inflation which gets completely out of hand, runaway inflation or hyperinflation, can lead to the breakdown of the whole economy and undermine the political system. Let us look in more detail at these various effects.

Whilst inflation implies a rise in prices in general, i.e. in the average level of prices, not all prices (including the prices of the factors of production) move upwards at the same rate; some may not move at all, others only after an appreciable time lag. When the prices of consumer goods rise some people are better placed to increase the price of their labour than others. Strong trade unions are likely to ensure that the wages of their members rise as rapidly as, or even more rapidly than, prices in general. Providers of risk capital, who derive income from profits, may do well in a modest inflation for the prices of the goods and services may rise more than their costs, some of which, like rent for premises or interest on borrowed money, are relatively fixed in money terms. Other groups are not so fortunate, such as less well organized workers or people who derive income from payments fixed by contract or custom. Landlords of houses or farms, whose rents are fixed by contract, will lose real income until the contract term is up and the contract can be revised. Retired persons with annuities[1] or with government securities not redeemable for many years, if at all, will have a fixed money income whilst the prices they pay for goods and services increase. There is a tendency for transfer payments, e.g. retirement pensions, family allowances, students grants, to lag behind prices, though latterly in the United Kingdom many such benefits have been linked to an annual review. One characteristic of inflationary redistribution of income is that debtors generally gain at the expense of creditors: where a debt is fixed in monetary terms which have not sufficiently reflected the rate of inflation, then the debtor pays a diminishing rate of interest in real terms and the creditor loses.

In an inflation asset prices also do not all change to the same degree. With a modest rate of inflation the price of ordinary shares tends to rise, though heavy inflation may reverse this trend. In inflation land and house prices tend to rise more rapidly than prices in general. On the other hand, unless the inflation has been anticipated, the value of fixed interest securities falls. Assets in the form of

---

[1] An annuity is an annual income of a predetermined and fixed amount. The purchase of a life annuity is a common way in which people endeavour to provide for a regular income in retirement; they may buy it by paying premiums over a number of years or in a lump sum payment. A life annuity guarantees a fixed money income until death.

cash, bank balances, savings in the Post Office or Trustee savings banks remain the same in money terms thus falling in real value.

If inflation becomes rapid, say 10 per cent or more, and if it is unanticipated or at a rate greater than anticipated, then it becomes seriously disruptive to business. Firms engaged in construction, ship-building and the like, which work to large fixed price contracts which take several years to fulfil, find themselves meeting rising bills for wages and materials whilst their product price is fixed. Some go bankrupt. But such firms are not the only ones to suffer. The whole process of business accounting becomes more complex and misleading. Replacement of machinery and stocks requires an increasing capital investment in money terms, necessitating a rising proportion of profits, and the problem is accentuated where tax relief on investment is limited to historic or original cost.

Taxation and Inflation

The tax consequences of inflation require more detailed consideration. Let us examine, first, this question of depreciation allowances. Apart from any special investment incentives, the general principle is that firms are allowed to treat as a cost, deductible from revenues, a proportion of the cost of an investment in new machinery to allow for its depreciation each year, such that when the machinery wears out the total depreciation allowances equal the cost of the machine. But depreciation allowed for tax purposes has normally been based on historic cost (say, 10 per cent of the purchase price per year for ten years). With inflation, the sum of the depreciation allowances is quite inadequate to replace the machine. Or, putting the point in another way, each year profits tax has been levied on a sum in excess of real profit because the deduction for depreciation, based on historic cost, has been too small. The same argument applies to investment in stocks of materials and semi-finished products. Replacement cost is higher than historic cost and only historic cost is tax deductible.

In the absence of special remedial measures, inflation generates a haphazard redistribution of income through income tax. If income tax allowances and the size of the brackets for each tax rate are not adjusted in line with inflation, not only does the overall burden of income tax rise but the increase falls disproportionately on certain groups. In the United Kingdom the groups which have suffered most in recent years have been those with most allowances (e.g. the large family), the low income groups, whom inflation has lifted above the tax threshold for the first time, and those in or just below the higher rate, whom inflation has pushed into higher tax brackets. The inequity in the taxation of investment income has sometimes been even more than that of earned income. Consider a taxpayer with £1000 in a savings bank or deposit account on which he might receive 10 per cent (£100) in interest. If inflation is at the rate of 25 per cent (as during the period 1974–75 in the United Kingdom), at the end of a year, capital plus interest amount to £1100 but because of the 25 per cent price rise he needs £1250 simply to stay where he was. In other words the real rate of interest, after allowing for the fall in the value of his capital, has been negative. Yet tax will have had to be paid on the £100 of money interest.

Inflation similarly affects capital taxes like death duties and capital gains tax. For example, it effectively turns a capital gains tax into a wealth tax. Suppose the general price level rises 25 per cent in a particular year at the beginning of which a taxpayer bought shares for £1000 and at the end of which he sold them for £1250; under the United Kingdom gains tax 30 per cent of the money gain of £250, i.e. £75, would have to be paid in tax. Yet there would have been no gain in real terms. The capital gains tax, in that year, was therefore equivalent to a 6 per cent wealth tax (£75 as a percentage of £1250)—a rate twice as high as the maximum rate of wealth tax of any country in Europe.

Finally we should note that if a country has a higher rate of inflation than its competitors, it is liable to meet severe balance of payments difficulties.

How Inflation Creates Poverty and Redistributes Wealth

Let us look at two specific illustrations, drawn from United Kingdom data, of the results of inflation: firstly, how inflation may create poverty and secondly, its effect on the distribution of income and especially of wealth.

Imagine a small businessman, Mr Smith who, having worked hard all his life and put all his savings into the business, retired at the end of 1946 at the age of 65. He sold his business for £10,000 and early in 1947 put the proceeds into a newly issued government security, 2½ per cent Treasury Stock which he bought at 'par' (i.e. he paid £100 for every nominal £100 stock). He recalled how after the First World War a short-lived boom was followed by a long period in which the trend of prices was downward. With a guaranteed income of £250 per annum and with his capital behind him in case of emergency he seemed assured of a comfortable, though not luxurious, retirement. Yet because of inflation, before he died at the end of 1967 at the age of 85 his living standards had been slashed. By then the £250 per annum would only buy what £116 would buy in 1947; prices had more than doubled and the value of his income had more than halved. As to his capital, at the time of his death £100 of 2½ per cent Treasury Stock would fetch only £36 in the capital market. His £10,000 of stock would only sell for £3600 and this would only have bought what £1674 would have bought in 1947.

Mrs Smith, let us assume, was ten years younger than her husband and outlived him. She inherited the stock to provide for her widowhood needs. Eight years later, at the end of 1975, when she reached the age of 83, the £250 income per annum was worth less than one-fifth its 1947 value; it would buy about what £48 would have bought then; and on the last day of 1975 the stock was selling on the market for £17. Mr Smith's £10,000 had become £1700 which was worth only the equivalent of £330 in 1947. Thus, *unanticipated* inflation forced Mr and Mrs Smith into poverty or dependence on supplementary benefit.

The second example concerns both the distribution of income and the distribution of wealth and relates to house purchase. A house which cost £5000 in 1960 would typically sell for about £30,000 in 1975—a sixfold rise compared with a rise in retail prices over the same period of between two and three times. This rise in house prices partly reflects the attractiveness of a house as a form of investment in an inflationary period, but also the other factors discussed in Chapter 14 (e.g. tax concessions to owner-occupiers and lack of houses to rent) which stimulated demand for a product of very inelastic supply. It may seem from those figures that the purchaser of the house has had a capital gain in monetary terms of £25,000, or 500 per cent, and a real gain of rather more than half that. But that understates the gain. The typical owner-occupier buying a house for £5000 is unlikely to have paid more than £1000 (20 per cent of the purchase price) from his own resources—he will have borrowed the rest. Let us assume, to keep the illustration simple, that he has repaid none of the borrowed £4000 but simply paid interest on it. Then his money capital gain will have been not 500 per cent but 2500 per cent. If he sold the house for £30,000 he could repay the borrowed £4000, leaving £26,000—a £25,000 gain on an investment of £1000. Nor is this all. During the fifteen years in which he has been paying interest, because of a combination of unanticipated or insufficiently anticipated inflation, government attempts to keep down interest rates to home-buyers and tax concessions on mortgage interest, the *real* rate of interest he has paid has been very low or even negative.[1] To the lender it has also been low, and sometimes negative even before tax has been deducted from the nominal interest. There has, in effect, been a transfer of income from both taxpayer to borrower and from lender to borrower. Inflation and government policy have combined to redistribute income from small savers in building societies, who are often poor, to owner-occupiers, who are generally amongst the better-off. Moreover the growing wealth of owner-occupiers may well have given a new face to inequality. As the statistics in Chapter 11 showed, the share of the top 5 per cent of wealth holders has fallen substantially since 1960 and before. But a potentially more serious division amongst wealth holders has been emerging which would separate them into two nations—the wealthiest 50 per cent who are owner-occupiers and the less wealthy half of the nation who are not.

Hyperinflation

There is no precise rate at which inflation becomes hyperinflation, but we can say that it is a higher rate than that ever experienced in the United Kingdom. Hyperinflation occurs when all confidence in the currency is lost, and people seek to change money into goods as fast as they can; savings in monetary form become valueless; there is a reversion to barter; economic life breaks down; and the political system may collapse also. Germany experienced hyperinflation in 1922–23: between July and November 1923 wholesale prices in Germany rose over one million fold. Many historians believe that the inflation paved the way for Hitler's rise to power. It is almost impossible to imagine what this rate of inflation implies but the following extract from a contemporary historian gives something of the flavour.

[1] R. L. Harrington, 'Housing—supply and demand', *National Westminster Bank Quarterly Review*, May 1972, calculated that, over the period 1949–69, the net real rate of interest to housing borrowers (assuming they paid standard rate income tax) was negative in seven years and in no single year did it exceed 2½ per cent.

A man who thought he had a small fortune in the bank might receive a politely couched letter from the directors: 'The bank deeply regrets that it can no longer administer your deposit of 68,000 marks, since the costs are out of all proportion to the capital. We are therefore taking the liberty of returning your capital. Since we have no bank notes in small enough denominations at our disposal, we have rounded out the sum to 1 million marks. Enclosure: one 1,000,000 mark bill.' A cancelled stamp for 5 million marks adorned the envelope.[1]

Causes

Unemployment

We can distinguish three causes of unemployment. Firstly, unemployment which arises because of a lack of complementary resources with which to set workers to work. This kind of unemployment is very important in developing countries. It often takes the form not of actual unemployment but of under-employment and of employment where the addition to output from the marginal workers is very low. In advanced countries unemployment from this cause is spasmodic—arising when there is some breakdown in equipment or, more likely, in the flow of materials. Thus, if workers supplying car components go on strike this may lead to unemployment on the assembly line; or strikes of power workers may cut off or reduce power supplies to industry, leading to unemployment.

A second category is unemployment which arises from changes in the structure of the economy resulting particularly from changes in demand for products or from changes in technology. Some workers are no longer needed in their previous line of production, or have not the appropriate skills for the new technology, and become redundant. The more advanced an economy, the more it is liable to structural unemployment.

Thirdly, unemployment arises from instability and insufficiency of effective demand. By effective demand we mean desire backed by purchasing power. A high and sustained level of employment requires a high and sustained level of aggregate demand (or total expenditure) for goods and services. In the private sector of the

[1] Source: Konrad Heiden, *Der Fuehrer: Hitler's Rise to Power* (1944), quoted in Fritz K. Ringer (ed.), *The German Inflation of 1923*, Oxford University Press, 1969.

economy employers will employ workers if they think that consumers (or, if the product is a producers' good, other producers) will buy the product the workers help to make at a price which will yield a profit. Thus the demand for labour, which determines the level of employment, is a 'derived demand'—derived from the demand for goods and service. In the public sector the state also exercises a demand for consumption goods and services such as drugs for the NHS and the services of teachers, and for investment goods such as roads and schools. In a self-contained economy the aggregate private demand for consumption and investment together with government demand determine the level of employment. Where there is international trade then demand for export adds to domestic employment, but the purchase of imports creates employment in other countries.

This third type of unemployment is the most important in advanced countries and was the prime reason for the inter-war unemployment. Unemployment resulting from insufficiency of effective demand may arise in several ways. For example, the decisions to save and to invest may get out of step.[1] If some people decide to save more than others wish to invest, then there is a bigger decline in demand for consumption goods and services than there is an increase in demand for investment goods (which are usually producers' durable-use goods). In that case unemployment occurs, income and output fall. Or again, unemployment may be 'imported'. Supposing there was a slump in the USA; the relative prices of American goods would be likely to fall and Americans would make increased efforts to export to Britain and to other third markets where they compete with British goods. Thus American imports into Britain would be likely to rise (replacing some home-produced goods) and British exports to the USA and in competing third markets to fall. The reduction in demand for British goods would generate unemployment.

Unemployment also tends to feed on itself. If workers become unemployed their income is likely to drop (from a wage to a dole) and their demand for consumption goods and services to fall; then fewer workers are needed to meet their demands, so more workers become unemployed and income and output fall further. Also reduced demand for consumption goods may lead to a disproportionate reduction in demand for new investment by producers.

[1] The reader may find it convenient to refer to the circular flow of income, output and expenditure in Chapter 3 and, in particular, to Figure 3.3.

Inflation

Inflation may result from any upward pressure on prices in general. It is usual to distinguish between demand (or demand-pull) inflation and cost (or cost-push) inflation. Demand inflation is the upward pressure on prices when aggregate demand is in excess of the aggregate supply of goods and services and supply is inelastic—it cannot be readily increased and an increase in price will call forth a proportionally smaller increase in supply. If, for example, there was already a very high level of employment, the main effect of a further increase in aggregate demand for goods and services would be a rise in prices because there would be little spare capacity and few workers who could be brought into employment to meet the demand. Such a demand inflation might be generated in a number of ways—a consumption boom (a decreased willingness to save) without a corresponding fall in investment demand; an investment boom without a corresponding increase in willingness to save; increased government expenditure without the necessary curtailment of private demand; an export boom without an adequate curtailment of home demand.

Cost inflation results where the pressure on prices arises from an increase in costs. Costs may increase as a result of a general rise in import prices of raw materials; increased costs of labour—wage and salary increases; increased costs of capital—rises in interest rates; or higher profit margins.

Although it is convenient to distinguish between demand inflation and cost inflation, once an inflation gets under way both elements are commonly present; what started as a demand inflation may be aggravated by cost inflation as trade unions push for higher wages to keep pace with (or ahead of) the rising prices of consumer goods and services.

Inflation, like unemployment, feeds on itself. If people expect inflation, then they build an allowance for it into their economic bargains. Workers press for higher wage increases to allow for expected price increases. Lenders require a higher rate of interest if they anticipate inflation.[1] Industrialists build a margin against

---

[1] This is why, in our example above, the value of Mr Smith's securities fell. They were irredeemable securities, yielding £2.50 each, and he bought them for £100 when few people expected inflation. But once people anticipated inflation, they wanted a higher monetary return to compensate. If they expected an annual 2½ per cent rate of inflation then (ignoring the effect of tax)

inflation into tenders for contracts. These actions necessarily generate further cost inflation—and carry the danger of an accelerating rate of inflation.

Inflations are associated with an increase in the supply of money. How far an increase in the amount of money should be regarded as the invariable 'cause' rather than a consequence of inflation is disputed, but it is very unlikely that an inflation could proceed far without an increase in the money supply.

Hyperinflation results from a combination of a big increase in the amount of money and accelerating inflationary expectations. In a hyperinflation prices rise much more than proportionaly to the increase in the amount of money because money changes hands more rapidly as expectations of accelerating inflation undermine confidence in the currency. In economists' language, in hyperinflation there is an enormous increase in the 'velocity of circulation' of money.

Remedies

With both unemployment and inflation there are two aspects to examine by way of remedy: in so far as they may be inevitable or necessary, arrangements to make them easier to live with; in so far as they can be eradicated, measures to eliminate them.

Easing the Lot of the Unemployed

No advanced economy can function efficiently without some unemployment. That unemployment may not appear in the statistics; for example, in the extreme form of command economy everyone is always on the state's payroll. But unemployment will exist if the economy is dynamic and progressive; there will be changes in products and methods of production which in turn mean that some people will not be employed, or at least not effectively employed.

The essential concern should be to ensure that unemployment is short term so that it is not always the same people who are unemployed; that the unemployed should not suffer a severe fall in living standards; and that they should be helped to find new jobs, appropriate to their abilities, by assistance to increase their occupational mobility (by retraining if necessary) and their geographical mobility.

they would require £5 interest per annum on £100; then a security which only offered £2.50 would fall to a price of £50 in the market—and so on.

In the United Kingdom the income of the unemployed, partly as a result of policy measures and partly by accident, is generally not much below their earnings. A worker who loses his job after more than two years with an employer is entitled to redundancy pay. In addition, the 1960s and 1970s have seen a narrowing of the gap between net unemployment pay or supplementary benefit, and net average wages. This is because of rising benefit rates, including benefits from a graduated insurance scheme; a more generous provision for children under social security than is available in work; the fact that unemployment pay is untaxed income, and income tax on those in work has been increasing; and latterly the rise of social security benefits in line with rising prices when wage-rates have been held back by income policies. Indeed, when account is taken of the lower expenses of the unemployed, who do not have to travel to work, and the income tax refunds to which they may be entitled, the issue of current concern is that some unemployed can actually receive a higher net income than in work, at any rate for a period. This may be a disincentive for them to seek work, and may tend to raise the unemployment figures if only because the unemployed look around longer before taking a job. Unemployment pay is not taxed solely because of administrative difficulties. A switch to a weekly non-cumulative system of income tax, as under the Conservative proposals for a tax-credit scheme, would correct this anomaly.

Curing Unemployment

General unemployment arises from a deficiency in aggregate effective demand. Keeping unemployment below an acceptable minimum necessary for the smooth running of the economy thus requires a willingness of government to step in, if necessary, to maintain the level of monetary expenditure, or effective demand. They can do so by budgetary and monetary policy.

By means of budgetary policy the state can buy more goods and services itself without increasing taxation; it can stimulate private consumption demand by reduced taxes without cutting its own expenditure; the state can increase private investment demand by tax concessions or cash grants. Alternatively, or additionally, it can use monetary policy to reduce interest rates and, by increasing the cash reserves of the banks, make more credit available so that people are encouraged to borrow and spend.

Making Inflation Easier to Live With

There are many ways in which a government could make inflation easier to live with. Indexing the tax system is one (e.g. tying personal allowances to an index of retail prices and widening the rate bands regularly to maintain their real value) so that the hidden redistribution of income is checked. Another would be for the government to make widely available an 'indexed bond', a security which carried a return in real terms, even if a small one (e.g. a rate of interest guaranteed at 1 per cent above the rate of inflation, with only that 1 per cent subject to income tax). This would go a long way to remedy an inequity between public sector employees, many of whom enjoy a guarantee that their future pensions will rise in line with prices (because the government can always raise additional taxation) and private sector employees who just cannot be given that guarantee by firms which, in the absence of an inflation-proof investment, cannot be sure that the return on their pension funds will keep pace with inflation.

The United Kingdom government has taken a few tentative moves in this direction, but is still a long way behind other governments in, for example, its indexing of the tax system.

Curing Inflation

The measures to be taken against demand inflation are the obverse of those to promote employment: demand can be cut back by reduced government expenditure, or private demand can be reduced by higher taxes or higher interest rates and tighter credit.

The same measures, sometimes with a little help from incomes policies, can be used against cost inflation. A reduction in aggregate monetary demand necessarily leads to some rise in unemployment which can be expected to reduce the pressure exercised by trade unions for increased wage rates.

Demand management based on these principles appeared to work tolerably well from the end of the Second World War to the middle or late 1960s, but not since. What has gone wrong?

It must be acknowledged that there is no unanimity amongst economists about the reasons for the deterioration in the record on inflation and unemployment in the past decade, though there is much more common ground amongst them than is often appreciated.

This disagreement is not wholly surprising in view of the enormous complexity of the inter-relationships in a advanced modern economy —between prices, incomes, employment, consumption, saving, investment, tax payments, money supply, interest rates, imports and exports of goods and services, international movements of capital, foreign exchange rates and so on. It is even less surprising that policy-making governments have sometimes got things wrong. The tools with which they work are imperfect—the statistics are necessarily somewhat out of date and (as we pointed out on p. 19 about the unemployment statistics) often a very imperfect indicator of what has to be measured. Policy instruments such as changes in tax rates or the supply of money may operate over a long period and with varying time lags. Thus the initial timing of policy measures is crucial or policy becomes destabilizing rather than stabilizing. Above all, we are dealing with people's behaviour and the policy-maker is acting under the limitations (that we stressed in Chapter 2) which distinguish the social sciences; for example, we can rarely if ever conduct controlled experiments; and people learn from experience and react differently at different times to what are superficially similar circumstances.

Also matters were made worse in the 1960s and early 1970s by some particular difficulties and jolts to the economic system, largely outside the control of British policy-makers. The large foreign holdings of dollars, resulting from persistent American balance of payments deficits, gave an international stimulus to inflation; and the big rise in commodity prices in 1972–73 followed by the quadrupling of oil prices by the Organization of Petroleum Exporting Countries (OPEC) created serious problems.

Undoubtedly British governments made policy errors. It seems likely that governments did not appreciate the significance of the narrowing gap between net pay in employment and net pay in unemployment and that the target level of employment was consequently set above the minimum sustainable rate in the late 1960s and early 1970s. There seems little doubt, too, that the policy-timing of both Mr Barber and Mr Healey in their first year of Chancellorship left much to be desired. Moreover both generated or acquiesced in a big increase in the supply of money.

The main difference between economists on the causes of the recent acceleration of inflation is about the respective parts played by this growth in the money supply and the cost-push pressure exercised by trade unions. Monetarists, of whom the most notable is Nobel prize-winner Professor Milton Friedman, see the growth in the money supply as *the* causal factor. Money supply is more directly under the control of the government, and if it were not increased inflation could not last. Most monetarists see trade union wage pressure largely as an induced response to the inflation generated by this growth in the supply of money.

On the other hand, other economists see trade union pressure as the key factor, with government accommodating to the situation by increasing the money supply to avoid large-scale unemployment. This raises the question, why should trade unions have become more 'militant'? There are a number of possible answers, in particular, frustrated expectations about increases in real wages. From the second half of the 1960s the rate of growth of the British economy slowed down. Not only that, the proportion of growth going in government expenditure increased, and with it taxation, so that real take-home pay rose much less than the rate of increase in real GNP. Then, too, the rise in commodity and oil prices meant a worsening of the British terms of trade, reducing real living standards.

Either view about the role of money and the unions is compatible with the increased part played by inflationary expectations in the story. In the 1950s and 1960s expectations were sluggish. Subsequently people adjusted their expectations in the light of experience and incorporated an inflation component into their economic bargains. Trade unions were no laggards in this process. This, in turn, generated more inflation and, indeed, a tendency for inflation to accelerate.

Where do we go from here? If we are to return to a more stable situation inflationary expectations must be eradicated. This could be done by severe cut-backs in demand, for example, by reducing the rate of increase in the money supply appreciably below the rate of increase in prices. Interest rates would rise, investment would fall, unemployment would grow. The price level would be brought down (or the rate of increase markedly slowed up) but at the cost of heavy unemployment. A more gradual process of demand reduction with a series of targets in the form of successive reductions in the rate of inflation would do less harm to employment; the indexing of wage-rates might help to undermine the wage responses to inflationary expectations and some form of incomes policy could assist the move to stability and enable it to be accomplished with less unemployment. But the process will not be simple or painless.

Is an Incomes Policy Compatible with a Market Economy?

Economists differ in their views about the value of an incomes policy in dealing with inflation, reflecting their interpretations of the importance of the role of trade unions in the inflationary process. Monetarists think of such a policy, at best, as a means of gaining time whilst deflationary policies can work and possibly as helping to reduce expectations of the rate of inflation. Economists who ascribe a more positive role to trade unions in the inflationary process see an incomes policy as much more central to counter-inflation policy.

A temporary incomes policy would not seriously affect the market economy, but it may be questioned whether a more permanent policy, or succession of policies, is compatible with an efficient private sector in the mixed economy. As we have stressed before, especially in Chapter 4, a wage is both an income and a price. Will attempts to control it as an income prevent it from working effectively as a price? Changes in the relative price of different kinds of labour should provide the motivation for workers to transfer from making goods people want less to those they want more and should act as a guide and stimulus to the organization of production.

The short answer to the question 'Is an incomes policy compatible with a market economy?' must be that it all depends on the incomes policy. Some incomes policies could incorporate the necessary degree of flexibility. One such policy has been proposed by Professor J. E. Meade[1]—the kind of policy which could help to deal with a high rate of inflation in the way suggested above, whilst allowing prices to do their work.

Professor Meade suggests that the government should set a norm for the annual percentage rise in earnings of X per cent, but any group of employers and employees would be free to reach agreement on any wage or salary bargain whether or not it was above the norm. If, however, agreement were not reached, the matter would be referred to a tribunal with responsibility to determine whether or not the increase in pay claimed exceeded the norm. If the tribunal ruled that it was above the norm, then, if the workers tried to enforce their claim by industrial action such as a strike, sanctions would be taken against them, for example, the loss of accumulated rights to redundancy pay or a tax on any strike money paid out by their union. Where the claim was ruled *not* to be above the norm, there

[1] *Wages and Prices in a Mixed Economy*, Occasional Paper 35, Institute for Economic Affairs, 1971.

would be no curbs placed on the bargaining powers of the union concerned.

If this procedure were introduced when there was a high rate of inflation, say 20 per cent per annum, the norm might initially be set at 15 per cent, then subsequently reduced to 10 per cent and so on.

Such a policy would enable the price system to fulfil its efficiency functions; if there were a genuine shortage of workers in a particular occupation because of a change in economic conditions such as a shift in demand or a technological innovation, employees and employers in that industry would agree to an above-norm increase.

SUMMARY AND CONCLUSIONS

Unemployment wastes resources and, if long-term, creates human misery. Inflation which is unanticipated or insufficiently anticipated leads to a haphazard redistribution of income and wealth, and if the rate of inflation is high creates serious dislocation in an economy—bankruptcies and unemployment. Hyperinflation can lead to the breakdown of the whole economic and political system. The most important single cause of unemployment in an advanced economy is insufficiency of aggregate effective demand (or monetary expenditure). Government action can remedy the deficiency by budgetary and/or monetary policy. Inflation arises from an excess of aggregate demand or from cost-generated inflation. Measures to curtail demand were reasonably successful in dealing with inflation in the United Kingdom until the later 1960s. In analysing the acceleration of inflation in the past decade economists differ in the roles ascribed to the money supply and to trade union pressure. Inflationary expectations are an important part of any explanation of accelerating inflation. An incomes policy could be a useful component of a counter-inflation policy, and an appropriate form of incomes policy is compatible with an efficient private sector.

16 Economic Growth and the Environment

In Praise of Economic Growth

Until a few years ago almost every economist would have automatically accepted a higher rate of economic growth as a national economic objective. The typical economist would have been prepared to make two admissions. He would have acknowledged that the measure of economic growth, the rate of increase of real GNP, like so many other statistics, was less than perfect;[1] but interpreted with care, and especially for comparing adjacent years, he would have argued that it served well enough. Further, if pressed, he would have agreed that economic growth was not really an end in itself but a means to an end, or rather a means which contributed to a great many ends, so that it was not unreasonable for it to stand proxy for the lot.

Let us illustrate from the issues discussed in this volume. To start with, the higher the rate of economic growth, the more easily we can provide for the needs and comfort of the increasing proportion of retired people in the community without cutting back on the living standards of the rest. We can more easily reduce inequalities in the distribution of income, in the context of economic growth, for then it is possible to narrow differentials by pulling the lowest up without having to pull the highest down in absolute terms. Indeed on this issue it is worth remembering that the empirical evidence on international comparisons surveyed by Professor Lydall points to the conclusion that the degree of inequality in a country 'tends to diminish as income rises'.[2] Much the same arguments hold for the relief of poverty. It is easier to establish a decent minimum income level and find acceptable administrative arrangements which enable it to be properly implemented if all real incomes are rising. This is true not only of an absolute but a relative measure of poverty; for example, if one wished by a series of annual adjustments gradually

[1] See Chapter 3, p. 38–41.
[2] Above, p. 140.

to pull up the poverty level to a specified and higher proportion of the average industrial wage (with appropriate allowance for family circumstances) this could more easily be done if the average increase in real income still permitted an annual real increase to the rest of the community. Similarly it would be easier to find the extra resources for the NHS or other social services in a rapidly growing economy.

Problems of unemployment and inflation are also eased in a growing economy. With rapid growth the adjustments to changes in demand or technology can be made with less unemployment. The most painless way for effecting changes in the distribution of the labour force between industries is for the expanding industries to take on an above-average proportion of the labour force newly entering the market, whilst the declining industries do not replace retirements and other reductions by natural wastage. In an expanding economy the same relative decline of a contracting industry becomes a slower absolute decline than in a no-growth economy; thus a larger proportion of the decline in its labour force can be brought about by natural wastage rather than by redundancy. As to inflation, we saw that attempts in the United Kingdom to increase the 'social wage' (that is to raise public expenditure) above the rate of economic growth, leaving only a small annual rate of increase in disposable income, may well have helped to precipitate cost-push inflation through trade-union pressure for higher take-home pay. M. Panić[1] has pointed out that the countries with the lowest rate of inflation in recent years have been those with the highest incomes per head and has hypothesized that inflationary pressures are generated by an 'aspirations gap'; such a gap is likely to widen if a country's rate of growth slows up.

The advantages of growth are not confined to the matters discussed in this book. Economic growth, generating higher incomes per head, enables a country more easily to assist the developing countries of the Third or Fourth World. Further, it is a fact of life that Britain's voice in the councils of the world will carry more weight if it is backed by a growing economy; if you believe that, on the whole, British influence in international affairs is beneficial, this consideration is important.

It is, therefore, hardly surprising that much of national economic policy in the past thirty years or so has been, and still is, concerned with trying to increase the rate of sound economic growth. What has

[1] M. Panić, 'The inevitable inflation', *Lloyds Bank Review*, July 1976.

worried politicians and economists has been the comparatively slow rate of British economic growth compared with the other advanced mixed economies. The National Economic Development Council (NEDC) was set up in 1961. Its foundation and the experiments in indicative planning which followed, including the establishment of the Department of Economic Affairs and The National Plan of 1965, were specifically to improve the rate of economic growth.[1] That remains the basic objective behind latest government attempts for *The Regeneration of British Industry* (Cmnd. 5710, 1974). Again, increased resources have been devoted to education, especially scientific education, in the post-war period partly because of the belief that education would contribute to economic growth; and it may be that the NHS has attracted less public resources than education because its potential for contributing to growth was thought to be less.

The Case Against Growth

The objections to growth can be grouped under two heads—arguments questioning its desirability and those questioning its continued possibility. To some extent, though the distinction should not be pushed too far, the difference is between the philosophical and the physical objections to growth. Often, the same objectors are to be found in both camps. Because of the uncertainties surrounding future growth possibilities, it is natural to find those who dislike growth, or the kind of society it generates, taking the pessimistic view of its future possibilities and using 'doom' arguments to support their opposition.[2] Value judgments play a significant part in the growth controversy.

The objectors to the desirability of growth question whether growth, with its accompanying technological life-style, has made anyone happier.[3] They put forward the 'relative income hypothesis'

---

[1] See C. T. Sandford, *National Economic Planning*, Heinemann Educational Books, 2nd edition, 1976, especially Chapters 4 and 5.

[2] Professor Stephen Cotgrove has pointed out in a recent broadcast 'Which utopia?', BBC Third Programme, 3 December 1976, that those opposing the growth society have very different objectives—some wish to see a return to a more ordered, hierarchical and less libertarian society; on the other hand 'eco-freaks' seek to break away from the present mode of society towards a still more libertarian way of life.

[3] A notable economist amongst these objectors is E. J. Mishan, see, for example, *The Costs of Economic Growth*, Penguin Books, 1969, and 'Economic growth: the need for scepticism', *Lloyds Bank Review*, October 1972.

—that what matters to a person in society is not absolute command over material goods but his relative income position—and this attitude of 'keeping up with the Joneses' is both immoral and futile since everyone has to keep running just to stay in the same place. The growth objectors also stress the diseconomies of growth, the external detriments such as congested living, countryside spoiled by motorways, quiet rent by aircraft noise, and the like.

The strongest attack on growth has, however, come from those, mainly scientists, who consider that it is impossible to maintain high growth rates and that the attempt to do so will result in catastrophe. The argument is essentially in world terms and it was given prominence by the publication of *The Limits to Growth*,[1] a report by an MIT research team for the so-called Club of Rome, which has launched an ambitious project on the 'predicament of mankind'. With the aid of a computerized model the research team investigated on a world scale the inter-relationships between population, food production, industrialization, pollution and consumption of non-renewable natural resources, all of which are increasing according to a pattern of 'exponential' growth (like compound interest). Their conclusion was that 'If the present growth trends in world population, industrialization, pollution, food production, and resource depletion continue unchanged, the limits to growth on this planet will be reached some time within the next one hundred years. The most probable result will be a rather sudden and uncontrollable decline in both population and industrial capacity' (p. 23). Whilst the report recognized that the model was imperfect and over-simplified, the authors declared they did not expect their broad conclusions 'to be substantially altered by further revisions' (p. 22).

The claims made for the *Limits to Growth* model have been as extreme as some of the criticisms of it. Undoubtedly there is a high degree of arbitrariness in the values assigned to the variables and to the designation of the inter-relationships. Also the estimations of the total reserves of resources were dubiously arrived at and are far too low. But we shall concentrate on three major limitations of the model.

First, the model insufficiently allowed for the effects of technology in improving resource utilization. It is useful to distinguish between renewable and non-renewable resources. The prime example of a renewable resource is land. As we saw in relation to Britain, by improvement in technology—machines, fertilizers, better crop

[1] D. H. Meadows, *et al.*, *The Limits to Growth*, Pan Books, 1974.

rotations, etc.—the productivity of the land has been increasing and continues to increase. If technology leads to an increase in productivity as rapid as the required increase in food supplies, then the 'day of reckoning' can be indefinitely postponed.

A non-renewable resource is something like oil or fossil fuel, of which the supply is necessarily finite, and which is exhaustible. But even here if, as a result of technology, the efficiency of utilization rises at a more rapid rate than the growth rate, the rate of consumption of the non-renewable resource declines.

Moreover, though useful, the distinction between renewable and non-renewable resources is not absolute. Some non-renewable resources can be renewed by recycling. Renewable resources can be diminished by misuse. And some non-renewable resources may be replaced by renewable resources, e.g. oil replaced by solar energy. Moreover it may be possible to substitute man-made capital for natural resources. The fact that improvements in resource utilization as rapid as the growth rate could indefinitely defer doom does not however, prove that technology will generate such improvements.

A second major deficiency, as Professor Meade has pointed out,[1] lies in the degree of aggregation of the model, which generates misleading conclusions. Let us illustrate by reference to pollutants. The *Limits to Growth* model assumes that industrial production emits a stream of pollutants of various kinds, at a rate proportional to the level of world industrial activity. Natural ecological and meteorological systems, e.g. wind, water, bacteria, drain away and eliminate these pollutants. But the point arises at which the increase in pollution exceeds the capacity of the natural cleaning agents to deal with it. Then there is a crisis—an explosive rise in environmental pollution which chokes economic and other human activity. In an aggregated model in which different places and different kinds of pollutants are lumped together, this critical point must be reached at the same time for every part of the world for every pollutant. Remedial action is taken too late and the effect is catastrophic. But, as Meade says,

Atmospheric pollution in London rises unobserved to a crisis level in which smog kills a number of people; and belated action is taken to prevent that happening again; then the mercury danger reaches a critical level in a particular Japanese river, there

[1] J. E. Meade, 'Economic policy and the threat of doom', in B. Benjamin (ed.), *Resources and Population*, Academic Press, 1973.

is a local catastrophe; action is taken to deal with that; and so on. . . . What in the real world might well take the form of a continuing series of local pollution disasters or of shortages of particular non-maintainable resources for which substitutes have not yet been found or of localised population control by a particular famine in a particular phase of development in a particular region, are bound in an aggregated model to show up as a single collapse of the whole world system in a crisis of pollution, raw material exhaustion or famine.[1]

Thirdly, the limitations of the model which arise from aggregation link up with what to the economist is the most glaring deficiency—the price mechanism is ignored. Yet the function of prices is to act as warning lights about particular scarcities to promote product substitution and economy of source resources. A particular resource shortage generates a rise in its price; the price rise leads producers to economize in its use; to substitute other cheaper factors of production for it; to search for new sources of supply both of this material and substitutes. At the same time the rise in the price of the products containing the particularly scarce resource encourages consumers to substitute other products. The price mechanism exercises a powerful influence in favour of activities which avoid the use of the scarcest resources.

A Rational Reaction

The quality of the output of a computer model is no better than the quality of the input. As one American critic of the *Limits to Growth* model pungently put it: 'Garbage in, garbage out'. In the light of the model with all its deficiencies, what should our reaction be? Again, it can be pointed out that, whilst serious scarcities of particular resources arose in the past such as the timber and charcoal shortages of early eighteenth-century Britain, substitutes have always been found. Similarly, past prophets of resource exhaustion have almost invariably been confounded as have population forecasters; the National Coal Board in Britain has just started drilling a fantastically rich coalfield at Selby in Yorkshire, yet a century ago the famous economist, Stanley Jevons, was concerned about an imminent exhaustion of coal reserves in Britain.

But it would be wrong to dismiss the doomsters. What has happened in the past is no necessary guide to the future. We face the

[1] *Ibid.*, p. 134–5.

possibility of the exhaustion not of one resource but of many. The power of exponential growth cannot be denied and catastrophe could come very suddenly. To quote an illustration of exponential growth from *The Limits to Growth*: a lily plant may double in size each day and if allowed to grow unchecked would cover the pond, choking off all other forms of life in the water in thirty days; yet, on the twenty-ninth day it covers only half the pond. Growth at 3 per cent per annum implies a doubling of output every twenty-three years and an eight-fold expansion in seventy years. The world population growth is frightening; at present growth rates it doubles about every thirty years; yet even if there were an immediate and substantial reduction in fertility (say to replacement family size) in the countries with the highest birth rates, population would still go on growing at a high rate for thirty years because of the big increase in potential parents from the earlier high birth rates.

The sensible reaction in the light of the evidence and the uncertainty would seem to be agnosticism and practical caution. To quote Professor Meade again: 'The disutility of doom to future generations would be so great that, even if we give it a low probability . . . we would be wise to be very prudent indeed in our present actions.'

Some Possibilities for Action

We cannot attempt to outline any comprehensive programme for action here. Apart from limitations of space, that would require scientific knowledge the author does not possess. But certain general lines of approach can be indicated.

On the negative side it would seem quite wrong to seek to check all growth. But there are a number of positive things that can be done. Let us give some examples.

First, the acceptance of a concern for the future as a 'pure public good' (as defined in Chapter 5) together with a willingness to see an increase in public expenditure related to the protection of the future.

Second, following from the first, increased measures to combat pollution and to conserve the scarcest resources. The economist would stress a high priority for the use of taxes both on the polluters and on the scarcest resources; that way the dynamism of the price system is employed for social purpose.

Third, the encouragement of anti-natal policies in the countries with rapidly-growing populations—where the case for a population policy is very different from that in contemporary Britain.

Finally the encouragement of international action. Some measures of pollution control can only be successful if jointly undertaken, for the effects of industrial pollution in one country can wreck the policies for protection of the environment which are promoted in another. Similarly with conservation; especially joint action is needed for resources treated as in common ownership, like fisheries, which will be exhausted if there is no international agreement to prevent over-fishing. In economists' terms, this is very much the problem of externality effects, where action by the fishermen of one country has detrimental effects on others.

Is There an Oil Crisis?

Oil is a non-renewable resource. Its price has risen quite disproportionately in the past five years, quadrupling in a few months after the Yom Kippur war of 1973. Is this the sign of a rapidly diminishing vital resource?

First let it be said that there undoubtedly has been, perhaps still is, an oil crisis in one sense. The rapid rise in oil prices gave an immense jolt to the delicate mechanism of international trade and payments. It brought about huge international transfers of purchasing power. The industrial countries lost at the expense of the oil producing countries; but the developing countries without oil lost still more. The international repercussions of the oil price-rise were immense and are still with us.

But this is not really the point we are concerned with here. Does the price rise herald a world oil shortage because a vital natural resource is nearing depletion? The immediate answer to this question must be 'no'. The rise in the price of oil was a deliberate act on the part of a cartel, a monopoly of suppliers, to charge what the market would bear. The price does not reflect any increase in production costs such as would arise if the most readily accessible supplies had been exhausted and it had been *necessary* to go to more inaccessible and costly sources. Arab oil can be obtained at just as little real cost as before the price rise. Having said this, however, we must add a qualifier. There is a sense in which the price rise was only possible because of the depletion of oil supplies—American oil. It is not long since the USA was a net exporter of oil. Had she remained so OPEC could hardly have operated as such a successful cartel.

There is, also, another aspect of the price rise. In line with what we should expect from an appreciation of the workings of the price system, the rise in oil price has set certain wheels in motion. Thus, it has stimulated the search for new sources of oil supplies. We can see this particularly with North Sea oil which has become profitable to seek out and drill despite high production costs. In the massive oil rigs of the North Sea, we see examples of how technology, following price changes, can help to alleviate shortages. Again the high price of oil has undoubtedly encouraged the use of substitutes such as coal and North Sea gas, and the search for new forms of energy including improvements in atomic power, research on solar power and other possibilities. On the demand side the high price of oil has led to some reduction in demand for petrol, economies taking various forms including a marked consumer preference for the low consumption car. In other respects the high cost of energy, feeding through into electricity prices, has made consumers much more economy-conscious. And so on. It could be, that acting for purely selfish motives, the Arab oil sheiks have done the world a good turn by raising oil prices so much, so soon. There is more time to prepare for and fend off a much more serious possible future energy shortage.

SUMMARY AND CONCLUSIONS

Economists, most of the population, and certainly the politicians, have almost invariably regarded economic growth as desirable until very recently. Growth provides higher living standards and offers more scope for pursuing desired social policies. It remains a specific objective of British economic policy. A ripple in this pool of unanimity was caused by a questioning of the desirability of growth; a big splash, with heavy shock waves, resulted from the forecast of eco-catastrophe if growth was not deliberately checked. The Club of Rome's report on *The Limits of Growth* has significant defects, however; failure to allow sufficiently for the effects of technology in increasing the efficiency of resource use; defects of aggregation; failure to recognize the significance of the price system. Yet the prospect of doom is so appalling for future generations that there is no room for complacency. Concern for the future should be clearly recognized as a pure public good and policies on conservation and pollution adopted accordingly, using taxation where possible to utilize the merits of the price system. Countries with high birth rates need to adopt anti-natal policies. International cooperation is needed for effective action against some forms of pollution and to ensure some forms of conservation.

Selected Bibliography

Books and Articles

A. B. Atkinson (ed.), *Wealth, Income and Inequality*, Penguin, 1973.
The Tax Credit Scheme and the Redistribution of Income, Institute for Fiscal Studies, 1973.
Unequal Shares, Allen Lane, The Penguin Press, 1972.
Poverty in Britain and the Reform of Social Security, Cambridge University Press, 1969.
The Economics of Inequality, Clarendon Press, 1975.

A. B. Atkinson and A. J. Harrison, *The Distribution of Personal Wealth in Britain*, Cambridge University Press, 1977.

D. J. Bartholomew and E. E. Bassett, *Let's Look at the Figures*, Penguin, 1971.

P. T. Bauer and A. R. Prest, 'Income differences and inequalities', *Moorgate and Wall Street Journal*, Autumn, 1973.

W. Beckerman, 'Why we need economic growth', *Lloyds Bank Review*, October 1971.
An Introduction to National Income Analysis, Weidenfeld and Nicolson, 1968.

M. Blaug (ed.), *Economics of Education*, volumes 1 and 2, Penguin, 1968.

M. Blaug, *An Introduction to the Economics of Education*, Penguin, 1972.

Samuel Brittan, *Participation Without Politics*, Institute of Economic Affairs, 1975.

C. V. Brown and D. A. Dawson, *Personal Taxation Incentives and Tax Reform*, P.E.P., 1969.

Martin Buxton and Edward Craven (eds.), *Demographic Change and Social Policy, The Uncertain Future*, Centre for Studies in Social Policy, 1976.

M. H. Cooper and A. J. Culyer (eds.), *Health Economics*, Penguin, 1973.

Bernard Crick and William A. Robson (eds.), *Taxation Policy*, Penguin, 1973.

Robert Dorfman, *Prices and Markets*, Prentice-Hall, 2nd ed., 1972.

J. Flemming, *Inflation*, Oxford University Press, 1976.

M. W. Flinn, *British Population Growth 1700–1850*, Macmillan, 1970.

J. K. Galbraith, *The Affluent Society*, Penguin, 1962.

B. B. Gilbert, *The Evolution of National Insurance in Great Britain: the Origins of the Welfare State*, Michael Joseph, 1966.

P. Gregg, *The Welfare State*, Harrap, 1967.

C. D. Harbury and P. C. McMahon, 'Inheritance and the characteristics of top wealth leavers in Britain', *Economic Journal*, September 1973; and C. D. Harbury and D. M. Hitchens, 'The inheritances of top wealth leavers', *Economic Journal*, June 1976.

R. L. Harrington, 'Housing—supply and demand', *National Westminster Bank Quarterly Review*, May 1972.

M. M. Hauser (ed.), *The Economics of Medical Care*, Allen and Unwin, 1972.

J. R. Hicks, *The Social Framework*, Clarendon Press, 4th edition, 1971.

H. V. Hodson, *The Diseconomies of Growth*, Pan/Ballantine, 1972.

Institute for Fiscal Studies, *Conference on Proposals for a Tax-Credit System*, 1973.

Dudley Jackson, *Poverty*, Macmillan, 1972.

Aubrey Jones (ed.), *Economics and Equality*, Philip Allan, 1976.

W. A. Laing, *The Costs and Benefits of Family Planning*, P.E.P., 1972.

T. Liesner (ed.), *Housing Finance*, Institute for Fiscal Studies, 1975.

Harold Lydall, 'The economics of inequality', *Lloyds Bank Review*, July 1975.

D. F. Lomax, 'What attitude to growth?', *National Westminster Bank Quarterly Review*, February 1974.

J. E. Meade, 'Poverty in the welfare state', *Oxford Economic Papers*, 3, **24**, November 1972.

The Intelligent Radical's Guide to Economic Policy, Allen and Unwin, 1975.

D. H. Meadows, *et al.*, *The Limits to Growth*, Pan, 1972.

E. J. Misham, 'Economic growth: the need for scepticism', *Lloyds Bank Review*, October 1972.

A. A. Nevitt, *Housing, Taxation and Subsidies*, Nelson, 1966.

W. A. Niskanen, *Bureaucracy: Servant or Master*, Institute of Economic Affairs, 1973.

A. T. Peacock and J. Wiseman, *The Growth of Public Expenditure in the United Kingdom*, Allen and Unwin, 2nd edition, 1967.

G. H. Peters, *Cost-Benefit Analysis and Public Expenditure*, Institute of Economic Affairs, 3rd edition, 1973.

D. Piachaud and J. H. Weddell, 'The economics of treating varicose veins', *International Journal of Epidemiology*, 3, **1**, 1972.

George Polanyi and John B. Wood, *How Much Inequality?*, Institute of Economic Affairs, 1974.

J. A. Roberts, 'Economic evaluation of health care: a survey', *British Journal of Preventive Social Medicine*, Vol. 25, 1974.

C. T. Sandford, *Economics of Public Finance*, Pergamon, 2nd edition, 1977.

National Economic Planning, Heinemann Educational Books, 2nd edition, 1976.

C. T. Sandford, J. R. M. Willis and D. J. Ironside, *An Accessions Tax*, Institute for Fiscal Studies, 1973.

An Annual Wealth Tax, Institute for Fiscal Studies/Heinemann Educational Books, 1975.

J. Sheehan, *Economics of Education*, Allen and Unwin, 1973.

J. F. Sleeman, *The Welfare State, its Aims, Benefits and Costs*, Allen and Unwin, 1973.

M. E. H. Smith, *A Guide to Housing* (and *Supplement*), Housing Centre Trust, 1971 (and 1974).

R. Wager, *Care of the Elderly*, I.M.T.A., 1972.

E. G. West, *Education and the State*, Institute of Economic Affairs, 1965.

Brandon Rhys Williams, *The New Social Contract*, Conservative Political Centre, 1967.

Official Publications

Report of the Royal Commission on Population, Cmd. 7695, 1949.

A National Minimum Wage: an Inquiry, Department of Employment and Productivity, 1969.

Output Budgeting for the Department of Education and Science, Education Planning Paper No. 1, HMSO, 1970.

Proposals for a Tax-Credit System, Cmd. 5116, 1972.

Report of the Population Panel, Cmnd. 5258, 1973.

Select Committee on Tax Credit, vol. 1, 341–1, 1973.

Royal Commission on the Distribution of Income and Wealth, *Report No. 1. Initial Report on the Standing Reference*, Cmnd. 6171, 1975.

National Income and Expenditure 1965–75, HMSO, 1976.

Pension Age, Memorandum by the Department of Health and Social Security, September 1976.

Public Expenditure to 1979–80, Cmnd. 6393, February 1976.

Royal Commission on the Distribution of Income and Wealth, *Report No. 4. Second Report on the Standing Reference*, Cmnd. 6626, 1976.

Social Trends, No. 6, 1975, HMSO, 1976.

Supplementary Benefits Commission Annual Report 1975, Cmnd. 6615, 1976.

The General Household Survey, 1973, HMSO, 1976.

'Effects of taxes and benefits on household income', an article published annually in *Economic Trends*.

Index